W0254550

CAPITALISM
TO
PEOPLEISM

PRAISE FOR THE BOOK

'Ravi Chaudhry has brilliantly captured the need to reimagine our collapsing economic system with humanity and ambition. All great societal transformations require leaders, and all great leaders require wisdom and courage. *Capitalism to Peopleism* offers plenty of both.'

—Paul Polman, co-author, *Net Positive*; former CEO, Unilever

'Ravi Chaudhry has given us a gift of wisdom and empowerment with *Capitalism to Peopleism*. He documents and guides the evolving nature of how we understand the current economic model and provides a roadmap for how we can put people right at the heart of the economic system.'

—Chris Coulter, CEO, GlobeScan; co-author,
All In: The Future of Business Leadership

'This book is a pathway from a world teetering on the precipice of self-destruction to a world in which humanity has solved critical problems. It calls for the most profound and yet simple transformation—from profits to people as the organizing principle for economics and social affairs. People, planet, profit is the golden key and Mr Chaudhry provides the way to combine all three to the benefit of all.'

—Jim Garrison, Founder and President,
Ubiquity University; Director,
New Paradigm Institute, Washington, D.C.

'Ravi Chaudhry offers a visionary roadmap for transforming our global economic and governance systems. With incisive analysis and profound wisdom, he charts a course from the failings of modern capitalism to a more equitable, sustainable future. This is not merely a critique, but a masterful blueprint for action, challenging leaders to evolve from knowledge to wisdom and embrace a new era of "survival of the wisest". Chaudhry's concept of Peopleism provides a compelling framework for reinventing democracy and business to truly serve all of humanity.'

—Iain Patton, Founder, Ethical Team PR, U.K.

'This is one of the most transparent and compelling analyses of the current state of leadership I've ever encountered. What I find particularly encouraging is the author's optimism in suggesting potential ways forward. He extends an invitation to all leaders to recognize the growing power of collective wisdom and its increasing ability to address global challenges effectively, while valuing the unique contributions of each individual in the process. Ravi Chaudhry conveys it clearly: it is not too late for leaders to reconnect with the people, to reinvent what it means to be elected or appointed, and to understand that leadership is not about serving just a select few, but entire communities and the planet as a whole. We all share one family— humanity, and one home—our planet Earth. It is time to shift from *capitalism to peopleism.*'

—Dr.hc. Violeta Bulc, Founder and Curator, Ecocivilisation Movement; former Deputy Prime Minister of Slovenia; former European Commissioner

'*Capitalism to Peopleism* is a ground-breaking book that challenges the status quo and presents a visionary path forward. It offers profound insights into the failures of current systems and introduces Peopleism, a transformative governance model rooted in equity and sustainability. Essential reading for leaders and change-makers, it empowers individuals to shape a better future with wisdom, compassion, and inclusive leadership.'

—Tomas Björkman, Founder, Ekskäret Foundation, author, *The World We Create: From God to Market*

'*Capitalism to Peopleism* leverages Ravi's vast experience in leadership and consulting to guide readers through a journey of self-discovery and societal evolution. This ground-breaking book challenges the status quo, addresses the existential crises facing our world, and advocates a shift from outdated capitalist principles to a transformative model of Peopleism.

Drawing from historical and contemporary contexts, Chaudhry presents a compelling vision of a future dominated by wisdom-led leadership and compassionate governance. He empowers readers with the tools to foster collaboration, bridge the divides, and champion the rights of all. *Capitalism to Peopleism* is a clarion call for change, inspiring seasoned leaders and aspiring change-makers to prioritize people and the planet over profit. Let's join Chaudhry in shaping a future that aligns with our shared values and aspirations. Our journey towards transformative leadership starts here.'

—Joshua Chimakula Ngoma, Founder and Chief Enabler, Enterprising Africa Regional Network (EARN); author, *It's Time for Africa: Embracing Our Ancient Roots and Charting a Prosperous Tomorrow*

'*Capitalism to Peopleism* is a work of incredible original thinking, '*inspiring a leadership transformation*', before human civilization runs out of time. Ravi Chaudhry reveals how everyone can access the wisdom inherent in each of us and help co-create a 'Safe New World' for all of us. An essential read for those who care about their future.'

—Rinaldo Brutoco, Founding President and CEO, World Business Academy, USA

'*Capitalism to Peopleism* resonates deeply with the core values of the Globally Responsible Leadership Initiative. This transformative work champions the principles of responsible leadership, ethical governance and sustainable development. Chaudhry's call for integrating human-centric values with economic and political systems aligns seamlessly with our mission to foster globally responsible leaders. His concrete proposals for democratizing democracy and fostering inclusive, equitable societies are not only timely but essential for addressing today's global challenges. This book is a must-read for anyone committed to creating a more just and sustainable world.'

—John North, Executive Director,
Globally Responsible Leadership Initiative, South Africa

'*Capitalism to Peopleism* is one of the most significant books of our time. It distils how humanity stands at a watershed moment in history, defining the leadership and governance models needed to create a world that works for everyone. An extraordinary book that bridges the author's unparalleled experience, practice, and wisdom, charting the path to a Wisdom Economy that serves the well-being of every individual, organization, society, and our natural environment. This book is a must-read for every aspiring and accomplished leader.'

—Peter Matthies, Founder, Conscious Business Institute; author,
Plan BE: A Professional's Guide to Authentic Success

'Citizenship, Ownership and Leadership are the three pillars of any society. In the new era of planetary boundaries, resource and economic disparities and multi-cultural societies, reinventing what it means to be a citizen, an owner, a leader is what all countries should be working on. Ravi Chaudhry's book aims straight at these pillars in a coherent, holistic exposé with clear recommendations for action. Such wisdom and experience are shining through his words. For readers outside India, his writings are doubly enlightening, since they are underpinned by Indian philosophy and practices, which the whole world ought to know better.'

—Marcello Palazzi, Co-founder and Chairman,
Progressio Foundation and Leaders for Good Cooperative, Netherlands

'Ravi Chaudhry's admirable—and necessary—search for a holistic but achievable vision for national governance led him to the *Gitanjali* of Rabindranath Tagore, which envisages a State in which *citizens enjoy access to learning*, knowledge and skills; are *encouraged to think and express their views honestly*; and to *display respect for all*, whatever their race, gender, religion, caste, or other status. This is a splendid triad of socio-political virtues.

Ravi describes the ethos of the State he seeks, as 'enabling every resident to pursue her quest to achieve her highest potential'. Facilitating the actualization of the potential of each person is the founding ethos of all great civilizations. The sole reason for the existence of any government is to enable the well-being of the citizens and other residents. If we distil that responsibility to its essence, it requires the State to provide *equity*, *security*, and *sustainability*, the last of which is, of course, *intergenerational equity*.

Ravi's splendid book discusses these themes and unpacks their implications in today's world. It is both timely and important at a time when narcissism and privilege have come to define the social systems of the advanced economies and are misdirecting those of many emerging societies.'

—Sean Cleary, Executive Vice-Chair, FutureWorld Foundation;
Managing Director, Centre for Advanced Governance, South Africa

'Ravi's book is an essential read for anyone seeking a solution to the existential challenges we collectively face. His central thesis that we "must make way for the primacy of people and the preponderance of nature" should be everybody's call to action!'

—Thierry Malleret, Co-founder and Managing Partner,
Monthly Barometer and the Summit of Minds, France

'Ravi Chaudhry raises a profound issue in this book. Given the unprecedented advances in science, technology and productive capacities, why is the world threatened by a growing array of existential challenges? He reminds us of a fact most often forgotten by both theorists and practitioners: economy, business and technological development are social institutions founded to promote the welfare and well-being of society in a manner that preserves the rich, productive capacities of the natural world which supports our existence.

When theory and practice are divorced from this objective truth, they undermine the very purpose for which these institutions exist. He points out the misuse and abuse of all forms of social power—economic, political and social—that undermines democracy, equitable development, and the security of all. He calls for leadership based on wisdom and time-tested universal values that are enshrined in our constitutions, but widely misapplied and misinterpreted in practice. Rather than lofty unattainable ideals, he asserts the value of these values as the essential wisdom needed by leaders in all fields to promote sustained peace, prosperity and sustainable development. The conclusions he comes to are of fundamental relevance to present and future leaders of business, technology and government.'

—Garry Jacobs, President, World Academy of Art and Science;
Chairman and CEO, World University Consortium

Also by Ravi Chaudhry

Quest for Exceptional Leadership: Mirage to Reality
(1st Edition—2011, 2nd Edition—2016)

CAPITALISM TO PEOPLEISM

Inspiring a Leadership Transformation

RAVI CHAUDHRY

SIMON &
SCHUSTER

London · New York · Sydney · Toronto · New Delhi

First published in India by Simon & Schuster India 2024

Copyright © Ravi Chaudhry, 2024

No reproduction without permission.

The right of Ravi Chaudhry to be identified as author of this work has been asserted by him in accordance with Section 57 of the Copyright Act 1957.

1 3 5 7 9 10 8 6 4 2

Simon & Schuster India
818, Indraprakash Building,
21, Barakhamba Road,
New Delhi 110001.

www.simonandschuster.co.in

Simon & Schuster: Celebrating 100 Years of Publishing in 2024

Hardback ISBN: 978-81-972789-4-5
eBook ISBN: 978-81-974895-4-9

Typeset in India by SŪRYA, New Delhi
Printed and bound in India by Replika Press Pvt. Ltd.

The views and opinions expressed in this book are the author's own and the facts are as reported by him and which have been verified to the extent possible, and the publishers are not in any way liable for the same.

The author has made all reasonable effort to contact copyright-holders for permissions. In case there are omissions or errors in the form of credits given, corrections may be made in future editions.

Simon & Schuster India is committed to sourcing paper that is made from wood grown in sustainable forests and support the Forest Stewardship Council, the leading international forest certification organisation. Our books displaying the FSC logo are printed on FSC certified paper.

No part of this publication may be reproduced, transmitted or stored in a retrieval system, in any form or by any means, electronic, mechanical, photocopying, recording or otherwise, without the prior permission of the publisher.

This book is sold subject to the condition that it shall not, by way of trade or otherwise, be lent, resold, hired out, or otherwise circulated, without the publisher's prior consent, in any form of binding or cover other than that in which it is published.

Dedicated to

Present and future global leaders in society and business who have the conviction and courage to uphold these timeless truths:

- The core essence of humanity that flows in each of us is essentially the same.
- Responsible leadership with good governance is the only way to ensure equitable and enduring growth for all.
- Credible and autonomous 'oversight institutions' are indispensable for genuine democracy and sustained societal prosperity.

Contents

PART THREE | Transition from Capitalism to Peopleism

PART FOUR | The Safe New World: Where Every Person Matters

An Invitation to 'Shape Your Future before It Shapes You'

> *The world is moving so fast these days that anyone who says it cannot be done is generally interrupted by someone doing it...No one ever gets far unless he accomplishes the impossible at least once a day.*
>
> —Elbert Hubbard (1856–1915)[1]

A Personal Invite

The deficit of responsible leadership has been conspicuous for as long as one can recall, but it has always been accepted as a fait accompli by both: those who govern and those who are governed. However, the events of the last four years have stirred up the status quo and the fault lines of leadership are clearly visible. These events have not only shaken up but also awakened the people. Perhaps for the first time ever, most leaders in business, politics and society are deeply concerned about how these sudden twists could impact their future.

This book addresses the concealed anxieties of the leaders today and outlines a pathway to help them become better leaders and live better lives. It is about discovering one's potential to be 'the best of oneself', while also becoming a catalyst to bring out 'the best of everyone else' whose lives one touches. This is the only credible way to partially neutralize the deliberate or inadvertent adverse consequences of past actions. Concurrently, this book also lays down the agenda for the leaders of tomorrow.

Though focused on leadership in business and society, this is a book for all of us, as our future is invariably determined by the decisions and actions of our leaders. At each step, we will take calls on what our leaders must do and what we as citizens and consumers need to do, individually and collectively, to shape our future before it shapes us.

While preparing for this endeavour, I thought it necessary to create conditions so that we can readily and naturally collaborate with each other. To start with, I have done four things:

- I have completely emptied my mind of all my past biases, beliefs, and assumptions, with no remnants of pre-conceived notions whatsoever.
- I am conscious that I am a product of my upbringing and my culture. I tend to notice only the things I think are important to me, and remember only those 'important' things. All others, I simply ignore. Even when I pay attention to the things I like, most of my attention is directed towards what I am looking at. *I have resolved to start paying more attention to where I am looking from.* Then alone can I take full cognizance of the perspectives of others. Then alone can I ask the right questions.
- I am nudging the adult in me to become a child once again, knowing well that a child loves everyone around her; a child is content and happy with what she has; and every child dreams. A child does not see any barriers and she believes everything is possible.
- I am aware that I do not know the answers to all the questions that concern us. With utmost humility, I look forward to collaborate with a diverse group of stakeholders to ensure that the answers we are looking for will meet theirs as well as our aspirations.

With these premises, there is a much better chance that we will find the right answers to the many vexing questions that confront us all the time. We shall begin with a brief overview of what has happened since 2020.

Four Years of Persistent Challenges

The popular saying goes: 'There are decades when nothing happens, and then there are weeks when decades happen.'[2] Collectively, we have come through a series of such periods since 2020.

It is worth reflecting how something that did not exist until 2020, the Covid virus, acquired the inconceivable power to humble the entire might of the planetary economy that is worth US$ 85 trillion. Nothing that futurists could imagine had prepared humankind for such an overarching clutch of events that would leave a large majority of seven-and-a-half billion people so hapless and helpless for so long.

People in every nation were confined and isolated for long periods of time. More than a billion people were reported to have been infected with the disease and at least 10 million people lost their lives.[3] Powerful governments found themselves incapacitated. Many of the best-managed corporations felt suddenly debilitated. The veneer of impregnable supremacy in virtually every domain developed cracks as the entire human race struggled to meet the persistent challenge of this miniscule adversary and its mutations.

Soon, it became clear that the adversary was not the issue. We would get a respite from the adverse effects of Covid, which eventually happened in 2023. The concern was that another adversary could appear at any time, either in the same incarnation or a different one and with even greater ferocity. The issue is whether we realize that these pandemics, as also acts of war or terrorism, and extreme weather events, are not accidents or results of planetary configurations, or random acts of nature, but more of a reprimand to the human race stemming from our collective misdeeds of the past.

It was, in effect, a forewarning of even more adversity. Worrying about Covid was bad enough, but the multiple spectres of wars, inflation, climate change, the perils of unrestrained Artificial Intelligence (AI), and many other dire concerns also continue to trouble us now. It is time to completely transform how we live, with a total revamp of the human relationship with nature as well as relationships among humans.

The Biggest Leadership Challenge Today

If we study history over the centuries, we find that sometimes calamities or catastrophes have led us to a better world. From the formation of small kingdoms to nations, and after the Second World War, to the formation of the European Union (EU), the Association of Southeast Asian Nations (ASEAN), and the worldwide phenomenon of globalization that enabled strangers in different countries to become friends and collaborate in joint ventures. But these transformations take time, and it always feels like things are at their darkest before dawn. Now, too, the world will move on. As always, the aftermath will inevitably lead to a new set of winners and losers.

Three hundred years earlier, the Enlightenment and the Industrial Revolution tore down the foundations of an ancient order. Seemingly permanent kings, religious heads, tribal chiefs and feudal lords were all thrown out.[4] Since 2020, multiple new hammers have been chiselling our world once again. Naturally, our concern is where we will be in the new matrix of champions and also-rans.

We were all living our lives and running our businesses in relative stability, reasonably well. In a flash, the sense of continuity and familiarity which is the bedrock of our emotional security vanished. Virtually everything around us changed. But our past beliefs, prejudices and habits still stay with us, which make it difficult to accept the new reality. We develop a feeling of dis-ease. To ensure that the dis-ease does not become a disease, we have to review our beliefs, discard our prejudices, and change our habits. But that is not easy. We keep learning all the time and yet we do not change. For successful executives, 'The past is never dead. It's not even past.'[5]

> This is the biggest leadership challenge today: the unwillingness or the inability to face reality.

Strangely, when one learns, one does not change. You change only when you absorb. Let me share an ordinary experience. I made myself a cup of coffee and added a little sugar. But when I sipped it, it was not sweet. Since I had not stirred the coffee, the sugar had not been absorbed.

Likewise, change happens only when the learning is absorbed. Till then, one is not even aware that one is unaware of the new ground realities.

A character named Mike in Ernest Hemingway's novel *The Sun Also Rises* is asked how he went bankrupt.[6] He responds, 'First gradually, and then suddenly.' The same fate awaits those who persistently disregard the new reality.

What Is the New Reality?

This is the end of the era of 'business-as-usual'. You can feel the change. The silent brunt of Covid is likely to last for a long time. The embers of the wars in Ukraine and Gaza will not be doused soon. The uneasy relationship between the US and China is a constant source of uncertainty. Erratic supply-chains may drag inflation longer even as AI technologies hold the potential to severely lessen new job opportunities and give rise to unforeseeable problems. One thing is certain: the things that have changed could change even more, and the things that have not yet changed will also begin to change. No industry and business will be spared the impact. Some will disappear. Some will revive and recover. A few may thrive.

However, the ones that survive will certainly need to renew themselves. They must accept the new expectations from society. The unrelenting adversity experienced by billions of people over the last few years has awakened humanity to two stark realities:

- *Rapid acceleration of pre-existing trends* such as automation and digitization, heightened surveillance from state and non-state actors, rising nationalism, a noticeable retreat from globalization, and a new amphitheatre of geopolitics, all of which could lead to unpredictable economic impacts; and
- *Unobstructed exposure of global fault lines* such as the deficit of responsible leadership in business and society, irresponsible capitalism, worsening inequality, and lack of justice, all of which have brought to the fore the long-ignored and perpetually overlooked societal expectations from leaders.

It has become more obvious that capitalism as it is practiced today is concerned only with itself and is fixated only on profits and growth. It is blind or oblivious to environmental and social realities.

> Corporate objectives and societal expectations are like the two tracks of a railway line; they seem to converge in the distance but in reality, they never do.

All this has exposed the fragility of our global economy, our frail public health structures, and our deeply corrupted systems of governance. The burden of this mis-governance does not much impact the well-off, it is borne primarily by the poor and the marginalized communities. Societies need a bigger meta-story. People are yearning for meaning in their lives. Organizations that realize the importance of having a higher purpose will benefit themselves and their stakeholders. One has to create a purpose, share the purpose, and live the purpose with humility and continuous reflection and introspection. There can be no divergence between one's organizational purpose and one's personal commitment, nor between a leader's personal agenda and the aspirations of society.

Leaders that embrace these ideas in what they think, what they say, and what they do are likely to emerge as the new winners in the next decade. The heartening part is that this process is neither difficult nor unlikely. Quite effortlessly, it leads one to the intuitive discovery that 'when you change the way you look at things, the things you look at also change'.[7] This realization makes it naturally easy for leaders to relate and collaborate.

A Rare Watershed Moment in History

The world today is traversing a 'watershed moment', a definitive moment in history that completely changes the future trajectory of the human race. It is a divider in time and space beyond which the things that mattered till now will never be the same again. It is a moment when history ceases to determine our future.

Usually, a watershed moment is recognizable in hindsight—for instance, the gradual transitions from the Hunter-Gatherer Economy to the Agricultural Economy, followed by the Industrial Economy, leading to the Information Economy and thereafter to the Knowledge Economy. Humankind is now on track to transition to a new era of the Wisdom Economy. We are perhaps the first members of the human race who are able to recognize a watershed moment as soon as it arises. This is an exceptionally precious and rare occasion that bestows on us a collective opportunity to consciously choose the type of future we want. It is a choice that comes once in many lifetimes. To make the best of it, for all of us, we must recall two important truisms:

- There is nothing inevitable about our future. We have access to a multiple array of resources to influence it. We can even outline the detailed contours of our future and take charge of our own destinies.
- We have been used to incremental change so far—often two steps forward and then a step backward and a step sideward. This won't suffice anymore. This is a time for big leaps, a time for transformational change.

At this watershed moment, we must raise relevant and fundamental questions deep within ourselves and answer decisively: What do we want our future to be? Let us call it a 'Safe New World'. This book is an earnest attempt to provide clarity on what we should seek and how.

The Legacy of Huxley's *Brave New World* and Orwell's *1984*

Aldous Huxley and George Orwell were both intellectual giants and prolific writers. Huxley's *Brave New World*,[8] written in 1932, and Orwell's *1984*,[9] written in 1949, were both speculative fiction, projecting what the future may look like. It is a coincidence that the future both these books portrayed was a dystopian one. Each one used a different context and a different script but, in substance, both the novels focused on complementary, overlapping warnings. Many reviews rightly emphasize that the authors wrote their books in an attempt to try and prevent the imagined dystopias from coming true.

Somehow the world today has become a mix of the futures

that Huxley and Orwell vividly highlighted: authoritarian regimes, unmitigated surveillance, indiscriminate social stratification, the ever-present risks of nuclear war, biological and chemical weapons, human control through bio-engineering and psychological conditioning, and similar other dire scenarios.

Even though Huxley specifically warned, 'This is possible: for heaven's sake, be careful about it,' and Orwell explicitly cautioned against leaders who tell blatant lies and asked us to 'reject the evidence of your eyes and ears', it did not help.[10] I wonder if the portraits of the future in science fiction and speculative fiction, while they imagine alternative trajectories, actually make those futures possible.

However, if a dystopian future can come true, so can a non-dystopian one. Somehow, many of our writers and philosophers have tended to dwell more on the ills of civilization rather than on its potential virtues. Is it because predictions of bad news and sad outcomes sell better? Or is it because publishers believe that pessimism is serious philosophy and optimism is just wishful, impractical imagining? In either case, the Latin proverb, 'Fortis imaginatio generat causum' (A strong imagination begets the event) holds true.

In my submission, I have refrained from using the term 'utopia' because that implies an unattainable, idealist state. I sense all of us will be content with a meaningful, collaborative, sustainable and a genuinely equitable future.

A New Narrative for a 'Safe New World'

It is in this context that this book takes on the task of creating a new, contemporary narrative that will enable humanity to venture beyond the 'Brave New Worlds' envisaged in the last century. We shall all work together to outline the vision for a 'Safe New World' for humanity:

- A world that is safe to live in, and peaceful for everyone, everywhere;
- A world that is safe for all to learn, to question, and to reason;

- A world that is safe for everyone to think, to dream, and to speak without fear;
- A world that is safe from pandemics and deadly diseases;
- A world that is safe from famines, terrorism and wars;
- A world that is safe for children, women and all minorities; and
- A world that is safe for all the species that sustain eco-balance and life on Earth.

Are We Asking the Right Questions?

It is not unusual for successful and wealthy people to believe that they know the answers to all the questions of life. However, the unacknowledged reality is that all the questions have changed quite suddenly. And yet, the erstwhile beliefs and prejudices continue to hold sway. *What we know continues to be an impediment in being open to what we do not know.*

> To find the right answers, we must ask the right questions, and then keep questioning the questions till we have fully understood every aspect of the new reality that envelopes us.

What are the top-of-the-mind questions doing the rounds since 2020? If you ask the least well-off, the four billion people, over half the world's population, with little income, no savings, no stable jobs and uncertain prospects, you discern a palpable sense of resignation. Their frustration is fraught with simmering anger: 'Why us again? Why us every time? Is poverty our eternal destiny?'

If you look at the ignored minorities, you can still hear the reverberating echoes of 'I can't breathe', 'Black lives matter', 'Dalit lives matter', 'Jin, jiyan, azadi! (Woman, life, freedom!)', 'This religion is better than that' and other similar slogans from all over the world. You wonder: Where is racial justice? Where is social justice? What happened to education justice? And whither climate justice?

If you ask small business entrepreneurs and owners of service-sector industries that create 60 to 80 per cent of the employment in a nation, they wonder, 'If capital is not accessible to us, supply chains are choked, globalization is in retreat, and inflation is at a peak, how long before our fortunes start reviving?'

If you ask big business, their concern is, 'How can we cut costs even as we digitize person-to-person interactions, automate processes, and discover new, relevant business models, employing as few people as possible all along?'

As regards political leaders, you don't have to enquire, heads of authoritarian regimes as well as many professed democracies are using the opportunity to strengthen surveillance and hegemony, and deepen the 'deficit of democracy'.

Political analysts remind us that human history is an unremitting saga of discords and accords among nation states. At this juncture in the 21st century, when existing multilateral institutions, including the United Nations (UN), are virtually moribund, and when the strong winds of nationalism, protectionism and 'my-country-first-ism', are blowing across all continents, one encounters more discord among nations than at any time since the Second World War. The Russian attack on Ukraine, a sovereign nation, in February 2022, and the Israel–Palestine war, which began in Gaza in October 2023, have cast a dark pall on mankind's hopes for a gradual, peaceful convergence of political differences and ideologies.

There has been an ongoing dialogue on how we can make G-20 leaders genuinely, collectively accept that no country or region can hereafter be an island of seclusion; we will either all grow, or we will all perish. The G-20 summit in Indonesia in 2022 was dubbed as G-19, since Vladimir Putin, the president of Russia, did not attend. Putin and Xi Jinping, the Chinese president, both skipped the G-20 summit in India in 2023, making it a G-18. Though the African Union was invited to join this grouping to provide a greater voice to the global south, the outcome did not convey a sense of urgency to collectively acknowledge and address the perennial challenges the planet continues to face: ecosystem collapse, nuclear menace, technology's dangerous trajectory, financial exclusion and inequality. The emphasis was more on how not to challenge any member's stated positions and sensibilities. Other than making a few prosaic, high-sounding declarations, no common grounds were identified to make a decisive push towards a more united, better world.

This planet belongs to all of us. Territorial ambitions or military actions may create a façade of transient superiority for a nation but eventually, everybody loses. It is still within our capabilities to reverse course and begin envisioning a new charter to usher in a 'United Nations of Earth' in the 'Safe New World' that we envisage. The potential upside for both, those who lead and those who are led, is enormous.

The rays of light that provide hope in this endeavour are the ones emanating from a rapidly growing mass of people's organizations, civil society, a few business leaders and new groups of volunteers miraculously sprouting all over the world. They are generating a new agenda and the new contours of leadership required in the third decade of the 21st century. These are the millions of people determined to demolish the demons of today and tomorrow. They all believe in this axiom:

> The obstacles to shaping our future lie not outside but within ourselves.

Confronting the Global Divide and Governance Deficit

The well-off, barring a few, are capable of surviving all challenges. But for the less well-off, 53 per cent of the global adult population (about 2.8 billion adults that own a meagre 1.1 per cent of the planet's wealth), life will not continue as usual.[11] For them, better days seem far away. Grave deprivation is the norm; concerns about getting a job (or if they have one, retaining it), discrimination, forced migration, and the devastating consequences of natural disasters—one or more of these worries continuously pervade their lives.

Most economic commentaries and forecasts still tend to focus primarily on GDP forecasts, along with a generous sprinkling of the impact of geo-political risks on stock markets, currencies and asset valuations, while the vast majority remains stuck in a decades-old time capsule of stagnant wages and a dismal quality of life.

One seldom comes across a study that attempts to forecast the per capita income growth rate for the less well-off, the ones who make up 80 per cent of the population, which I believe should be the key criterion of the impact of the implementation of most of the 2030 Sustainable Development Goals (SDGs) in every country.[12] The usual classification of 'developed' and 'developing' countries is misleading. One country may be wealthier than another but to say that it is now 'developed' and therefore no longer 'developing' has an ironic connotation that these countries need to do nothing about their problems of inequality and poverty.

Irrespective of the average per capita income of a nation, as long as the gross income differential between the top 10 per cent of the population and the bottom 40 per cent, known as the Palma Ratio,[13] collectively exceeds 2, which roughly corresponds to a Gini co-efficient of 0.35, in my view, that country must be considered a 'developing' country on any measure of social equity. Based on this criterion, there are only five countries in the world today with a Palma Ratio of less than 2.0 that can be called equitably developed: Iceland, Czechia, Norway, Slovenia and Sweden.[14] China with a Palma Ratio of 5.03 and the US with a Palma Ratio of 5.19—corresponding to a Gini coefficient of about 0.48—have a similar level of social inequity. The corresponding figure for India is not readily available.

Regrettably, the fact that the richest only get richer and the poorest only get poorer is now looked upon as an inevitable consequence of economic growth. There is a serious apprehension that these feelings of inequity and insecurity will no longer be confined to the less well-off 80 per cent of the global population. Acceleration in the usage of new technologies such as AI, robotics and the Internet of Things is instilling fear among many people who are at the top 20 per cent of the income bracket. Meanwhile, a spate of unimaginable economic, social and political events continues to add fuel to the raging fires of 'lack of trust' and 'absence of hope' in most nations of the world.

The Edelman 2024 Trust Barometer reveals that 63 per cent of government leaders, 61 per cent of business leaders, and 64 per cent of journalists and reporters are believed to be purposely trying to mislead people by saying things they know are false or gross exaggerations.[15] *This 'lack of trust' between those who govern and the governed, and the accompanying 'absence of hope' for a better future, are the two prime viruses in our society today. Governments do not govern fairly, and the 'good governance deficit' continues to mount.* Incrementalism and mere tinkering with policy frameworks does not work. A transformational shift is necessary in the way nations are governed.

The Quest for a Truly 'Democratic' Democracy

When the Soviet Union collapsed in 1991 and the Berlin Wall fell in 1989, it was widely accepted that the West had won the Cold War and capitalism had finally defeated communism. In the words of Sami J. Karam, American publisher and author:

> This sweeping statement was only partially true. If one took capitalism and communism as the only two protagonists in the post-World War II struggle, it was easy to see that the latter had suffered a mortal blow. But there was a third, stealthier protagonist situated between them—a system best identified today as cronyism. Even if capitalism did win over the other two contenders in 1991, its victory was short-lived. In the years that followed, it is cronyism that captured an ever-increasing share of economic activity. The distribution of power and money around the world makes it amply clear: cronyism, not capitalism, has ultimately prevailed.[16]

Cronyism is a partnership of convenience; a collusion between business elites, government officials and regulators with the specific intention to confer unwarranted or unjustifiable benefits on private entities at the expense of public interest. This is usually done surreptitiously through preferred treatment in awarding government contracts, hidden incentives or higher tariffs, and often blatantly through policy formulations that make competitors irrelevant. This collusion makes a mockery of both democracy in government and competition in business, and has detrimental short-term and long-term effects.

After 1991, there was widespread expectation that capitalism would bring about the long-promised prosperity for the masses but capitalism did not live up to its promise. The real issue has not really been capitalism versus the socialist market economy; it has been more about ensuring that governments, in at least the constitutional democracies, actually function democratically. In a clearly elitist quest for the rights of the few, we have let a nexus of the well-off hijack virtually all norms of democratic functioning.

Whatever the prognosis, people have been raising fundamental questions: Can capitalism survive? Is the capitalism that has evolved a product of democracy as it has evolved? The question then becomes: 'Can true democracy be revived?'

> How can we rediscover the fundamental tenets of democracy to seek a transition to 'democracy as it should be'—for the people, not merely of the people and by the people. The latter two characteristics can never be sufficient conditions for a truly 'democratic' democracy.

This is the broad framework issue that the book addresses.

Is Responsible Leadership a Mirage?

We all live under the same sky but each of us has a different view of the horizon. Some of us may have a wide, broad view while others have a narrow, partial view. Some are conscious that the view they have is, at best, limited while quite a few assume, with characteristic over-confidence, that they have the entire view.

In all this viewership, an important aspect often gets neglected. What is the lens through which one is looking at the world? We are not referring to a Western perspective or an Oriental standpoint. It is not even a question of whether it is an elitist view or a bottom-of-the-pyramid perspective. The vital concern is whether the view is taken from the standpoint of one who is seeking personal gain or whether it is a holistic view aimed at addressing societal concerns.

There is a widespread public perception that those who lead belong to a self-centred, closed-circle, highly networked strata of global society who tend to think alike, irrespective of the country they live in and regardless of their own background. It is as if this is an essential pre-condition to join this small, exclusive decision-making group in the world that openly proclaims: conform or quit.

It could be argued that this is not entirely true. Indeed, there are quite a few exceptions. Regardless, what can no longer be ignored is that the chasm between the well-to-do and the rest has grown unremittingly, and the gap between 'what is' and 'what could be', or 'what should be' continues to become larger. There is a widespread cognizance of this gulf and yet no sincere attempt has been made to foster worldviews that could catalyse shared, corrective actions.

Noticeably, most of the leaders who have led us in the last few decades were unable to align themselves with societal expectations. They promised but barely delivered. They sought power and fought for it but, after securing power, displayed little responsibility or accountability. Barring a few individual exceptions, they collectively failed in country after country. Responsible leadership has become a mirage.

The dominance of the role of the corporation is incontestably perceived as a major handicap in transitioning to a better world. To shift from 'shareholder primacy' to 'planetary primacy', part-time 'corporate social responsibility' (CSR) must give way to 'socially responsible corporations' (SRC)—a shift from CSR to SRC.

A New Magna Carta—A Global Charter of People's Rights

This book identifies discernible signals that humankind has taken the first decisive steps in changing the course of future history. It is a call to create a new Magna Carta, a new Global Charter of People's Rights that will need to be enshrined as a non-alterable and inflexible component of every constitution in the world—a 21st century enunciation of how citizens hereafter will demand to be governed. Those in power may just have two choices:

- Willingly and transparently initiate serious work for improving the lives of the less well-off and create new benchmarks of inclusive development; or
- Be prepared for an unpalatable or even unthinkable fate.

There is a small time-framework for the heads of states—both democratically elected or heading dictatorial regimes—to voluntarily change course before the people they lead force them to do so. This book attempts to carve a new path and portray the constituents of a new policy framework. It explores in depth what the leaders today can do, without losing power, and how they could do it.

I do not believe that our collective wisdom will be incapable of finding solutions to the persistent problems that plague us. There is adequate knowledge to articulate what needs to be done, but the enduring reluctance of leaders to take the requisite actions is the root cause of the continued malaise. This will not last long. The leaders who wish to remain in power must volunteer to transcend from a state of indifference to a state of concern, with a commitment to implementing workable solutions. As they do so, they will be surprised to see how the future unfolds, not only for themselves but for all of humankind. By leading this transformation, they will become the proud pioneers in a global turn-around story; generating better lives and livelihoods, and shared, collective human happiness.

Quintessence of the Book

This book identifies the simultaneous emergence of two interrelated and interdependent phenomena. The first is the transition from the Knowledge Economy to the Wisdom Economy which, in its wake, is prompting a multitude of fundamental changes in how we govern and how we are governed. This triggers the second phenomenon, the *initiation of the pioneering concept of 'Peopleism'*, a system of governance that sensitively collates and meets the collective aspirations of all citizens, within sustainable resource parameters.

This book spawns a 'think-reflect-do' agenda to reorganize and synergize our collective, unused potential. 'One could be a pessimist by dint of reason or an optimist by force of will.'[17] Our endeavour is to choose a path from the perspective of a pragmatic 'possibilist' and a realist. The present reality is not being ignored; the focus is on visualizing a better reality than we have today.

It is an invitation to all leaders, and to all citizens who think they deserve better leaders, to join this quest—not just to imagine the future we yearn for, but also to create a path to get there. It is not about fantasizing a utopian world; it is about gathering courage and conviction and working relentlessly to mould our destiny into the shape we want. It is about not letting our future cave in under the legacy of history or the tyranny of custom. It is entirely up to us, people all over the world, to choose to ignore the possibilities or actually make it happen. But let us remember that while it may not matter as much to us, it will matter a lot to the coming generations.

Undeniably, we are all strangers to our future, more so now as we enter a new era when the forces of change are gathering momentum against the forces of status quo at an unprecedented pace.

This book identifies multiple silver linings that while we transition to a new future, we have, for the first time, the means to be consciously cognizant of many favourable scenarios that could emerge. Let us choose a scenario we really crave for and happily transition to the 'Safe New World', where *every person matters*. It is, after all, our future. The future of our children and grandchildren.

Author's Note:

This book uses the terms *he*, *she*, and *they* as well as *his*, *her*, and *their* interchangeably—to reflect inclusion of all genders.

PART ONE

Facing Reality

Outlining a Vision

Chapter 1

Paucity of Responsible Leadership

The State of Our World Today

To lead people, you have to understand them.
To understand them, you have to be close to them.
To be close to them, you have to love them.
If you don't love them, you cannot lead.

—Mother Teresa (1910–1997)[1]

Civilization: A Story of Human Progress

The history of civilization is the history of the unfolding of human progress; the story of bridging the chasm between what we are and what we can be. It is the story of human achievement and also the story of human folly. Planet Earth, as we know it today, comprises eight billion people living in 196 sovereign states. For centuries, all activities and efforts of individuals, institutions, corporations, governments and inter-government organizations have been aimed at making 'progress'.

What Do We Mean by Progress?

I look upon progress as a civilizational advance that leads to a tangible and sustainable improvement in the lives of a vast majority of people living in a particular community or nation. In today's context, this would refer to the whole world. Fundamentally, it implies an improvement in key measurable indices such as education, health, livelihoods and quality of life in a society that offers all individuals complete freedom to achieve their aspirations, as long as they are in sync with societal norms and they respect nature. This can happen only when there is a dominant preponderance of integrity, a culture of transparency, and an incorruptible system that ensures justice for all.

There are also other dimensions of progress rooted in one's faith or traditions. Sustainable progress is contingent on mutual trust and respect for diversity of all kinds. Progress is multidimensional. You feel it more than you see it. Progress is a consequence of change, but every change does not guarantee progress.

Progress is a trajectory. An upward trajectory is easily sensed because it makes each tomorrow better for a large majority. But the trajectory does not always go up, it also goes down. When it does so, it is no longer progress as it results in stagnation or the deterioration of lives and livelihoods.

When we take a wide overview across millennia and compare our chaotic, frenzied existence today with the ignorance, brutality and diseases suffered by ancient people, we have reason to be quite satisfied. However, while the averages seem very attractive, the lowest rungs of our society are still only marginally better than those people millennia ago.

While no one should denigrate or dilute the achievements of the human race over the millennia, a sensitive mind is understandably concerned about whether the direction of our progress is good enough, whether it is holistic enough, whether it is as inclusive as it can be.

The Role of Leadership in Our Lives

All of us, everywhere, are primarily a product of the collective leadership that directly or indirectly influences who we are, what we have become and what we can be. The policies and frameworks put in place by the collective leadership, and the mechanisms to implement them, largely determine how different entities and nations are stacked on the progress index over the centuries. It is important, therefore, to have a clear understanding of the role of leadership in determining our future.

Many experts tend to make the art and craft of leadership sound easier than it is in practice. Typically, they fail to take cognizance of the multitude of powerful forces, often conflicting with one another, that leaders have to contend with all the time. While 'win-win' outcomes are most desirable, the pressures of lobbies and personal agendas often lead to painful 'win-lose' choices.

The world often resists real change and resists it hard. The lives of great leaders confirm Machiavelli's observation that, 'Nothing is more dangerous or difficult than introducing a new order of things.'[2] The photographs of Abraham Lincoln in his final years depict the toil and pain etched into his face. 'Lincoln cared deeply and the price he paid was high. But leaders working far from history's grand stage have the same burden. Their aims may be more modest, but so are their means, so they often have to fight very hard for what they care about.'[3] This is a key operating attribute of leaders: 'what they care about'.

However, traditional leadership literature tends to focus on leadership attributes in myriad ways, such as leadership guided by one's vision, leadership focused on achieving articulated goals, leadership to create motivated teams, leadership to generate a culture of perpetual innovation, leadership to foster equity and justice, leadership to create first-rate new leaders, and so forth. There is also an emphasis on the leader's accountability for the tasks he sets for himself.

Despite all this, the rankings of national or corporate leaders do not take these attributes into account, they are primarily based on empirical criteria expressed in percentages—most of them money indices measured in gross terms—with relatively scant regard, at least until recently, for equitability or fairness.

In the post-Second World War period, spanning almost eight decades, many parts of the world grew up in an era of eternal hope, abundant optimism, and the confidence that we all control our own destiny. Today, no matter where we live, we feel enveloped in a fog of complexity and are tossed around by the winds of uncertainty. We are driving, but our windshield is muddy. It appears we have more misgivings about the next few years than those felt by any human generation before us. Have our leaders let us down? Is it true that most of them don't really care about us? If so, why is that?

I could identify three relevant clues in historian and thought leader Yuval Noah Harari's analysis of the present times:[4]

- Liberal thought flourished on the basis that human beings are rational individuals, democracy was founded on the idea that the voter knows best, free market capitalism believed that the customer is always right, and liberal education was meant to teach students to think for themselves. All these hypotheses are no longer valid.
- Individuals in general and leaders in particular do not realize that they actually know far less than they think they know. We rely on the expertise of others for all our needs. We treat knowledge in the minds of others as if it were our own. Cognitive scientists Steven Sloman and Philip Fernbach call this 'knowledge illusion'.[5]
- Most people tend to be locked up in the echo chambers of like-minded friends and self-confirming news-feeds from social media where their beliefs are constantly reinforced and seldom challenged.

We take collective solace by saying that unthinkable events are the new norm. It does not even occur to us that these developments are unthinkable only in our 'knowledge illusion'. Our views are shaped by our 'communal groupthink'.

The thinker Nassim Nicholas Taleb introduced the term 'black swan events' for high-profile, hard-to-predict, rare events that are beyond the realm of normal expectations.[6] We must acknowledge that Covid was not a black-swan event. We knew that a coronavirus pandemic was imminent. Epidemiologists had been cautioning about such a pandemic since 2003, and a coronavirus detection technology was patented in the US in 2006, but most of us chose to disregard the signs.[7]

It is our reaction to the pandemic that had more of the black-swan characteristics. We panicked and over-reacted on the need to take short-term steps and under-reacted on vital long-term measures. We kept people in the dark by denying the equally severe outcome of Covid, long after initial cure, now referred to as Long Covid (or post-acute Covid syndrome). This has put at risk the health of surviving generations all over the world. It is estimated that as many as 17 per cent of patients who get Covid go on to develop post-acute Covid syndrome.[8]

As far as climate change is concerned, we had dire warnings as early as 1988.[9] But most of us ignored them and now we continue to ignore their impact. *To choose to be ignorant is never bliss. It is an invitation to bring forward an imminent calamity.*

Could better leadership have avoided some of the hardships we faced and the threats we encounter today? This is not to apportion blame or point fingers but to ensure that we now choose a path that never lets our leaders lower the trajectory of our progress hereafter. This decade offers us a once-in-many-lifetimes opportunity to reshape our destiny; an opportunity to completely transform ourselves, our families, our communities, and help evolve a new thought process in all those who lead us.

The Future of Democracy

Many of us rejoiced in the latter years of the 20th century when the Berlin Wall fell, the Soviet Empire fragmented, and capitalism defeated communism. Much to our dismay, capitalism is now well on track to defeat democracy.

David Runciman, professor at Cambridge University, urges in his book *How Democracy Ends* that we better take seriously the idea that democracy may come to an end at some point.[10] According to him, this is not pessimism, it is realism. He argues that:

> The beginning of the 21st century is a lot like the end of the 19th century—financial crisis, technological change, rising inequality and populist revolt. Concentrations of wealth and power have always been a perennial feature of democratic life; what is now different is that even the control of technology is with large dominant entities. Complex problems demand technical solutions. But powerful, international elites have scant interest in the concerns of ordinary

> people. The new tech monopolies virtually permeate the whole world and directly and effectively influence most of what we do or don't do, and how we live.

Many elected leaders devalue the virtues of democracy and may continue to do so till it becomes an empty idea.

Runciman provocatively asks: Can you imagine a post-democratic America? It will call itself, he says, 'a democratic country while behaving like a country that doesn't know what it is anymore.' He lays out three possible alternatives to democracy: pragmatic authoritarianism (China-ish), epistocracy (rule by enlightened elites) or 'liberated technology' (hail, robot overlords).[11]

None of these options holds any appeal. This book is an endeavour to look for other acceptable and feasible alternatives before it is too late for us, the residents of this planet, to get our leaders to reinvent how they lead.

The Impact of Wealth Concentration

Pope Francis has repeatedly warned that, 'Terrorism grows when there is no other option, and (will do so) as long as the world economy has at its centre the god of money and not the person. This is fundamental terrorism against all humanity. And as long as inequality grows, so does the political influence of the rich.'[12]

The evidence that concentrated wealth contributes to concentrated power suggests that reducing inequality becomes more challenging even as it becomes more urgent. A vicious cycle of rising disparities has taken deep roots across the world; this is not what one would expect of enlightened, democratic leadership.

Across most of human history, one comes across a recurring theme that the masses in every age have no choice but to meekly accept the whims and oppression of the rulers, irrespective of whether it is a democratic system or an autocratic regime. Inequality is the 'default consequence' of the actions of most governments. Barring very few exceptions, benevolent rule has remained an eternal mirage.

Logically, in at least the democratic countries, one assumes that the rich and the well-to-do cannot be so powerful that they can perpetuate their rule. They should be easily outvoted by the victimized majorities that are frustrated with them. Yet this does not happen. Quite naturally, the current democratic system defies solutions. The rulers do not even look upon inequality as a problem. Poverty is a problem, yes, but inequality seems acceptable to them because they feel fully entitled to the wealth they have amassed. They ignore the fact that accumulation would not have been possible without the laws and regulations specially crafted by the state.

The 21st century has irrevocably changed our world, continuously altering how we live on almost every level except democratic politics. It remains impervious to change. However, it is now all set for a makeover.

Multiple Existential Threats

A recent report by the U.S. National Intelligence Council notes:

> Runaway artificial intelligence, engineered pandemics, nanotechnology weapons, and nuclear war, [are] four key sources of existential risks—threats that could damage life on a global scale and challenge our ability to imagine and comprehend their potential scope and scale. Dual-use medical research could, in principle, be employed to identify or create pathogens that are more transmissible and lethal than anything in nature. Unlike nuclear weapons, bacteria and viruses are self-replicating. Once a new pathogen has infected a single human being, there may be no way to put the genie back in the bottle.[13]

Apart from that, we continue to be increasingly vulnerable to four other equally grave challenges—climate change and ecosystem collapse, an exclusionary global financial system, inequality and the absence of good governance. Any one of these eight threats is enough to create unprecedented risks and unfathomable hazards.

It suddenly dawned on us in 2020 that new potential epidemics, coupled with the incalculable collateral damage, could perhaps be the deadliest of all for the simple reason that the human race is least prepared to cope with them. In reality, we are equally unprepared to deal with any of the other threats as well.

Political leadership in every country spends a lot of energy in building capabilities to ensure that it can handle any external aggression or internal insurrection. It fails to realize that political risk is no longer limited to external hostilities or internal uprising; it can emerge from any of the threats mentioned above, in any part of the world, and with the inexorable ferocity of a tsunami or an earthquake.

It is also abundantly clear that the abuse of nature or eco-balance can lead to calamities no one may be able to control. And yet, both national governments and international organizations are repeatedly caught unawares. Inexplicably, they spend far more resources and funds on disaster mitigation than on disaster prevention which would cost much less.

The Silent Majority Unearths a Shared Unity

The forgotten victims of the global operating systems comprise the large majority that could not become a part of mainstream prosperity. These people are no longer willing to accept inequality as their destiny. Many of them all over the world are increasingly discovering a common bond that extends to all sections of societies, except the elite, and is fueled by disgust towards the continuation of pro-rich policies and rampant corruption everywhere, be it in politics, business or sports. They are being united by new forces at play: a knowledge-based civil society, instant connectivity, and a youth that is apprehensive about its future.

For decades, many democratically elected leaders as well as most dictatorial regimes have been united in pursuing virtually similar policies in their single-minded mission to foster GDP growth in their respective countries. It never mattered if most of the growth was confined to the top 10 per cent of the population. Recent protests and trends in voting behaviours in many parts of the world are unmistakably a revolt against 'a government of the elite, by the elite and for the elite'.

What we hear today is a clarion call to wake the ruling elites from their political complacency and remind them unambiguously that while their prosperity has continued unabated even beyond the global financial crisis of 2008, the less-fortunate citizens in their countries still face harsh times. Those grappling with the tough realities of life are not looking at ideas of 'left versus right' or the nuances of geopolitical equations. They are seeking a departure from the conformist, predictable political and economic ideologies that are no longer relevant. The silent majority is beginning to speak up.

Even those who were a little more tolerant or indifferent to their own misery till now have learnt from the Covid fallout that the design of the financial stimulus and the urgency to get economies back on track in 2020 ensured that the better-off were back to normal sooner than those who were rendered jobless and moneyless, one more time. The issue now is not if the leaders will wake up tomorrow and do something to correct this course. It is more likely that they will themselves discover that it could be perilous for them to ignore these signals.

Three Preambles of the New Reality

I sense three emerging preambles that are shaping a new Global Charter of People's Rights. Leaders who can understand and enthusiastically accept and embrace the new ground realities will still have a good chance of continuing to remain in power.

> PREAMBLE ONE
>
> People all over the world have more that unites them than divides them.

They all cherish an equitable society and prefer to live in sync with nature. They all seek 'justice' that encompasses four inviolable attributes:

- Transparent, broadly accepted version of fairness in the way people are dealt with;
- Uniform establishment of the same rights for every human being;
- Equality before the law and equality in access to every opportunity for better lives and livelihoods; and
- Not only public justice, but also justice in private.

In practice, this manifests as social justice, gender justice, racial justice and, above all, a justice that is 'just', a justice with dignity.

PREAMBLE TWO

Lack of equity and not the clash of civilizations is the root cause of most global fractures.

The term 'clash of civilizations' gained recognition when sources of information were scarce and the vast majorities tended to rely on widely disseminated beliefs about their religions and antecedents. Today this 'doctored knowledge' is beginning to be disputed and ideologies are being questioned. The young, the marginalized and the deprived are not interested in debating academic issues, nor the fractured zones of totalitarianism or religious divides. Their concerns are focused on the question of 'opacity versus transparency', 'elitist versus all-inclusive', 'top-down versus bottom-up' and 'authoritarian versus collaborative'. This is a world-wide phenomenon; sadly, the political class is seemingly stuck in a stationary time capsule.

PREAMBLE THREE

The poor in the world will really matter hereafter.

The rich and the powerful cannot continue their hold on power indefinitely. We are beginning to enter an era where those with the voice and the money will have to care for those without. The problems of poverty and inequality can no longer wobble along.

Barring conspicuous exceptions, those in power have been more concerned about retaining their power and have been either unwilling or incapable of making democracy work for every citizen. In most so-called functioning democracies, only a few dozen persons of political pedigree tend to decide who is fit to be fielded as a candidate for election. This has been most noticeable in Asia, Africa and Latin America but also, surprisingly enough, in the US as well. In effect, this has led to 'strongman leadership' in more democracies than ever before and perpetuated high numbers of people with near-criminal antecedents among those elected. These practices have been repeatedly challenged and will no longer be acceptable to the masses.

John Keane, professor at the University of Sydney, puts it across quite explicitly:

> Democracy goes beyond the mathematical certitude of election results and majority rule. It is a whole way of life. It is freedom from hunger, humiliation and violence. Democracy is saying no to every form of human and non-human indignity. It is respect for women and tenderness with children. Democracy is public and private respect for different ways of living. It is humility: The willingness to admit that in the end nobody is invincible, and that ordinary lives are never ordinary. When democracy begins to resemble a fancy mask worn by wealthy political predators, self-government is killed and society is subordinated to the state. People are expected to behave as loyal subjects, or else suffer the consequences. A thoroughly 21st century type of top-down rule called despotism triumphs.[14]

There are enough signs that the new Global Charter of People's Rights will not let this indifference and injustice continue for long.

Shared Responsibility and Shared Power

Many of these issues are now global problems, and the resolution of global problems can only come through 'shared global responsibility' among nation states to evolve a unified global approach. That is possible only if shared responsibility is accompanied by shared power. For national leaders eager to strengthen their hegemony, this is a hard reality to accept because shared power inherently implies surrendering a part of national sovereignty.

The Economist Intelligence Unit's Global Democracy Report classifies 167 nations into four categories: full democracies, flawed democracies, hybrid regimes and authoritarian regimes, based on five parameters—electoral process and pluralism, the functioning of government, political participation, democratic political culture and civil liberties.[15] The findings reveal that more than half the world's population (54 per cent) lives in ninety-nine countries that are authoritarian or hybrid regimes. Forty-six per cent reside in sixty-eight 'so-called' democracies, of which only 6.4 per cent, living in twenty-one countries, enjoy full democracy. It is quite worrisome that as many as fifty-three nations (including Brazil, France, India, Italy, Spain and the US) have been gradually downgraded from 'democracies' to 'flawed democracies' over the last few years.

It is time for the rulers in the 146 nations that are not full democracies to acknowledge that irrespective of whether they are authoritarian rulers or elected leaders that love authoritarianism, their ability to continue in power is contingent only on accepting the principle of 'shared responsibility and shared power', which essentially means embracing three 'shared beliefs and commitments':

- Resolute belief that we now live in a world where each nation is vulnerable to any incident in any part of the world. Irrespective of how efficiently we can scramble national economies back on track, we cannot ignore the fact that no country or a group of countries can hereafter be an island of seclusion. We will either grow together or we will perish together.
- Commitment to an attitude of 'give and take'. Since taking is easier than giving, this basically implies a willingness to give, to sacrifice something, to let go of what you have been holding on to in the larger interest of peace and stability for both, the people within and nations outside.
- Commitment to setting a personal example to nurture a spirit of trust with citizens, and trust among nations; trust that all parties will fully honour all their obligations.

Nations that wish to be the sole hegemon will discover to their peril that the old rules of isolationist leadership may no longer work in the new world. They stand to gain a lot of domestic and overseas prestige if they voluntarily exercise the option to reach out for an understanding with their own people. The immediate dividend will be to make them more acceptable as they seek global collaboration while leading to more sustainable outcomes at home for both themselves as well as for their citizens.

This transformation in the leadership mindset in 21st-century diplomacy can no longer be postponed. The way is already paved for the demise of absolute power as a prelude to shared decision-making processes. Citizens' interests on a global scale, will become the default priority and the paramount focus in the new processes. This is the only practical way forward to reduce the frequency and scale of global disruptions and make it easier for 'global unifiers' to be at the forefront of national and international dialogues.

> The Stone Age did not end because we ran out of stones.
> It ended because we came up with better
> ideas and implemented them.

Fortunately, even today, the world is not short of ideas; it is short of holistic leadership. It is not short of talent; it is short of talent with purpose. It is not short of meaningful discussion; it is short of meaningful action. It would not be prudent to wait for another pandemic, or a Lehmann moment, or the emergence of an organization like the ISIS (Islamic State), or a nuclear disaster, or a tsunami, or another unwarranted attack on a peaceful sovereign state or region, to think about a unified global approach. Leaders must collaborate constructively, motivated by a vision of common good rather than one of common danger.

Beyond Nationalism and Regionalism

Close interactive partnerships can lead to sustainable gains far in excess of the unilateral gains secured by any national display of raw power when exercised on a platform of shared initiatives, shared responsibilities and shared power in an environment of trust, a give-and-take attitude, and an acknowledgement of one's vulnerability in the global context.

The present moment is a timely opportunity to replace the current structure of post-Second World War global institutions with a new post-Covid configuration of global organizations, collectively controlled, with no veto power. Leading nations within the G-20 group are best placed to come forward with new proposals. Of course it is difficult, but here it is relevant to recall economist William

Edwards Deming's words: 'Learning is not compulsory. Neither is survival.'[16]

The good news is that we have a window of opportunity where responsible, conscientious leadership can still prevent further global catastrophes. Political and business leaders need to be cognizant of the new ground truths, not for philanthropy but for sheer survival. There is no alternative to changing course. If we do not, we may be overwhelmed by even more severe and uncontrollable transformational forces. It is time to rise beyond the notions of nationality and regionalism. It is time to reach out to the idea of 'beyond me and my nation'.

Let us make our planet a great place to live
for every individual everywhere.

Reviving Responsible Leadership

A leader is a person whose thoughts, words and decisions to act, or not to act, have a discernible impact on the thoughts, feelings and behaviours of a large number of people around him, as well as on the trajectory of their future lives and livelihoods.[17]

One comes across all kinds of leaders: authentic leaders, autocratic leaders, bureaucratic leaders, charismatic leaders, transactional leaders, transformational leaders, laissez-faire leaders, participative leaders, situational leaders, good leaders, great leaders, and others. Some are quite effective, some are often effective, and some are seldom effective.

We need leaders who can be effective most of the time while ensuring that all the decisions and actions they take have a positive impact on the lives and livelihoods of all citizens and stakeholders, not temporarily, but sustainably. This is a key feature of responsible leadership.

Responsible leadership is not just being held responsible for what we do, but also for what we do not do; being held responsible for not just what we say, but also for what we do not say.

A responsible leader leads and works with both implicit and explicit transparency; transparency not merely of her actions but also of her thoughts, transparency not just in chosen domains, but complete, total transparency.

One cannot be a responsible leader partially. Either you are one or you are not. In practice, a responsible leader's sense of responsibility is mirrored in her ability to undertake all tasks with sensitivity, understanding and commitment, with implicit acceptance of personal accountability for everything she does or does not do. Essentially, this 'ability to respond responsibly' stems from the DNA of one's character. It is about winning the trust and respect of others and that happens only when a responsible leader perceptibly demonstrates three distinct personal traits:

a) *Capability*: Credible skills to perform and deliver results. If someone is honest and responsible, but unable to lead and perform, no one would trust her at all.
b) *Service above Self*: An ever-present commitment to give priority to the interests of others, rather than one's own.
c) *Integrity*: Keeping the promises you make to yourself, and to others, while ensuring all the time that each promise emanates from deeply cherished values and principles.

Without these three qualities, you can never earn trust. You may earn fear and compliance, but not trust. We are trusted not because of our polished exteriors or our expertly crafted communications, but because of our way of being.

Life is not about having more, but being more. That is why we are called human beings, not human havings.

The sooner societal and business leaders align themselves with people's expectations and imbibe the newly minted contemporary ethos, the easier it will be for them to remain longer in power.

Profile of an Exceptional Leader

Leadership, going forward, will be a totally different ball game. What led to success until now may no longer be relevant. In the turbulent world ahead, multifaceted challenges, new trends, new technologies and unpredictable risks are simultaneously coalescing together. Responsible leaders in the years ahead will need to acquire 'inner agility', an innate ability to respond quickly to changing contexts, the ability to identify and respond to foreseeable problems before they become problems. Inner agility is about readily disrupting one's own thinking well before one is forced to do so.

In practice, inner agility is about 'reinventing oneself as a leader'. This means lifting one's vision to new heights and raising expectations of one's own performance. Inner agility can be acquired, nurtured and sustained, provided one has imbibed four irrefutable insights:

1) No one is infallible, no one can have all the answers. If one needs help, one should seek it, but without pride and arrogance.
2) Past experience and knowledge may not be relevant to cope with the future. One should keep learning as if one will live forever, and live each day as if it is the last day of one's life.
3) The quality of leadership is never static. It either improves or deteriorates every day. If one can look within to discover the infinite potential that lies inside each of us, one will be surprised at the ease with which one can continue to scale new peaks of leadership performance—day after day, year after year.
4) One must seek out a personal North Star, a set of non-negotiable convictions, and embark on a relentless quest within, on 'how I can serve better the people I lead'.

This is the profile of a responsible leader likely to have strong odds to become an exceptional leader, and continue to function as one.

Facing Reality and Reinventing Oneself

I am quite aware that many readers will feel there is virtually no chance that the existing leadership will display a willingness to conform to the new template of a responsible leader. Still, it is my firm belief that a love for power will make leaders do so. Once they start perceiving real threats to their ability to remain in power, they will seriously consider change and do whatever is required.

Leaders in many countries are quite cognizant that they are in power not because they have the support of people but because people are scared of them. It is possible to convert the feelings of fear to feelings of support. It does not require giving up one's leadership stature; it merely calls for making an attempt to align with the aspirations of the ignored and the excluded. The next chapter explains that if one really resolves to do that, it is not difficult.

Chapter 2

Seven Billion Dreams and Aspirations

Aligning with the Ignored and the Excluded

No one is above or below.
It's the injustice governments create that disorders
the world and sets a few above the many below.
The world isn't naturally like this.
The true world, the great mirror of the dream of those who
gave birth to the world, is very big, and everyone is free as a bird.
Right now, the world is flawed.
It doesn't reflect the dream world where the first gods lived.

—Subcomandante Marcos[1]

We the Governed: How Do We Feel?

When children sleep hungry and parents feel helpless
When the young have no jobs and the old no savings
When honesty is punished and the wicked remain free
When poverty endures and the wealthy only grow

When work is not honoured and sloth is treasured
When talent does not count, but mediocrity thrives
When goods are aplenty, but only for the rich
When laws are enforced, but only for the poor

When justice is delayed and equity denied
When freedom is clipped and hope can't fly
When citizens feel trapped and dreams never born
When progress is distant, and all seems lost

Though the sun rises, there is darkness all around
And the moon is forever behind the clouds
In such ominous hours of doom,
There must be some who relate to the gloom

These are the folks that are truly human
Never at ease with the status quo
They feel what others don't
They imagine what others don't

And eager to build bridges
Between the few haves and the many no-haves
They are human in thought and human in speech
They are human in action and human to the core.

But where are they?
Have they the courage to do what others don't?

There are seven billion of us, waiting for such humans to steer our destinies. We live in every nation of the world. The well-off see us but do not really notice us. Occasionally, we appear on magazine covers or in photographic exhibitions but that is more to give awards to the journalists and photographers who expose our conditions. Generally, we are known more for showing up in the statistics.

- 700 million of us, almost 9 per cent of the world's population, live in extreme poverty on less than $2.25 a day, (based on 2017 purchasing power parity). Covid dealt the biggest setback to global poverty-reduction efforts since 1990 and the wars in Sudan, Ukraine and Gaza have made matters worse. Just over half of us live in Sub-Saharan Africa. The world is not likely to meet the global goal of ending extreme poverty by 2030; nearly 600 million people will still be struggling in extreme poverty by then. The outlook is also grim for the nearly 50 per cent of the world's population who live on less than $6.85 a day—the measure used for upper-middle-income countries.[2]

- More than 2 billion of us don't have access to clean water at home. This means that we (mostly women and girls) collectively spend some 200 million hours every day walking long distances to fetch water instead of getting an education.[3]
- About 1.6 billion of us, more than 20 per cent of the world's population, lack adequate housing, of which 1 billion live in urban slums and at least 150 million of us, about 2 per cent of the world's population, are homeless. Yet, around 15 million of us are forcibly evicted from our homes each year.[4]
- The world's richest 1 per cent, those with more than $1 million in assets, own 45.8 per cent of the world's wealth. We, adults with less than $10,000 in wealth, make up 52.5 per cent of the world's population but hold just 1.2 per cent of the global wealth.[5]

Every government, every institution and virtually every transnational entity speaks of us as a key component of the inclusive growth that they are committed to. They show concern and re-emphasize all the time that the prevailing situation is not acceptable. Whenever there is even a marginal improvement in just one of the many indices, that becomes a cause for global celebration and self-laudatory accolades and press conferences. We, however, are seldom a part of the celebrations, and rightly so, as we are never involved in the process anyway and seldom asked if there indeed has been a positive change in our ground realities.

What Are the Ground Realities?

Here are a few illustrations of the four Ds that pervade our lives—deficiency, deprivation, dispossession and denial.

- Forty-two of the fifty-four African countries are in poverty. Twenty-seven of the world's twenty-eight poorest countries are in Sub-Saharan Africa; 440 million people live in poverty there. 256 million Africans sleep hungry every day.[6]
- Multidimensional poverty encompasses multiple deprivations, other than income, experienced by poor people—lack of

education, poor health, inadequate living standards, disempowerment, poor quality of work, the threat of violence, and living in environmentally hazardous areas, among others. As per the Multidimensional Poverty Index (MPI) Report, 1.1 billion people across 110 countries live in acute multidimensional poverty.[7] Sub-Saharan Africa (534 million) and South Asia (389 million) are home to approximately five out of every six people living in poverty.[8] 566 million (about half) are children under eighteen years of age.[9]

- 9.2 per cent of the world's population—735 million in 2021—were affected by hunger, an increase of 122 million since 2019.[10] More than 3.1 billion people could not afford a healthy diet in 2021, causing deep concerns about the future of the state of global health.[11] Malnutrition is a major threat to children's survival, growth and development.[12]
- On any single night in the US, in 2022, 552,000 people experienced homelessness across the nation, which is equivalent to about seventeen out of every 10,000 people (0.2 per cent of the American population). Six of the ten people experiencing homelessness (61 per cent), were staying in sheltered locations, and nearly four in ten (39 per cent) were unsheltered. About 13,000 of these homeless people die every year.[13]
- In 2021, 95.4 million people in the EU, representing 21.7 per cent of the population, were at risk of poverty or social exclusion, i.e. lived in households experiencing at least one of the three poverty and social exclusion risks (risk of poverty, severe material and social deprivation and/or living in a household with very low work intensity).[14]
- Farmer suicides underscore the continuing agrarian crisis in India. The figure reached a six-year high of 11,290 in 2022, when fifteen farmers and fifteen farm labourers died by suicide every day, according to a report by the National Crime Records Bureau of India.[15] The reasons why farmers commit suicide have remained unchanged over the decades: floods, drought, debt, use of genetically modified seeds, poor health, use of lower quality pesticides, low produce prices and epidemics.

Four Shades of Human Misery—All Dark

- *Dark Red*—victims of violence: lack of human rights.
- *Dark Blue*—alive but no quality of life: poor health, poor hygiene, sub-par housing.
- *Dark Grey*—scarce opportunities to acquire education, skills and jobs: no hope, no future.
- *Dark Black*—apartheid against the poor (certainly in spirit) continues even to this day, even in societies where it is constitutionally illegal.

Denial of these basic necessities and rights to the poor is not an accident of history, nor a mistake stemming from ignorance; it is the consequence of purposeful policies aimed at ensuring that the demands of the deprived are limited to minimal basic needs so that they do not cross the threshold of fundamental freedoms en masse.

Except for a few honourable mentions, leadership in several countries is perceived as being morally bankrupt; not because the citizens of these countries are so but because the functioning of democracy has been effectively hijacked by elitist leaders. Colonialism is history but the existing rulers in many countries—whether democratically elected or autocrats—continue to act as if they are the new colonial masters: neither accountable nor responsible to citizens.

A large segment of the media also becomes an unwitting collaborator of the self-styled 'home-grown colonial masters'. Excluding a handful of cases, neither television nor the print media takes forward the people's struggles. Most of the time, they focus on relatively insignificant matters or happenings that took place last evening or this morning, thereby limiting the debate to marginal issues of the day rather than portraying the agony of the vast majority on a host of diverse issues.

The global elite is blissfully oblivious in their sheltered world because the status quo is tilted in their favour. They are safely insulated from the bleak realities tormenting the less fortunate. Such injustice cannot be a part of the planet we want. In effect, the global elite has let the world down.

The business-politics nexus has succeeded in formalizing political processes and institutions that enable them to callously pursue policy frameworks to extract income and wealth from large sections of society to benefit a select few. The net result is that those in power do not represent the people they are supposed to represent. De facto, across the board, politicians brazenly abuse the power entrusted to them.

The Entire Societal Pyramid Is Inverted

- Globally, the effective income tax rates the richest people pay are much lower than those for the middle class. A big chunk of the earnings of the rich—the income from corporate dividends and capital gains—is either tax-free or taxed at a very low rate. Increases in asset valuations are taxed only if the assets are sold. However, they can easily avoid that as well by transferring their assets to their heirs, fully circumventing situations which could increase their tax burden. A study conclusively showed that a median American household earning about $70,000 annually paid 14 per cent in federal taxes and, as the earnings increased to $628,300, the income tax rate inched up to 37 per cent.[16] In contrast, the richest twenty-five Americans whose collective worth rose by $401 billion from 2014 to 2018, paid a total of $13.6 billion in income tax during those five years, equivalent to a tax rate of only 3.4 per cent.[17]
- The rich pay low interest rates on hefty borrowings, the poor pay hefty interest rates (two to four times) on micro-finance borrowings.[18]
- A major portion of a government's expenditure is allocated to perpetuating and preserving the lifestyle of the rich; money spent on the poor is classified as social-sector spending and is the first to be cut whenever governments face a financial crunch.
- Pride in proclaiming the success of 'trickle-down capitalism' implicitly acknowledges that, at best, wealth will travel down in a trickle while the flood of wealth stays at the top.
- Real concerns for the 99 per cent receive only 1 per cent attention from the 1 per cent elite.

The continuation of such deliberate indifference and blatant disregard for a large majority of people is patently indefensible.

Why Is Bad Governance the Norm?

> We the governed, the masses, are often perplexed why we are generally governed by people who are either unwilling or unable to understand the simple aspirations, the normal needs and the ordinary legitimate demands of ordinary people.

One could possibly understand such a lack of concern for the masses in dictatorial monarchies or totalitarian regimes. But how does one explain this in an ostensibly democratic society? The leaders in a functioning democracy are elected by the masses and yet the masses in all democratic countries are frustrated by the continued apathy and disinterestedness of their own elected leaders.

- Is it because the two-party political system (or even the multiple-party system in certain countries) unequivocally directs each elected representative to virtually stop applying his mind on any of the legislative issues and just toe the party line?
- Or is it because each electoral candidate is primarily financed by his or her political party and therefore has no option but to follow the diktats of the party leadership?
- Does that mean that the leaders of the political party (known as 'coterie' in certain countries) function as dictators and decide the position the entire party should take on every issue, irrespective of the views and interests of the people they represent and in total disregard of their constitutional responsibility to act for the larger good?
- Is this the outcome of capitalism and democracy working together? If so, does the blame rest entirely with capitalism, as it has evolved? Is the entire system of capitalism at fault or is it only certain types of capitalists who have given capitalism a bad name?

- Will reforming the excesses of capitalism and fault lines of democracy be enough or do we need to discover and evolve a new economic ideology and a new governing system?

These are the serious issues bothering millions of people on our planet. The youth and workers in every profession in most countries are angry and frustrated with the state of affairs. They wish to know why their lot, even after years of drudgery and hard work, has not perceptibly improved while the well-off appear to become better off every day. What is their crime other than that they were born poor?

On my lecture tours encompassing several countries, young students, middle-class housewives, shopkeepers, teachers, taxi-drivers, small businessmen and middle-level industrialists bombard me with penetrating questions related to these aspects. Is this a short-term aberration or has it become the established norm? Now that it is alarmingly perceptible, will our leaders become more caring rather than continue to be heartless partisans?

We live in an era of extreme emotional intensity. Decision-makers and those who have access to the ears of decision-makers tend to hold extreme views only to protect and perpetuate their power. They treat evidence that does not support their view with disdain and dismiss it as irrelevant.

The political skill of compromise and finding the middle ground, one that would be acceptable to a large majority of reasonable, thinking people, is no longer on anyone's agenda.

Capitalism: A System with Fatal Flaws

Jerry Mander, activist and author, describes capitalism as an obsolete system with several fatal flaws and asks:

> Why do very rich people want to be richer? What's the appeal of accumulating more wealth than can ever be used for personal or family purposes? Laissez-faire, the key precept of capitalism, has virtually become an economic strategy with only one purpose—to accumulate ever-expanding wealth for its owners by whatever means it can, including eliminating jobs and worker benefits, depressing wages, evading taxes, denying health insurance claims,

> and pillaging the retirement accounts of the elderly. Capitalism's greatest achievement is clearly in the area of wealth creation for a small minority of the population.[19]

The resultant inequality, in virtually every country in the world, stares us in the face all the time. Those who can do something about it intend to do nothing as the rest of the world watches helplessly.

In the US—the most unequal of the rich countries—wealth and income inequality has been soaring over the last forty years and is now approaching levels that prevailed prior to the Great Depression. America's high inequality primarily reflects the emergence of 'super-salaries', with the lion's share of income gains going to people at the very top. Economist Thomas Piketty, author of *Capital in the Twenty-First Century,* believes there is no natural tendency for inequality to decline when a country reaches economic maturity. Rather, he argues, 'increasing inequality is the natural state of a capitalist economy'.[20]

Factors That Perpetuate Bad Governance

Two well-entrenched tectonic ruptures continue to make a charade of good governance all over the world:

1) Crony capitalism has become a generator of unjust wealth, exploiting many and making wealth the only currency of life. The birth of the US was itself the outcome of a rebellion against the British corporations which had been deployed as instruments of abusive power by the British monarchy. But soon after the new nation was formed, American corporations also started calling the shots. Abraham Lincoln warned in 1864, shortly before his death, that, 'Corporations have been enthroned. An era of corruption in high places will follow and the money power will endeavour to prolong its reign by working on the prejudices of the people until wealth is aggregated in a few hands and the republic is destroyed.'[21]

   Rutherford Hayes, the nineteenth president of the US declared in utter disgust in 1876, 'This is a government of the people, by the people and for the people no longer. It is a government of corporations, by corporations, and for corporations.'[22]

President Theodore Roosevelt put it across even more bluntly in 1912, 'Political parties exist to secure responsible government and to execute the will of the people. Instead of instruments to promote the general welfare they have become the tools of corrupt interests...Behind the ostensible government sits enthroned an invisible government owing no allegiance and acknowledging no responsibility to the people. To destroy this invisible government, to dissolve the unholy alliance between corrupt business and corrupt politics, is the first task of the statesmanship of the day.'[23]

The virus of this collusion between industry and government has become the norm almost all over the world.

2) Those who acquire wealth and power also take over, by default, the custodianship of superior intellect—a phenomenon that has created distressing results by discouraging alternative thinking. In effect, this has led to the classification of all voices that speak against the prevalent system as merely misinformed dissent; those in power refer to them as anti-national and unpatriotic.

Put together, these deep-rooted practices supported by the elite have subverted our democratic system so badly that it is now just a democratic facade built on the foundations of human greed and infatuation with power. The key question is whether we can foresee a self-induced, miraculous swing in political and business realms. Or will change be prompted only by a spate of massive peoples' uprisings?

Governance through the Ages

Until the 16th century, bad governance was the prevailing norm. Good governance was scarce, discernible only when a ruler became benevolent of his own volition. Starting with King Ashoka in India (304–232 BCE), there were brief interludes in many nations when leaders ruled with benevolence and compassion. According to some historical accounts, Marcus Aurelius in the Roman Empire (2nd century CE), Emperor Kangxi of Qing Dynasty, China (17th century), Emperor Meiji (Mutsuhito) in Japan (18th and 19th centuries) and Mustafa Kemal Ataturk in Turkey (20th century), showed benevolent traits. They earned the people's respect and admiration and were considered kind and compassionate by a majority of the citizens.

In the 16th century, protest became a vehicle to seek better governance. The weapon of protest was born in Europe, made possible by the advance of science and technology. Peoples' protests eventually led to the Reformation in Europe (1517–1648), the Glorious Revolution in Britain (1688), the French Revolution (1789), and the American Revolution (1776). Protests in China were always thwarted, as they are even today. Japanese culture somehow abhorred protest and quietly followed the trends elsewhere.

Till the 20th century, most protests tended to be violent; it all changed when Mahatma Gandhi introduced non-violent protest. India and many other countries were re-born out of protest to end colonialism. Most of them are still discovering that it was just the starting point; the protests must continue to secure good governance from their new 'home-grown rulers'. Increasingly, even in many democratic countries, protests are dealt with as ruthlessly as they were in colonial times.

Mahatma Gandhi's message was emulated by Martin Luther King Jr. and Nelson Mandela. In the recent past, it became institutionalized as societal protest. Somehow, in Tunisia, Egypt and Syria, these led to only short-term successes; the script did not play out as envisaged.

Only short periods in certain nations have experienced good governance. But such periods did not last long because the rulers and leaders practicing good governance were usually succeeded by those who preferred to revert to greed and short-term populism. The hope of the masses that sincere dialogue would prevail over persecution never materialized, and yet the citizens continued to seek good governance even though most of the earlier attempts had failed. While the events of history may not give one confidence that the governance deficit can be sustainably bridged and a liberal, democratic, society created, I believe that the forces of transformation are only getting stronger and we are entering a new phase of human enterprise where rulers and leaders will be compelled to change.

In Sri Lanka, countrywide protests against gross economic mismanagement in 2022 led to the resignation of the prime minister. In Kazakhstan, after more than 200 people were killed during protests over fuel price rises in 2022, the government had to reverse the decision and resign. Increasingly, it is now the norm for people to protest out of necessity, even in the countries where fundamental freedoms are repressed and state violence is customary.

Transition to Good Governance

I discern four social forces that are rapidly catalysing and accelerating transition to good governance.

- *Knowledge-based civil society*, driven by enlightened and concerned citizens, is effectively prodding this transformation. Some of these NGOs (Non-government Organizations) have impeccable credentials and a set-in-stone sense of ethics. They have taken on the role of *progress accelerators*. I refer to them as the 'Institutions to Promote Consciousness'—IPCs.
- *Youth movements* that challenge the might of powerful governments are now progressively more widespread. 2.43 billion millennials (those born between 1981–1996) and 2.47 billion Generation Z (those born between 1997–2012), 4.9 billion of them together, supported by 24/7 social networking and cyber media tools, are deeply frustrated with political manipulations that tend to preclude their interests. They are no longer willing to accept their continued neglect as a fait accompli. Their technology-aided protests have now acquired the confidence and the capability to change the narrative, and it is becoming increasingly difficult to ignore them.

  Climate activist Greta Thunberg's 'Fridays for Future', a sit-down protest against the lack of action on the climate crisis, became an international movement with dramatic results. The Iranian women's movement in 2022 against the hijab was triggered by the custodial death of twenty-two-year-old Mahsa Amini, who was arrested for allegedly wearing her headscarf improperly. Though the regime has come down ruthlessly against protestors, the protest will not just wither away; the embers will remain warm.

The Yellow Vest protests in France initially erupted in 2018 because of inequitable taxation but gradually became a political movement for social change. As we observed in Zimbabwe, Egypt, Haiti, Columbia, Brazil, China, Germany, India, Indonesia, the Netherlands, U.K., the US, and over fifty other countries during the last three years, while the protests are triggered by a grudge against a draconian law, or the revelation of gross injustice, the real driver behind the protests is invariably the neglect of long-festering issues.

Time and again, people have expressed their wish for more democracy, in Lebanon and Thailand, Bolivia and Guinea, Hong Kong and Sudan, Turkey, Russia and Belarus. The international non-profit Civicus, which works in the area of citizen action, says, 'All of these protests carried the conviction that democracy requires free and fair electoral competition, the availability of genuine alternatives, respect for minority and dissenting opinions and the opportunity to debate a range of viewpoints before reaching informed decisions.'[24]

Populist movements around the world may disagree on the details but are united around one big idea: The political and economic elites running or influencing the governments are very powerful people who know exactly what they are doing, and are doing it on purpose. Most of what they do is often indefensible, greedy and exploitative.

There were successful mobilizations to defend democracy in the Czech Republic and Slovenia, where people voted out political leaders who fostered divisiveness in favour of broad-based alternatives. Progressive leaders promising to advance social justice also won power in Chile and Honduras.[25]

- *Enlightened stakeholders* such as employees, customers, investors and affected communities are becoming more active in determining whether the corporations and the institutions they are associated with are operating within acceptable ethical norms. With all the forces of social media at command, it is surprising that so little has been achieved. But this is now set to change. With the end of secrecy and the virtual end of privacy, misdeeds can no longer be concealed from public scrutiny.

In July 2021, an investigation revealed that an Israel-based surveillance firm, NSO Group, had been allegedly selling Pegasus, a spyware tool, to many governments. Pegasus was being used to target political dissidents, journalists and human rights activists. A number of repressive authoritarian regimes are reported to be customers. The spyware is so sophisticated that it can defeat encryption and security protocols in all cell phones to remotely gain control over the device and access a wide range of data, including geo-locational information, browser history, text messages, voicemails and cameras. There has been such uproar in the countries named in the report that a stream of multiple enquiries is underway.[26]

- *Women are beginning to play a greater role* in societal governance than ever before. It is their innate nature to care and to share, and they instinctively know that love and understanding triumph when everything else fails. They network better and they nurture creativity. As we see more of them as community leaders, politicians, entrepreneurs, educators and role models, they are likely to be effective catalysts in bridging the governance deficit, and provide momentum to the journey towards an equitable, sustainable world.

No One Can Deny Us the Future We Deserve

It is quite normal for everyone to dream about and hope for substantive progress in their lives. The onus rests with the people of each community and each nation to demand better governance and transparent leadership. *A thought with firm belief has the ability to alter the future course of history. And a thought with collective firm belief has the absolute and incredible power to bring about an irreversible change in the fortunes of nations and, gradually, the entire planet.*

Inequality, poverty and injustices continue because we have a democracy of the few, by the few, and for the few. The 'few' typically comprise only extended families and the coterie of those in power.

This scenario prevails in several countries of the world. The many who suffer will tell you that the crimes and injustices committed against them in the name of democracy are as vicious as those by some of the worst authoritarian rulers.

Continued injustice in any society is not only due to the unwarranted actions of a few unworthy people but also the silence of the many who are worthy people. The silent majority has now found its voice and will collectively activate an accelerated movement to secure the future they deserve. Martin Luther King Jr. put it vividly:

> History is the long and tragic story of the fact that privileged groups seldom give up their privileges voluntarily. Individuals may see the moral light and give up their unjust posture; but...groups are more immoral than individuals. We know through painful experience that freedom is never voluntarily given by the oppressor; it must be demanded by the oppressed.[27]

Paradigms of the New Civilization

A fundamental paradigm of the new civilization is the culture of oneness with respect for diversity. As the Fuji Declaration of 2014 expresses:

> Just as the myriad cells and diverse organs of our body are interconnected by their oneness and work together in harmony for the purpose of sustaining our life, so each and every living thing is an intrinsic part of the larger symphony of life on this planet. With the conscious recognition that we are all a part of a living universe consisting of great diversity yet embracing unity, we will co-evolve with one another and with nature through a network of constructive and coherent relationships.[28]

It is now time to align our individual aspirations and tap our internal strengths to discover unity with each human being and our shared destiny with all forms of life. Once we realize that, all of us will have the potential to transition to a life of peace, love and goodwill, not only for ourselves but for all succeeding generations. I see this as a natural progression as we gradually steer our efforts to reach the next phase of our civilizational growth. However, it is equally important to evolve a clear vision. This we shall do in the next chapter.

Chapter 3

A New Vision

The World Everyone Will Cherish

Deep down within the core of our being lies a creative power,
the capacity to create what is to be,
and the urge to make unremitting efforts
until we have given it shape in one way or another,
either outside ourselves, or within our own person.

—Johann von Goethe (1749–1832)[1]

A Vision for a Nation

My search for a truly holistic yet achievable vision for how a nation should be governed led me to the works of Rabindranath Tagore, the recipient of the Nobel Prize in Literature in 1913. His vision of what a nation should be is vivid and vibrant as well as profound and comprehensive. It comes from the serene depths of the heart.

William Butler Yeats, also a Nobel laureate in Literature in 1923, was a great admirer of Tagore's writings. In his introduction to the English translation of Tagore's major works, he speaks of Tagore's thoughts as having 'stirred my blood as nothing has for years! I have carried the manuscript of these translations with me for days, reading it in railway trains, or on the top of omnibuses and in restaurants, and I have often had to close it lest some stranger would see how much it moved me.'[2]

Tagore shares deeply held convictions and time-tested beliefs when he describes in simple yet passionate poetry his concept of life in a nation-state.

Where the mind is without fear and the head is held high;
Where knowledge is free;
Where the world has not been broken up into fragments
by narrow domestic walls;
Where words come out from the depth of truth;
Where tireless striving stretches its arms towards perfection;
Where the clear stream of reason has not lost its way into the dreary
desert sand of dead habit;
Where the mind is led forward by thee into ever-widening thought
and action—
Into that heaven of freedom, my Father, let my country awake.[3]

This verse of ninety words, the defining piece in his masterpiece, *Gitanjali*, portrays an unequivocal vision rooted in the strong, basic fundamentals a state must espouse. Each word has meaning and purpose. Together, they outline a comprehensive conceptualization of what a nation must become in spirit and substance.

All the lines in this verse focus only and entirely on how the citizens of a country should feel about living in the country and the impact on the mind of each citizen of what the state does (or does not do). The criteria for being a great nation lie not in the quantitative numbers of performance but on the qualitative thought processes of the citizens.

The laws and actions of all institutions of the state are so formulated and practiced that they create an environment that bestows on all citizens the freedom to think and express their views fearlessly; guarantees equal access to learning, knowledge and skills; and ensures tolerance and respect for all human beings, irrespective of race, gender, religion, caste, status or any other differentiator. The state is committed to the sanctity of the truth, and creates an ethos that enables every resident to pursue her quest to achieve her highest potential.

The essence of this vision emerges from the notion that the principal role of a nation is to empower all citizens to do their best, and be their best. This verse is a veritable treasure that portrays the

DNA of a nation—emerging entirely from the thoughts, actions and the aspirations of its citizens—that continuously fortifies these beliefs into a virtuous cycle.

A Government for All People

Aristotle wrote that 'in a democracy the poor will have more power than the rich, because there are more of them, and the will of the majority is supreme'.[4] In the same vein, Plato, Aristotle's teacher, warned that 'a democracy, though a charming form of government, should not end up dispensing one sort of equality to equals and another sort of equality among the unequals'.[5]

A government's prime priority must, therefore, be to deal with issues of poverty and inequality. The incessant debates on poverty reduction invariably focus on how to define and measure poverty so as to calculate the percentage of people living below the poverty line, rather than focusing on effective measures to eliminate poverty and raise the quality of life.

Many countries have gone virtually broke after evolving a system of handouts in which the poor were not helped enough to overcome poverty but were given just enough to survive in poverty. A government truly concerned about the poor should aim at ending the poverty trap rather than simply reacting to it. In the short term, that requires more public funding so that deprived children of this generation can enjoy the benefits of a healthy diet and quality education. There is no other way to end the vicious cycle of intergenerational poverty. The additional funding would be temporary, mainly for this generation of deprived children. The next generation of children will not need the same degree of help. American economist Jeffrey Sachs has often said that, 'the long-term costs of ending poverty would almost surely be far lower than the status quo of simply managing poverty'.[6]

Every child in every country should be enrolled in early childhood development programmes. Primary and secondary education should be compulsory and free, as also medical care including all treatment and medicines. Water supply, housing, public transportation, food, sports and cultural facilities should be subsidized and accessible to all.

The traditional capitalist approach was patterned on a trickle-down approach to growth. But I believe that asking the poor to wait for the trickle-down is morally unacceptable and strategically questionable. This is the big deception economists offer that everyone will be richer in the future, thus justifying gross inequality and humiliation.

The key criterion of a good leader is not whether he responds to the vocal majority and to lobbyists but whether he has the interest and sensitivity in listening to the views that are not articulated, as these are held by the people who have no access to the leader.

Another necessary attribute of a leader is to foresee today the problems citizens may face tomorrow. For example, there is a worrying forecast that the collective impact of the surging use of AI and robotics would tend to reduce employment opportunities in many countries for quite some time. If this happens, it may become necessary for governments to seriously consider putting in place a framework to guarantee the 'universal basic income' ideology many economists have been advocating. The World Bank is, in principle, supportive of this move.[7]

Respect for Human Rights

At the basic elemental level, the content and structure of most government policies and regulations stem from how deeply the culture of respect for human rights is embedded within a country's ethos. Those in leadership positions are particularly expected to respect human rights of all persons, in all their dealings and interactions. But, in practice, most leaders tend to be more focused on enhancing their own rights and privileges than accepting or displaying any responsibility for respecting the rights of others. While rights and responsibilities can be distinguished neatly, they cannot be separated from each other.

We have long lived in societies in which certain groups often insist on rights at the expense of others, without recognizing the responsibilities that they must simultaneously accept. 'Consequently, we have a preponderance of rights over responsibilities. Instead of the culture of human rights which is striven for, there is often an "unculture" of exaggerated claims to rights, which ignores the basic intentions of human rights.'[8]

The necessary balance between freedom and responsibility cannot be taken for granted; it has to be realized and nudged towards. A sensitive government must be the most vocal spokesperson of the human rights of the less well-off, especially the most discriminated and marginalized sections of society. Traditionally, human rights are perceived as certain acts which a government must perform to ensure that no part of society is discriminated against. The issue is narrowly seen as individuals versus the government. But a more liberal interpretation of human rights should also encompass two additional features—satisfying human needs, including claims and entitlements which the state needs to take care of and ensuring that the rights of each section of society are also collectively protected vis-a-vis all other groups of people.

A nation is a vast extended family, with all the obligations of family loyalty. As Paul Seighart, law reformer, puts it, 'The test of human rights is not whether the prosperous, with access to the law courts, are well protected, or whether living standards for the majority are improving, but whether the weak are helped by the strong. The ultimate measure of whether a society can properly be called "civilized" is how it treats those who are near the bottom of its human heaps.'[9]

Respect for Nature

The World Meteorological Organization (WMO) State of the Global Climate report confirms that 2023 was the warmest year on record—about 1.45 degrees Celsius (with an uncertainty margin of ± 0.12°C) above the pre-industrial 1850–1900 baseline.[10] This is not just an aberration. The past nine years, 2015 to 2023, were also the warmest on record. Carbon dioxide levels are 50 per cent higher than the pre-industrial era, trapping enormous heat in the atmosphere. This means temperatures will continue to rise for many years to come. Sea levels and greenhouse gases are at a record high while sea ice in the Antarctic is at a record low. These are more than just statistics. Extreme weather is destroying lives and livelihoods on a daily basis.

Severe heat waves, drought and devastating floods continue to affect millions and cost billions.

Ecologist E.O. Wilson's warning in 2012 is alarming, 'If global changes caused by HIPPO (Habitat destruction, Invasive species, Pollution, Overpopulation, and Overharvesting, in that order of importance) are not abated, half the species of plants and animals could be extinct or at least among the "living dead"—about to become extinct—by the end of the century. We are needlessly turning the gold we inherited from our forebears into straw, and for that we will be despised by our descendants.'[11]

It is in this context that the United Nations Human Rights Council adopted a resolution in October 2021, recognizing that a clean, healthy and sustainable environment is a human right.[12] This was overwhelmingly endorsed by the UN General Assembly in July 2022.[13]

Though the resolution is not legally binding on the 193 UN Member States, it is likely to prompt countries to enshrine the right in national constitutions. A few progressive nations, including Sweden, Ecuador, Norway and Costa Rica, have already done so. In April 2024, the Supreme Court of India also ruled that 'the right against climate change is a distinct fundamental and human right'.[14] But all this is only a beginning; the passage from intent to action is still to be paved.

The prevalent economic systems in the world do not acknowledge the carrying capacities of the planet. We continue to be governed on the basis that human beings are separate from the environment and can continue to progress even as the health of our planet continues to deteriorate. To undo the enormous damage done for over half a century, society will have to accept a new narrative of progress and start working towards totally eliminating the well-entrenched carbon economy, avoid wastage and over-consumption, and encourage a 'recycling and re-use' culture. Everyone knows there isn't nor will there ever be a vaccine for climate change, yet no decisive or substantive steps have been taken.

Meanwhile, the huge carbon footprints of military conflicts and military preparedness all over the world still continue to be exempted from international climate treaties since the Kyoto Protocol of 1997.

Though the 2015 Paris Agreement did away with this exemption, it was not made an obligation. Rather, the decision to report military emissions and how to calculate them has been left to individual countries. Meanwhile, the five biggest arms exporters of the world, the US, France, Russia, China and Germany, stand to gain the most from every military offensive.

The voluntary initiatives by some of the big global corporations to reach a net zero-carbon status started showing some promise, but their seriousness about meeting their pledges is open to question. Typically, the commitments pertain to results to be evaluated a decade or two later—long after the pledge-makers will be out of office. We have not come across many corporations specifically announcing what they will do in the next year or two.

In a stirring message beamed to the UN headquarters in New York, in September 2019, activist Greta Thunberg cautioned lawmakers, 'We can no longer save the world by playing by the rules, because the rules have to be changed. We need systems change—I ask you to please wake up and make the changes required possible. To do your best is no longer good enough. We must all do the seemingly impossible. Everything needs to change. And it has to start today.'[15] The Conference of Parties (COP27) in November 2022 at Sharm el Sheikh, Egypt, and the much-hyped COP28 dialogue in Dubai in December 2023 achieved no significant breakthroughs other than a different vocabulary to restate what needs to be done. Commitments from the relevant parties were neither sought nor secured. The only unanimity was to continue the dialogue at COP29 in Baku the following year.

There are no aliens or guests on spaceship Earth, we are all crew. We, the people, must set our own limits, and we must create our own solutions. Tomorrow's world will be configured by the decisions we take, or fail to take, today.

Media: A Trustee for the Masses

An effective system of political communication that informs and engages the citizenry is an essential prerequisite for a democracy to function well. James Madison, the fourth president of the US, observed in 1822 that, 'A popular government without popular information, or the means of acquiring it, is but a prologue to a farce or a tragedy, or perhaps both.'[16]

A paper by philosopher Jurgen Habermas and others elaborated that, 'The key factor that creates and sustains democratic societies is the emergence of a "public sphere" for democratic discourse. This public sphere is a "space" independent of both—the state control and business control; permitting citizens to debate on public issues, without fear of immediate reprisal from the political and economic powers.'[17]

The purpose of media is to portray the 'truth' from the perspective of all sections of society. Since much of the media is owned by corporations that are owned by shareholders seeking maximum returns, the 'truth' has become a victim rather than the purpose of media. The right to chisel and shape the ostensible 'truth' in media is virtually auctioned off to the highest bidders, i.e. those who provide the largest revenue through advertising. We also have situations where the media is owned and controlled by corporations blatantly linked to a specific political party, with the sole objective of being the mouthpiece of that party. In either scenario, the masses get effectively disenfranchised as far as the mainstream media is concerned.

In non-democratic societies, those in power habitually dominate communication systems to maintain their rule. In democratic societies, one expects that this would not be the case. On the contrary, mass communication systems in most countries have been controlled for decades by five to ten big profit-maximizing corporations who receive much of their income from advertising by other big corporations and governments.

Social media kindled hope that it would offer a viable challenge to traditional media, making it easier to reveal the 'truth' to the masses but, sadly, most social media entities are products of the same corporate culture. The challenge to reform the media will determine whether democracies will survive and flourish, or whether democracy itself will become a casualty. In many so-called democratic countries, this is already happening.

Democracy means people have the power to control their own lives and destinies; this cannot happen if we let the market insulate vast realms of important decisions from collective deliberation. Democracy can be deepened only if it is easy for ordinary citizens to understand important issues and effectively participate in exercising choices. Only then can societies initiate the social transformations that are difficult but also unavoidable. This change cannot be stopped, irrespective of the role traditional media plays. Media leaders have two choices: resist human progress and suffer the consequence of irrelevance or become allies in spearheading progress.

John Kenneth Galbraith, a leading economist of the 20th century, wrote in his book *The Affluent Society* that the world is characterized by private affluence and public squalor, dirty streets and clean houses. He called it 'a chronic problem in our society where the private choices of individuals and corporations in the market are more privileged over collective choices of citizens and communities in the public sphere.'[18] He reiterated that building a vigorous affirmative state by extending democracy into domains currently dominated by the market is an essential part of the solution.

The mainstream media, so far, has not portrayed the views and interests of the public sphere. This has to change soon. We are yet to see if the newly minted tools of AI will make matters worse or better. So far, it has been deployed more to camouflage misinformation as truth. It is open to question if AI can develop reliable filters to effectively separate facts from fiction. That could very well be the litmus test on the potential of AI to do good, and be good.

Economics that Works for All

There are serious concerns about whether the practice of economics has also become an unconscious ally in the perpetuation of status-quo policies that are premised on the primacy of the rights of certain specific people, and the maximization of the gross domestic product (GDP) as the prime indicator of progress. Perhaps one should call this approach 'ego-nomics', not economics. Author David Korten says, 'Ego-nomics makes GDP growth the economy's defining purpose and assumes that advances in the well-being of people and Earth will follow. Occasionally such advances occur. Usually, they do not.'[19]

The 2008 financial meltdown and the ensuing recession distinctly brought to attention what was till then a behind-the-covers thinking. The collective economic expertise of the Western world was unable to predict the disaster that should have been staring them in the face. The solutions proposed to deal with the disaster too focused on designing a stimulus that would let off the perpetrators without any accompanying corrections on how macroeconomic policies should be re-framed.

In effect, all data that contradicts prevailing thinking patterns continues to be ignored. The nuances of inequality do not even feature in macroeconomic forecasts and outlook. Barring a few economists calling for a revolution in economic thinking, the issues of poverty alleviation and less unequal societies are left to be dealt with only in World Bank reports and UN goals. Government policies and taxation structures continue to be skewed to sustain the status quo.

Amartya Sen, Indian Nobel laureate in Economics, has emphatically written that:

> The calamity of deprivation and penury can hardly be missed by those who have bothered to think about the subject, no matter whether they are themselves poor or not. Lives are battered, happiness is stifled, creativity is destroyed, and freedoms are eradicated by the misfortunes of poverty. George Bernard Shaw mentioned in the preface to his brilliant play, *Major Barbara*, that 'The greatest of evils and the worst of crimes is poverty.' If poverty is indeed an evil, then there must be some wickedness, or at least some culpability, behind poverty—some wrong-doing that allows such human tragedies to occur and persist. This raises the immediate question: who, then, are the wrongdoers?[20]

It is heartening that a new set of economic thinkers are highlighting the many explicit and implicit forms of discrimination and bias that are an established norm in the discipline of economics today. They are endeavouring to create an understanding of how economic policies influence not only economic outcomes but also social and political outcomes. They are seeking to position 'inequality' at the core of economic analysis and reach a new accord on why inequality continues to worsen. They are raising fundamental doubts on long-treasured, neo-classical economic theories that the market response is the same from everyone, rich or poor; that if policymakers increase the minimum wage, employers will hire fewer workers; that if there is a price rise, demand will fall.

We need to integrate these concerns into a new meta-story on the role of economics that works for all. To facilitate this process, it would be useful to bring to the fore new alternative thinking from leading economists in the global south. Excluding a small number, most of the ninety-three Nobel Prizes in Economics until 2023 have gone to economists living and working in the US and Europe. This apparent location bias should not become a barrier to identifying new approaches that will force us to evaluate the implications of different economic policies. However, one must acknowledge that some of the West-based economists such as Joseph Stiglitz, Riane Eisler and Elinor Ostrom have been trying to change the narrative.

Deeper structural issues such as the discriminatory impact of fiscal and monetary policies, the exploitation of labour and nature by economic activity, the abuse of monopolistic market power, and the use of political power to push selective economic interests are seldom highlighted as the key issues to contend with. The initiatives for change generally originate from civil society and a few enlightened leaders but mainstream intellectuals and academics in economics have not yet come to the forefront to pioneer a transformation to a contemporaneous approach to address the key aspects related to inequality and poverty elimination.

It is reassuring that the growth orthodoxy has been challenged by the winners of the 2019 Nobel Prize in Economics, Abhijit Banerjee and Esther Duflo. They argue that rather than chase 'the growth mirage', governments should concentrate on specific measures with proven benefits such as helping the poorest members of society get access to healthcare, education and social advancement. They point out that 'a larger G.D.P. doesn't necessarily mean a rise in human well-being—especially if it isn't distributed equitably—and the pursuit of it can sometimes be counterproductive. Nothing in either our theory or the data proves that the highest G.D.P. per capita is generally desirable.'[21]

Kate Raworth, English economist, also makes a persuasive case in her book, *Doughnut Economics*, that:

> [T]he performance boundaries of a modern economy must be set within two indicator panels. One panel is meant to ensure that the essential needs of the entire population are met, so that they can all lead a full and satisfying life. The other panel is meant to continuously track the health of Earth's regenerative systems, including eco-balance and bio-diversity. It is a collective human responsibility to ascertain that the policy frameworks never go beyond the permissible parameters related to both boundaries.'[22]

Indian economist Kaushik Basu puts it quite succinctly:

> The risk economists face now is that the ground is shifting faster than our understanding. We must call on economics' scientific imagination to rise to the challenge and examine not just the state of the world but the state of the discipline. As technology advances and the environment changes, some of the key assumptions underpinning mainstream economic thinking will become obsolete. To reverse the public's loss of confidence in the discipline, economists must get back to doing what made the field so valuable in the first place.[23]

Gender Equality and Parity

> Gender equality with full parity is the most significant unfinished social agenda of the 21st century. When every woman is empowered, with equal opportunities and fulfilment of her rights, we shall have empowered all of humanity.

The advancement of women's emancipation is not merely a matter of justice; it is of vital necessity to ensure the welfare of society. Women account for one-half of a country's talent base. A nation's competitiveness in the long term depends significantly on whether and how it educates and empowers its women. The question is not of women's upliftment; it is about total gender parity. Parity in every area: same pay for same work, respect for working mothers, justice in career advancement, equality of spouses with regard to family rights, and the recognition of everything that is a part of the rights and duties of citizens in a democratic state.

'Gender parity' is a pre requisite for 'gender equality'. While gender parity is a statistical measure that shows if male and female participation ratios and empowerment indices are equivalent in every domain and every indicator of progress, 'gender equality' is grounded in holistic criteria emanating from a universal belief in the principle of equivalence of mankind and womankind.

Women's parity will lead to a significant collateral benefit; we will see more women leaders and that will do the world a lot of good because the feminine style of leadership is generally more inclusive. The toughest tasks in the world are not in the realm of physical endurance or intellectual endeavours, the toughest tasks relate to simple everyday acts such as 'offering love even in response to hate' and 'to include one and all in one's umbrella of caring'.

A greater role for women in society will prove to be the most valuable single step to upgrade humanity to hitherto unimagined levels of understanding and sensitivity as it will lead to an explosion of progressive thought streams anchored in humanism and a new civilization of love and compassion. These values also comprise the foundation of holistic, conscious leadership—the only sustainable basis for relationships among people; the only way that will nurture each of us and naturally bring out the best in each of us.

It is my firm conviction that as women occupy their rightful place and space, all of us will discover that precious something which unites all hearts everywhere.

A unity that has been unfathomable will become a new reality. This will be the natural foundation of the Safe New World.

A Framework of Benevolent Governance

The entire mechanism of governance is meant to fulfil the primary purpose of a state: the welfare of the community, which means the welfare of every individual and group that comprises the community, and that includes all residents of the nation.

The composition and contents of this welfare must be defined by society itself. The state is never in a position to claim that the laws it formulates are based on fulfilling this social purpose. The judge of the adequacy of these laws is the individual citizen. Citizens must participate in the formulation of laws and should have the right to criticize them, amend them or reformulate them.

For citizens to be so empowered, liberty must always be the enshrined feature of all laws.

- Laws must never dilute citizens' empowerment to exercise liberty.
- Laws that bestow power on the state without a purpose lead to tyranny.
- Laws must ensure an enduring social precept that the citizen and not the state is the judge of whether all laws comply with these sacrosanct principles.

When that happens, the government will have demonstrated beyond doubt that it is genuinely committed to liberty, not just for a few but for all. The liberty or freedom we are speaking about is not looked upon as a destination; it is an ongoing venture. French philosopher Alexis de Tocqueville once made the profound observation that, 'Liberty cannot stand alone; it must be paired with a companion virtue, such as: liberty and morality; liberty and the common good; liberty and civic responsibility; liberty and justice.'[24]

Leaders who are committed to shape governments that genuinely endeavour to pair liberty with each of these complements are the ones more likely to continue as leaders in the days ahead.

> Liberty is equity, sustainability, transparency and justice all coalesced together.

Such an ingrained foundation of liberty is a vital pre-requisite to usher in a new framework of benevolent governance with unalterable priorities and objectives grounded in three core maxims:

- Provide complete *security* to every citizen and make sure that each citizen in the country feels that he/she is as safe and secure as anyone else, vis-à-vis any personal attacks, internal violence, pandemics, hostilities or external aggression;
- Create and sustain an environment for generating *secure livelihoods* for every citizen through a well-coordinated system of relevant education, abundant employment and entrepreneurial opportunities in an equitable and transparent manner; and,

- Inculcate a strong value system of *integrity and ethics* in both personal and public interactions.

Several equally essential complementary steps would need to be taken simultaneously to create a supportive framework to achieve these goals. The survival of the entire political class is contingent on their commitment to support the evolution and collation of these thought developments. As the DNA of virtuous traits gets firmly and irrevocably enshrined in the minds of citizens and leaders, 'the heaven of freedom' Tagore envisaged will become a reality in the Safe New World.

To Stop Wars, We Must 'Win the Peace'

After the Second World War, there has been widespread consensus that war is evil and nations must resolve their differences through dialogue and discussion. Nuclear weapons have also acted as a deterrent because it is clearly understood that their usage guarantees collective suicide. In any case, the primary resource of material wealth is no longer limited to commodities and mineral or agricultural wealth but industrial and technological prowess, which is a by-product of knowledge and creativity. As a result, geographic boundaries play a minimal role in accelerating progress or prestige in today's calculus of geopolitics.

It is for this reason that except for a few skirmishes, there has not been a significant direct war between superpowers in the past seven decades. Everyone believes it is foolish for any nation to even dream about annexing a neighbour by aggression. It has no purpose, and it serves no purpose. Still, the US has resorted to military aggression to demonstrate its hegemony for diverse reasons but never with a justifiable rationale. In each case, the country's military initiatives, including in Vietnam, Afghanistan and Iraq, have never achieved any of their avowed objectives.

The Russian aggression on Ukraine in February 2022, therefore, came as a shocking manifestation of jungle raj in the international arena. And the more recent full-scale military offensive by Israel on Gaza is already turning out to be the deadliest operation of the 21st century. More than 40,900 civilians—most of them children and women—have been killed and thousands more are critically injured and disabled.[25] While most political leaders in the Western world have unconditionally supported Israel, the reaction of the global youth was entirely different. The war has stirred their conscience.

We witnessed, in April and May 2024, perhaps the most widespread global protests ever by university students around the world, demanding that their university endowments divest from companies enabling and profiting from the Israeli offensive. Demonstrations that commenced in college campuses in the US soon spread to all continents.[26] This has proven, beyond doubt, that there is more that unites the global youth than what divides them. It also establishes that today's youth are pro-peace and have the courage to defend their ideals to bring about positive change.

It is my firm belief that if we can win the peace, there shall never be another war. Peace can only be won with non-negotiable adherence to three principles: Equity, Justice and Transparency.

> No one ever wins a war. It simply ends after everybody has lost. Peace is easier to win. It happens when everybody has won. It is possible, and it is good for both, the leaders and those who are led.

We must keep striving for peace for as long as it takes for humanity as a whole to collectively 'win the peace'. Peace for every individual, peace for every community, peace for every nation, and peace at all costs, at all times.

Let no nation hold the view that peace is a part-time pursuit. There can be no partial peace, nor a temporary peace. Peace is not a selective quest to pursue only when it suits one; peace is an essential pursuit, not only within a nation but all over the planet. Peace has to be sought out; not after the war is begun but well before, to ensure that wars do not take place.

Peace can never be won if any of the parties stubbornly stick to their positions. For lasting peace, all discussants must have open minds and open hearts and sincerely look for common grounds, howsoever small they may be. It cannot be one-way either, it has to be a joint endeavour. Martin Luther King famously wrote: 'Darkness cannot drive out darkness: only light can do that. Hate cannot drive out hate: only love can do that.'[27] If I may add: *Wars cannot end wars. Only peace can end wars. This will happen only when the power of love triumphs over the love of power.*

A Perceptible Concurrence on the Way Forward

There is a growing consensus that to 'win the peace', we need better managed, better led, more accountable institutions as well as a more equitable way of sharing the gains from technological progress in a revamped version of the globalized world. Other than a few beneficiaries of the status quo, the rest of the world is irrevocably aligned with the call for transformational change.

There is concurrence that the rules of the game are clearly rigged to benefit a small but powerful and well-connected group at the top of the income and wealth pyramid. It is not surprising that political leaders in most nations are not even attempting to reach an accord on what a better future should look like. Since the world has been in the grip of a pandemic, and more so since the war in Ukraine started, the realization that our systems are too fragile and vulnerable to meet the challenges of the 21st century has taken deeper roots. Only the voices from civil society leaders, thought-leaders, youth and a large number of volunteer organizations from diverse backgrounds are coming together to articulate a shared vision of our future.

It has been heartening to see millions of citizens displaying the values of compassion, caring and sharing, and doing whatever they can with their meagre resources whenever a calamity strikes fellow citizens. In the words of Sahana Chattopadhyay, writer and coach:

> There is an extraordinary power at work—the extraordinary power of ordinary people. Their plain human courage. And it takes the breath away. People without any privilege, power, or wealth are giving of their time and effort to save their nation from collapse. They are coming together in self-organized teams and communities across cities and towns and villages to answer and amplify desperate calls for help. They are not waving any political banner. They claim no credit. They charge no money. Their affiliation is to humanity and dignity for all. They have risen as citizens, neighbours, and communities to help strangers in need.[28]

Quite obviously, the question arises: Why can't the rulers do what their subjects are doing so willingly, so naturally?

This collective rising of ordinary citizens around the world reinforces the belief that a Safe New World is no fantasy. But it would be naive to presume that it will come about smoothly, let alone emerge on its own. Efforts to strengthen democracy and accountability must go hand in hand with an expansion of the state's responsibilities. Striking the right balance will be difficult even in the best of times.

In a time of unparalleled polarization, crumbling democratic norms and dwindling institutional capacity, these efforts may appear to be a tall order. But like the generation that lived through and after the Second World War, we have no choice but to try. *In spite of all the complex problems we face today, it is human nature that if people have clarity on the collective goal they wish to achieve, an understanding of the role that they can play, and access to the requisite means, they will ensure that they will not regress, they will progress and prevail.*

This—just this—is our vision; nothing else, nothing less.

Chapter 4

Crystallizing the Questions

Capitalism, Democracy, Autocracy

What people think of as the moment of discovery
is really the discovery of the question.

—Jonas Salk (1914–1995)[1]

Can True Democracy Be Revived?

Two questions came up in the opening chapter:

Can capitalism survive?

Can true democracy be revived?

Examining the two questions together, one begins to wonder if *democracy as it is practiced is the product of capitalism as it is practiced.* Or is it that each is the consequence as well as the cause of the other?

It appears that the gradual debasement of the cardinal principles of democracy has distorted and abused capitalism, leading us all to the vital question: *Can democracy and capitalism in their present state co-exist?* For reflection on this key issue, I put forth two alternative, apparently contradictory, hypotheses:

First: Capitalism, as it has evolved, will continue to flourish, and democracy, as it functions today, will continue to survive because those in power have virtually infinite power and money to ensure this.

Second: Capitalism, as it has evolved, is unlikely to survive for long. Societal pressures are already changing the contorted version of democracy as it is practiced, to seek a transition to 'democracy as it should be' that is, *for* the people, not merely *of* the people and *by* the people. The latter two characteristics are not sufficient conditions for a truly 'democratic' democracy.

Prima facie, it appears that no argument or scholarly advocacy can alter the views of those who don't wish to see the other view, or block the images for those who see the other view. Those who hold on to the first view are not really concerned with the contents or discontents of democracy; their sole interest is to continue the current format of capitalism that has stood them in good stead for many centuries. As a result, they are unable to decipher the new realities that are emerging.

Those who hold the second view are beginning to gather a critical mass and believe they are more likely to prevail, notwithstanding the Covid interlude that provided another opportunity for status-quo loyalists to strengthen their position while silencing dissident voices.

Till just a few decades ago, democracy looked as though it would dominate the world. The United Nations Charter (1945)[2] and the Universal Declaration of Human Rights (1948) established rights and norms that countries were called upon never to breach.[3] However, democracy has been going through a very rough patch since the beginning of this century. In nations where autocratic rulers were dethroned, their successors either failed or took inordinately long to create credible democratic regimes. Even in established democracies, cracks in the system have long been visible and citizens have become increasingly disillusioned with the games politicians play.

Robert Skidelsky, British economic historian, expresses concern that the practice of capitalism has created a civilization in which people feel perpetually unsatisfied. Governments all over the world have created systems saddled with incentives that encourage the accumulation of wealth with no regard for our capacity to enjoy it. We have been pushed into a system in which 'the production and consumption of unnecessary goods has become most people's main occupation'.[4] Perhaps capitalism has neither the propensity nor the disposition to create a better life for all.

Democracy, at birth, was ostensibly meant to give voice to 'we the people'. Unfortunately, that did not happen and 'a few people' went about deciding what 'we the people' should think and what our voice should be. In spite of that, why do people still want democracy? Put simply, people believe that democracy has the basic structure that will permit them to speak their minds and shape their own destinies and their children's futures. That so many people all over the world are prepared to risk so much for this idea is a strong confirmation of its continuing appeal.

I sense that we are on the threshold of the rebirth of democracy as it should be, a re-emergence from the ashes of democracy we see today. The questions we need to probe are:

- How can true democracy be revived?
- What does it entail?
- What are the options?
- What are the related issues we must also examine?

Capital, Capitalists and Capitalism

The word 'capital' has been in use since the 12th century to refer to funds, stock of merchandise, sums of money, or capital assets owned by an individual or a firm. It is often interchanged with wealth, goods, assets or property. The term 'capitalist' is used for one who is the owner of capital.

Gradually, the system evolved by capitalists to deploy or use their capital began to be called 'capitalism'. Conceptually, there is nothing wrong or inappropriate about capitalism. It has been, it is, and it will continue to be a necessary and vital cog in the functioning of communities and governments as well as international trade and commerce.

How people and analysts perceive the outcome and impact of capitalism is a factor of how capitalists, the owners of capital, operate and use the system. Deliberately or unwittingly, governments have found it convenient and beneficial to help capitalists in maximizing their profits and have virtually become their accomplices by stealthily subverting the system to their mutual advantage. With this nexus, it has become easier for capitalists to misuse and manoeuvre the system.

While this is currently the perceived norm, one must simultaneously acknowledge a few incontestable facets:

- Capitalism as a system is an inherent part of our lives.
- We need capitalists to operate the system and make it work. That is the basis of entrepreneurship.
- There are many 'worthy capitalists' who do not resort to any abuse of the system.
- The problems highlighted relate to the actions of certain 'unworthy capitalists', the ones who do not pursue responsible leadership practices.

Whatever we call them, the actions of the not-good capitalists, some of whom happen to be major capitalists, have indiscriminately defiled the entire system with such disastrous consequences for a majority of the people that there is a vehement call to put an end to these appalling practices.

Over the last three centuries, those who highlighted and opposed the actions of these unworthy capitalists came to be called socialists and communists. They argued that the system, without checks and balances, hurts workers, as businesses make more money by arbitrarily reducing the wages of workers who toil to manufacture products or provide services. Business owners become rich while workers remain poor and exploited.

The concept of socialism gathered momentum as a response to consistent negation, by unworthy capitalists, of even the modest demands for a little more consideration and justice for the working classes. Socialism was a desperate effort to rein in the unworthy capitalists. The mass revolutions that followed since then, in the 18th, 19th and 20th centuries, merely helped create what came to be called socialist or communist states. As it turned out, these states became equally authoritarian as their leaders also caught the virus from unworthy capitalists.

In consequence, unworthy capitalists continue to flourish. Masses continue to agitate and protest but nothing really changes, while governments, in so-called democracies as well as authoritarian regimes, continue to be willing co-conspirators to perpetuate the prevalent system.

So let us sharpen the questions within the following four parameters:

- Capitalism as a system is necessary.
- Worthy capitalists are a nation's assets.
- If there were no unworthy capitalists, the 'democracies-in-name' could start functioning as 'truly democratic' democracies.
- We must make it easy for unworthy capitalists to transform themselves and become worthy capitalists.

What Is Unworthy about Unworthy Capitalists?

First, all unworthy capitalists are not completely bad. In fact, there are quite a few good things they do. Our focus is to share with them the actions the world perceives as unethical and unjust. These are the things society considers dishonourable. It is as if these capitalists are unable to access their conscience or any other in-built mechanism to help them distinguish between right and wrong.

If they stop doing the wrong things and embrace the principles of worthy capitalists as enumerated below, they will still make enough money because they are fundamentally entrepreneurial. By doing so, they can be sure of greater customer loyalty, improved employee morale, community respect, and a sense of peace and tranquility within. These assets are not readily countable but they are the ones which eventually count. As a reward, they will secure what I call a sustainable 'Triple Top Line' of joy, peace and contentment.[5]

TEN PRINCIPLES OF WORTHY CAPITALISTS

1) Do not lobby with governments to seek undue favours. Governments have to be just and fair to all *people*.
2) Make **political contributions** openly. Support the political party likely to be the best for all *people*.
3) Willingly pay all taxes. Shun tax havens; taxes are the only government resource to provide good governance to all *people*.
4) Pay more, not less, than **minimum wage** to all employees. Ensure all suppliers and service providers do the same. Value the aspirations of all *people*.

5) Respect diversity and demonstrate it in employment, development and promotion policies, irrespective of gender, race, caste, colour, or religious affiliation of *people*.
6) Display **transparency** and accuracy in all communications, product specifications, advertisements, press releases and annual reports; earn the most valuable and sustainable asset—the trust of the *people*.
7) Treat nature judiciously, not as an expendable resource. Nature belongs to the 'commons' and nurtures all *people*.
8) Preserve the environment, share a verifiable plan to get to a zero-carbon footprint within ten years or earlier. This is the only way to mitigate climate-change risks for all *people*.
9) Recognize that the corporation owes its **existence to the** society in which it functions. It must therefore discharge a primary role in sustaining and advancing the system that gives it life, and make it relevant and inclusive for all *people*.
10) Start following these precepts today. We are in a short window of opportunity when the early converts will become new role models for all *people*.

There is one specific aspect I wish to highlight; one particular word that figures in all the ten principles: PEOPLE—a word that points to the trajectory of our future. As we assiduously pursue these principles, we will observe a tangible shift.

A Shift in Focus from CAPITAL to PEOPLE

A shift from a system that excludes many to a system that includes all. Capital will stay and retain its pre-eminent status as always. But 'people issues' will be prioritized over 'capital issues'.

Capitalists will continue to make money by deploying their capital, but within the ten parameters listed above. It would be a gradual shift from the prevailing capitalistic system to a new Peopleistic system. In this transition, all capitalists will uphold and promote 'Peopleism' as the new system of governance.

Capitalists (owners of capital) and non-capitalists (with no capital) will both be Peopleists.

This is the overarching premise of this book, and the subsequent chapters describe how this single shift will usher in a world that has been eluding us for a long time. This is an idea whose time has come. Will all capitalists accept this new template? It is very likely that, this time, they will. Many of them certainly will, especially as they begin to understand that there may be no other choice.

Stakeholder Capitalism: An Irrevocable Advance

Milton Friedman, the recipient of the 1976 Nobel Prize in Economics, wrote in 1970 that the sole purpose of a firm is to make profit for its shareholders. Since then, this has been the corporate dictum all over the world, and Friedman has been the 'unofficial custodian' of social unconsciousness in business. It took business leaders forty-nine years before they publicly acknowledged that business must also discharge a holistic purpose.

In August 2019, the Business Roundtable in the US—ostensibly the 'association of chief executive officers of America's leading companies working to promote a thriving U.S. economy and expanded opportunity for all Americans through sound public policy'—issued a new 'Statement on the Purpose of a Corporation', signed by 181 CEOs, committing to lead their companies for the benefit of all stakeholders—customers, employees, suppliers, communities and shareholders (the BRT Statement).[6]

The statement called for abandoning the 'shareholder primacy' model of the corporate purpose in favour of a more socially responsible 'stakeholder primacy' model, in which corporate responsibility does not stop at generating profits for shareholders but extends beyond that to generate positive societal impact as well. Many questions relating to this statement remain unanswered: Is this meant to be another hype to buy time, or is it likely to be a promise this time? And what is the plan to do away with the legal provisions in some jurisdictions in the Anglo-American world that mandate shareholder primacy—for example, the corporate law of Delaware?[7] Most observers feel that as long as executive pay remains tied to stock prices, shareholder interest will, by default, continue to remain supreme.

Barely a year after the commitment of corporate chieftains to the BRT statement, the Covid pandemic provided the first opportunity to test if they really meant it. Like in other crunch situations before, the verdict was mixed. Many companies did not bat an eyelid while implementing pay cuts and layoffs even as they used the cash grant given by the government for Covid relief to buy back their shares and pay out dividends. According to a report, 'Marriott International, the world's largest hotel chain, which earned $1.2 billion in 2019, began furloughing most of its American workers, jeopardizing their access to healthcare, while it paid more than $160 million in quarterly dividends and pursued a raise for its chief executive.'[8]

Caterpillar, Stanley Black & Decker, Steelcase, Levi Strauss and World Wrestling Entertainment are among the many other companies that laid off workers just before declaring dividends for shareholders.[9] However, it is heartening that some of the signatories of the BRT statement, including Bank of America and Wells Fargo, vowed to avoid layoffs, while JPMorgan Chase promised to pay cash bonuses to employees earning less than $60,000 per year. They are helping to create new corporate norms.

The coming years will determine whether worthy capitalists will outnumber unworthy capitalists and create a real turnaround. It will all come down to whether the BRT really means business in accelerating this transformation, and whether governments are amenable to making laws that can no longer overlook or condone such behaviours. Whether or when it happens depends on when the corporate boards and CEOs acknowledge and accept the new tenets of doing business.

The New Tenets of Business

The New Tenets of Business relate to the New Reality of Business and encompass the inescapable societal expectations from corporate leaders. These comprise three non-negotiable components, shaped by the new ecosystem of the 'ease of doing business'. Those who enthusiastically embrace these tenets will be pleasantly surprised by the level of customer appreciation and societal approbation they gain.

First Tenet: Environmental, Social and Governance (ESG) Issues

An enterprise is an initiative of shareholders who contribute capital to provide products or services to existing or new customers. By itself, capital alone cannot achieve any goals; one needs multiple inputs from many others such as employees, suppliers and peripheral communities who, in many ways, have a stake in the functioning of the enterprise. This tenet essentially means that their collective interests, along with social and environmental justice, must hereafter become the foundational rock of corporate governance. The interests of specific stakeholders must not take precedence over the interests of other stakeholders. The allocation of surplus generated in the enterprise has to be equitable and acceptable to all stakeholders.

Second Tenet: Diversity, Equity and Inclusion (DEI)

In substance, this starts with 'employees first', and is mirrored on a day-to-day basis by fairness and respect towards all employees, irrespective of gender, colour, race or background. In particular, women and minorities should be fully at ease, and there should be interactive dialogues with young activists and trade unions. In general, this reflects a perceptible corporate ethos in which diverse people feel intrinsically included as an inherent part of the institution. Adherence to this tenet becomes the magic wand to create a corporate team spirit that empowers the corporation to successfully face any crisis and resolve any dilemmas.

Third Tenet: Corporate Character

The reverberations of corporate character are distinctly discernible in everything an organization does or does not do. It shows up in ethical corporate citizenship and in the transparency and humility of leaders in all their relationships and operations.

On the first and second tenets, the United States Security and Exchange Commission (SEC) has got into the act to outline the reporting mechanism for companies quoted on the stock exchange, based on the belief that unless you regulate and measure, nothing really gets done. Similar regulations have also been announced by regulators in the EU and India.

Experience suggests that legislative action, at best, brings about incremental hype, not real change. Transformational change generally comes about through two ways—either the corporate CEOs and boards are self-motivated to change or else there are strict regulations to punish the offenders. So far, there is little possibility that industry owners or leaders can be held culpable for such digressions. This time, it appears the punishments will emanate from different sources—the customers and society at large—which could be far more effective.

Fortunately, a change is already discernible. Quite a few corporate leaders are beginning to accept that while traditionally profit has been considered the sole corporate objective, it will not be the norm hereafter. This is not a matter of choice. For those who wish to prevail, or even survive, it will be mandatory.

Jamsetji Tata, the founder of the Tata Group in India, said this with unambiguous clarity 150 years ago when he established the first Tata enterprise:

> In a free enterprise, the community is not just another stakeholder in business, but, in fact, is the very purpose of its existence.[10]

This twenty-three-word 'belief' reflects the altruistic and humanitarian business ideology that has been the defining hallmark of the Tata Group throughout its history. In all Group companies worldwide, it is the endeavour never to dilute this commitment. In the process, they have proved, beyond doubt, that it is possible for a company to do well and to do good.

Transition from Autocracy to Democracy

According to a report by Freedom House, a non-profit based in the US, 'In 1973, only forty-four out of 148 countries were classified as "free". Fifty years later, eighty-four out of 195 countries are "free". Each country followed its own path to secure political rights and civil liberties; eventually it led to popular self-government through credible, competitive, free, and fair elections.'[11]

A big wave of democratization started when many military dictatorships ceded power to elected civilian leaders: Greece in 1974, Spain in 1977, Argentina in 1982, Brazil in 1985, Uruguay in 1984, and Chile in 1990, soon followed by Taiwan, South Korea and South Africa. The fall of the Soviet Union in 1991 brought freedom to many Central and East European states. In 2004, Czechia, Estonia, Hungary, Latvia, Lithuania, Poland, Slovakia, and Slovenia all joined the EU, with Romania and Bulgaria following in 2007. Despite pressure from illiberal forces since the mid-2000s, the gains of democratization have mostly held.

But somewhere along the arc of time, virtually all nascent democracies have been influenced by the nexus between governments and capitalists in the established democracies and, gradually, they too adopted similar policies and structures. This substantially increased the playing field for the big capitalists everywhere.

Two distinct patterns emerge from the above:

- The fight for freedom persists over time. People everywhere treasure it more than anything else and are willing to fight for it and,
- Autocrats are far from infallible. Their shortcomings and errors provide openings for democratic forces and eventually they all meet the same fate; they lose power and leave behind a fractured legacy.

Authoritarian leaders will need to accept the new reality that they cannot continue to be isolated outposts in a democratizing world.

Can Autocratic Leaders Become Benevolent Leaders?

The question then arises how, in these circumstances, when even the leaders in 'ostensible democracies' act undemocratically, can one expect leaders of established autocratic regimes to show a change of heart?

That might actually happen. When you have too many despotic heads of states, there will be a premium for benevolent autocrats.

The wise among them will sense increasing resistance within their own countries and they may realize that actually they have nothing to lose by becoming benevolent. They are already sole masters (most of them are men). Effective opposition does not exist anymore. All they have to do is start a new chapter of governance by simply transforming themselves from whatever they are and reincarnate themselves as 'benevolent leaders'.

In case they continue to be as they are, people will continue to resent them for whatever they feel is absent in their lives. Real power is not a factor of whether people kneel in their presence; real power lies in whether people speak highly of them in their absence, not just when they are alive, but also after they are no more.

After seeing the collapse of autocratic rulers in so many countries, there are conclusive lessons on what not to do, and what not to be. Alberto Fujimori in Peru, Hosni Mubarak in Egypt, Ben Ali in Tunisia, Robert Mugabe in Zimbabwe, and many others may have survived if they had voluntarily become benevolent leaders. In fact, it is not difficult to imagine the jubilation among the masses, and the simultaneous emergence of a genuine trust in the new benevolent avatar of the old aggressive persona.

Challenges in Personal Transformation

There is a widely held perception that those in positions of power tend to be materialistic and solely focused on their own interests. This is not entirely true because we equally come across feelings of generosity, empathy and a deep sense of compassion as well. Quite frequently, in my dialogues with leaders in business and government, I have sensed that whenever I explain relevant values in an unobtrusive, experiential way, they respond positively and sensitively. Often, I am surprised by how readily some of them relate all this to their own lives and invariably feel the urgency of thinking about their purpose in life, and why they do what they do. I get the signals that they are not averse to change, and this is a positive sign for a better future.

Management theorists Richard Boyatzis and Annie McKee highlight the difficulties of personal transformation:

> Facing our own shortcomings is hard work indeed. When we see who we really are and do not like it much, it hurts. Contrary to popular belief, it is not change itself that is so hard; what is hard is being honest with ourselves, and admitting that we need to change. Maybe that is why so few people do it, and why so few people are really great human beings and great leaders.[12]

Personal transformation is certainly possible, provided one believes one is doing so voluntarily, as the remarkable instance of King Ashoka demonstrates.

About fifty years after the misadventures of the Macedonian emperor Alexander the Great in India, King Ashoka of the Mauryan dynasty ascended to the throne in 270 BCE. He secured the crown after brutally killing several rival princes. In the ninth year of his reign, Ashoka attacked the state of Kalinga (now in Odisha) on the eastern coast of India, possibly looking for a sea route for trade. The conquest of Kalinga resulted in the death of over 100,000 people, and another 150,000 were deported from the kingdom. The scale of devastation and the resulting misery had a mind-numbing impact on Ashoka.

He was so repentant that instead of enjoying the spoils of war, he announced the renunciation of all wars in his kingdom. He embraced Buddhism and rigorously applied its teachings to politics and governance. He proclaimed a state policy based on compassion, non-violence and tolerance, and spread these Buddhist ideas through emissaries sent all over Asia, including China, Indonesia, Japan, Thailand and Sri Lanka. H.G. Wells wrote in his *Short History of the World* that, 'Amidst the tens of thousands of names of monarchs that crowd the columns of history, the name of Ashoka shines, and shines almost alone.'[13] He earned this tribute because he was the first great ruler in world history to reject the false glory of conquest and devote his remaining life to benevolent rule.

Ashoka's edicts were engraved in rocks all over India, and remain a magnificent testimony of his conversion to honesty and truthfulness in his administration. His first pillar edict puts it concisely, 'This world and the other are hard to gain without great love of righteousness, great self-examination, great circumspection, and great effort.' His other edicts advocate the virtues of concord and courteous dialogue between religions and communities. His commitment to creating an equitable and compassionate society led to the construction of hospitals, support for education and the establishment of a humane legal system.

Many historians believe that Ashoka's propagation of the virtues of the Hindu-Buddhist concepts of karma and dharma and their tolerant and liberal belief systems have contributed significantly to the relatively peaceful coexistence of different religions and identities in Asia.

In our lives, we all encounter moments when we are in a contemplative mood. These are the moments when one imbibes these thoughts of change and begins discovering a whole new worldview. These are the moments when traditional, established beliefs seek revalidation and one senses that there is virtue in being transformed—not for the sake of others, but in one's own self-interest. I foresee these changes taking place soon as the current autocratic leaders begin to grasp that there are only two possible scenarios: either they become benevolent and leave behind a strong likeable legacy, or they prepare to be replaced by a benevolent leader from within their own ranks.

The New Transitions in Process

As we crystallize the relevant questions, and keep questioning the questions, we can specifically observe signs of three tangible shifts beginning to take place in our world today:

- *Shift from a focus on capital to a focus on people*
- *Shift from unworthy capitalists to worthy capitalists*
- *Shift from autocratic rulers to benevolent rulers*

As these three shifts start maturing concurrently, we will observe a natural progression in democracy in many countries, ushering in a momentous positive change. History tells us that change means more of the same, only incrementally better. Now we can look forward to transformational changes in our attitudes, our habits, and the ways our institutions function. The sunrises of tomorrows will herald the discovery of the virtues of new freedoms and new collective enlightenments.

The Wide, Spacious Corridor to Liberty

Daron Acemoglu and James A. Robinson put forth in their book, *The Narrow Corridor: States, Societies, and the Fate of Liberty*, the proposition that:

> Liberty is hardly the 'natural' order of things. In most places and at most times, the strong have dominated the weak. The corridor to liberty is narrow and stays open only when a delicate and precarious balance is struck between state and society. Today we are in the midst of a time of wrenching destabilization. We need liberty more than ever, and yet the corridor to liberty is becoming narrower and more treacherous. The danger on the horizon is not 'just' the loss of our political freedom, however grim that is in itself; it is also the disintegration of the prosperity and safety that critically depend on liberty. The opposite of the corridor of liberty is the road to ruin.[14]

I believe that Peopleism is a credibly viable system of governance that has the potential to not only create a strong and stable balance between state and society, but to also make the corridor to liberty wide enough and spacious enough to accommodate everyone, everywhere.

It is in our individual interest, as well as in our collective interest, to pursue the path of Peopleism to achieve the future we desire. We know of no other path; this is the only way to avoid the road to ruin.

PART TWO

Transition from Knowledge to Wisdom

Chapter 5

The Human Story Till Now

A Chronicle of Four Watershed Moments

It's amazing what ordinary people can do
if they set out without preconceived notions.

—Ben Stein[1]

Five Stages of Economic Progression

In the panoramic arc of history from prehistoric times until now, one can discern five stages of economic progression in our civilizational journey.

- Stage 1: *Hunter-Gatherer Economy*
- Stage 2: *Agricultural Economy*
- Stage 3: *Industrial Economy*
- Stage 4: *Information Economy*
- Stage 5: *Knowledge Economy*

Each stage was differentiated by a specific key determinant that had the greatest impact on the lives of the people that inhabited the planet at that time. The transition to each succeeding stage was a defining moment in human history. I refer to each of them as a 'watershed moment', a divider in time and space beyond which the things that mattered will never be the same again. It is a definitive moment in history that sets a completely new trajectory for the future of the human race with a new set of norms, a new compendium of values and beliefs and a new era of governance. It is a moment when history ceases to determine our future.

We will quickly scan the four transitions.

The Hunter-Gatherer Economy

Since the appearance of *Homo erectus* around two million years ago, and *Homo sapiens* about 300,000 years ago, 'hunting and gathering' was the survival strategy deployed by human societies for several centuries of the Stone Age. This prehistoric age is usually referred to as the era of the Hunter-Gatherer Economy, which was the starting point for the evolution of human progress. This period also witnessed the first demonstration of human intelligence—the development of stone tools.

Sometime around then, the early *Homo sapiens* slowly developed the skill of speech. Starting with articulate expression, sounds gradually started taking shape as words and speech evolved as the medium of communication. The default belief of the human race in this period was that one 'lives to eat'. People believed that the purpose of existence was only to feed themselves by hunting animals and gathering plants. They had no interest in learning or knowing how plants grew and how animals lived and bred. They were perfectly satisfied with things as they were and neither intervened nor interfered with the animal and plant kingdom.

Around 300,000 years ago, man discovered fire. Fire enabled man to see in the dark, become more climate-tolerant, helped him eat things that were otherwise inedible, and made it possible to make harder and more durable tools.

About 100,000 years ago, climate change triggered large-scale *Homo sapiens* migrations across Africa. Many of them travelled from East Africa to what is now the Middle East, from where some went to Europe, and others to India and China. Gradually, they spread to America and Australia.[2] Wherever they went, they continued to live by hunting animals and gathering plants. Hunting and gathering was humanity's first successful collective adaptation, spanning almost 95 per cent of recorded human history.

During most of the period of the Hunter-Gatherer Economy, human beings were both the hunter as well as the hunted. About 70,000 to 80,000 years ago, humans displayed the first tangible signs of learning by experience. Some of the hunter-gatherer groups began to specialize, concentrating on hunting a smaller selection of relatively larger game and gathering a smaller selection of food. This development was facilitated by the creation of specialized tools such as hooks, bone harpoons and fishing nets.

First Watershed Moment: Transition from the Hunter-Gatherer Economy to the Agricultural Economy

The gradual transition from the Hunter-Gatherer Economy to the Agricultural Economy started about 12,000 years ago, ushering in the first big threshold transformation in human life on Earth. Humans started domesticating certain types of animals, starting with goats and sheep, and discovered the art of identifying seeds, beginning with wheat, that could be sowed, leading to a harvest of adequate plant foods and meat on demand. This was a big revolution in how humans lived and marked the beginning of the Agricultural Economy as well as the beginning of the human manipulation of the lives of select animal and plant species. With the confidence generated by the conquest of animals, the fear of surprises declined and humans tended to be more aware and observant of what was happening around them.

Humans began devoting more of their time and effort to new pursuits. They worked the whole day: sowing, watering, weeding and herding sheep and goats to nearby pastures. Over the next 4,000 to 5,000 years, humans in different parts of the world, influenced by their unique geographic and climatic features, added more animals such as pigs, horses and camels to the ranks of domesticated animals, and more agricultural products such as rice, maize, potatoes, millet, barley, peas, lentils, olives, grapes and cashews. It is interesting to note that most of what we eat and drink today was pretty much identified and evolved over 3,000 years ago.

It would be fair to say that we owe our attitudinal traits to our ancestors in the hunting and gathering economy, and our dietary habits and sense of palate preferences and tastes to the farmers in the Agricultural Economy.

The Agricultural Revolution enabled humans to live in relatively secure, permanent habitats, with a more settled way of life. It led to the concept of 'home', which became the prime catalyst to form the emotional and psychological foundations of society. A cluster of 'homes' transformed humans from their life as wanderers and settled them long enough in one place to enable them to build schools and community centres and later, as religions evolved, to build places of worship.

Thus began the story of progress fueled by human brain power. The nomadic, perilous life of hunters and gatherers was slowly replaced by the more settled and less strenuous life of farmers. The supply of food increased along with the ability to store food for future use. This fostered a population explosion as well as the formation of elite groups of land owners.

As the number and size of agricultural societies increased, they expanded into lands traditionally used by hunter-gatherers. This process of agriculture-driven expansion led to the development of the first forms of government in agricultural centres such as the Fertile Crescent in the Middle East, Ancient India, Ancient China, Olmec in Mexico, Sub-Saharan Africa and Norte Chico in Peru.[3]

Around 10,000 BCE, just after the beginning of the era of agriculture, Earth was home to about 5 to 8 million nomadic foragers. By the 1st century CE, only 1 to 2 million foragers remained, mostly in Australia, America, and Africa, while the number of farmers worldwide increased to 250 million.[4]

From then on till the year 1800, per capita income spent on food, clothing, heat, light and housing remained virtually the same; short-term gains in income through better techniques were inevitably lost through population growth. Thus, the average person in the world of 1800 was no better off than the average person of 100,000 BC. Life expectancy was no higher in 1800 than for hunter-gatherers—about thirty to thirty-five years.[5]

It is relevant to point out that while hunter-gatherer societies were egalitarian with little variation in material consumption across the members, inequality became pervasive during the agrarian economy that dominated the world till 1800. Landowners kept becoming better off while the masses subsisted on the bare minimum. One cannot help but question if inequality has been the only inevitable consequence of material progress.

Beginning of Scientific Inventions

The era of scientific inventions started gathering momentum in the 13th century.

Salvino D'Armate in Italy is credited with inventing the first wearable spectacles in 1284, making it possible for people beyond the age of forty to continue to have normal vision.

While Chinese alchemists are believed to have discovered gunpowder in the 10th century, its commercial usage as a weapon was facilitated in Europe by Roger Bacon of England and Berthold Schwarz of Germany between 1294 and 1326.[6] Immense firepower made Europe the leader in colonization. Many historians consider this as the most important development in the story of the fall of humanity.

The year 1454 saw the first printed documents bearing a printed date, at the Press of Johannes Gutenberg in Germany. These and similar other varied multifarious inventions encouraged a culture of continuous research and development of new products. In 1769, James Watt demonstrated, beyond doubt, the potential power of the steam engine, transforming forever the limitations of human energy and virtually launched the Industrial Revolution that heralded the second civilizational transformation from the Agricultural Economy to the Industrial Economy.

Second Watershed Moment: Transition from the Agricultural Economy to the Industrial Economy

The Industrial Revolution started displacing millions of people, first in England, and then in North America, Germany, Italy and France, out of their homes and farms into cities and factories. The impact was replicated in Japan and later in China, the Soviet Union and India in the subsequent century. Meanwhile, the flurry of life-changing inventions continued in the 19th and the 20th centuries: the internal combustion engine in 1860, the telephone in 1870, electricity in 1879, the aeroplane in 1903, air-conditioning in 1906 and the contraceptive pill in 1960.

The Industrial Economy transformed society and government by catapulting the owners of machinery and the controllers of commerce beyond the owners of land and titles, creating a new set of elites. It transformed religion by spawning a culture of scientific enquiry and questioning superstitions and blind beliefs. It transformed social norms and morals by the rigours of competitive economic life, postponing marriage, multiplying contacts and opportunities, liberating women, reducing the family and weakening religious and parental authority.

All this initiated a long trail of developments—capitalism, socialism, the imperialism that followed when industrialized nations needed foreign markets and foreign food, the wars that were fought for these markets, and the revolutions that emerged from such wars. Even the First World War and the vast experiment in Russia were corollaries of the Industrial Revolution.[7]

As we peruse the journey of humanity, it is important to keep asking how human progress impacted the soft traits of humans. Did we become morally superior, or did we become greedier? Did we become more compassionate and caring, or did we become more selfish, with little regard for the effect our actions would have on the society or the environment?

The impact of the evolving human traits on societal values, political structures and governance frameworks was quite phenomenal. What we experience around us is never an accident of history, nor a mere play of destiny; these are the outcomes of the prevailing value-beliefs in society. The masses started feeling that they were being exploited; they felt neglected and uncared for. Yet the rule of the new elites continued uninterrupted.

Third Watershed Moment: Transition from the Industrial Economy to the Information Economy

The development of the internet by the United States Department of Defense in the 1970s, and the subsequent adoption of personal computers a decade later, marked the onset of the third threshold transformation to the Information Age, also referred to as the Computer Age, the Digital Age and the New Media Age, which enormously accelerated the transmission and processing of information. The World Wide Web, initially used by companies as an electronic brochure for their products and services, became a worldwide interactive exchange mechanism for swift global messaging and information access.

Electronic mail (e-mail), which permitted near-instant exchange of information and communication, was widely adopted as the primary platform for workplace and personal connectivity. The digitization of information had a profound impact on traditional media businesses such as book publishing, the music industry and major television and cable networks. Companies with businesses built on digitized information became valuable and powerful in a relatively short period of time. Just as landowners held the wealth and wielded power in the Agricultural Age, and manufacturers such as Alfred Sloan and J.P. Morgan accumulated vast fortunes in the Industrial Age, the Information Age created its own breed of wealth-generators, and at a scale never seen before—from Microsoft's Bill Gates to Amazon's Jeff Bezos.

The key components of industrial production till then were capital, labour and land, and the spirit of entrepreneurship. The Information Economy introduced a vital new fifth element—digitization—with substantive impacts on the character of all other components.

The internet became a fulcrum of this transition, rapidly contributing to accelerating the spread of data exchange and changing forever how people learnt, lived, communicated and undertook research and development work. The new tools of information technology significantly reduced the cost of transactions in the production and distribution of goods and services, enabled better supply chain management and helped create a new spurt of initiatives in e-commerce.

Young people started discovering new entrepreneurial roles in old professions; nimble small operators became the beneficiaries of a new wave of 'outsourcing'. All this effectively increased management efficiency, quickened the pace of globalization, and facilitated the rapid growth of transnational corporations (TNCs).

Fourth Watershed Moment: Transition from the Information Economy to the Knowledge Economy

As the quantum of information continued to explode, and became virtually accessible to one and all, it became equally clear that while 'big data' is necessary for institutions and governments, it is not sufficient for them to be successful. It became quite a challenge to analyse and process the enormous data into meaningful nuggets of relevant knowledge. Quite understandably so, because information is always '*in formation*'.

That provided the seeds for the evolution of the Knowledge Economy, the fourth big transformation, shaped by the power of connectivity to share data and information faster and further, and also accompany it with analysis and implications. By 1995, technology had enabled all people to tap into each other's creativity. This gave a fillip to the emergence of the Knowledge Economy, bringing together powerful computers and technology-savvy entrepreneurial minds, leading to the rapid diffusion and application of knowledge across various sectors and regions. We witnessed a profusion of new knowledge streams through a seamless confluence of inputs from diverse disciplines—a process that spawned an amazing acceleration in disruptive innovation and research and development in new domains.

The Knowledge Economy provided a renewed impetus to promote youth entrepreneurship. There was an exponential growth in college and university enrolment around the world as stepping stones to amassing wealth. In its wake, a series of creative advances substantively expanded the role of the service sector in the structure of the global economy. A convergence of knowledge from infotech, biotech and biomimetics unleashed an avalanche of new cutting-edge technologies with unprecedented possibilities.

While information per se was democratized, the powers that controlled the flow of knowledge weaponized this new resource to further strengthen the framework of status-quo economic policies to retain most of the new wealth among the already rich; a small percentage of the population. Naturally, the collective prowess of the Knowledge Economy could not prevent the colossal failures of the regulators to prevent chaos in the world economic system in 2008—

from mortgage crises to the EU debt crises, which had a cascading, adverse impact on millions of people all over the world.

Where Has the Knowledge Economy Taken Us?

At the end of it all, are we more intelligent than we were a couple of millennia ago? I think it would be fair to say yes.

Does our character as a human race also rate better? Anecdotal evidence suggests that on this specific aspect, we have probably retrogressed. We still exploit the working classes but we soothe our consciences with 'welfare work'.

While human beings have triumphed over matter, the case for human progress strikingly fades when one realizes that they have still not been able to find a way for humans to control their baser instincts. Unless virtue takes precedence over deceit as the default character in our leaders, we, as a planet, are doomed to less than mediocre leadership.

Inadvertently, but sadly, the arrival of the Knowledge Economy has created two dilemmas:

- In general, those who have knowledge do not have power, and those who have power do not have knowledge.
- In some cases, people with knowledge do have power, but most of them are doing whatever they can to ensure that neither their power nor knowledge is shared with others.

The result is clear for all to see: increasing inequalities, persistent unemployment, terrorism and continuous migrations. A deficit of trust has ruined democracy. The paramount task of governments today, in most nations, appears to focus more on the self-interest of those who govern and not of those who are governed. American philosopher William J. Durant summed it up well:

> In every developing civilization, a period comes when old instincts and habits prove inadequate to altered stimuli, and ancient institutions and moralities crack like hampering shells under the obstinate growth of life. Our culture is superficial today, and our knowledge dangerous, because we are rich in mechanisms and poor in purpose. We have a hundred thousand politicians, and not

> a single Statesman.We move about the earth with unprecedented speed, but we do not know, and have not thought, where we are going, or whether we shall find any happiness there for our harassed souls. We are being destroyed by our knowledge, which has made us drunk with our power. And we shall not be saved without wisdom.[8]

For the reasons outlined, Knowledge Economy-based governance systems will neither be acceptable nor tolerated by the masses hereafter. The only avenue to avoid an unimaginable global cataclysm is to make a gradual shift to the next transformation: the fifth civilizational transition from the Knowledge Economy to the Wisdom Economy.

Five Phases of Human Enterprise

Viewing the unfolding narrative of history from a different lens, I have analysed that there have been five phases of human enterprise over the centuries.[9] I find those phases to be aligned with the five stages of human progression described above. This gives a strong credence to the onset of the fifth watershed moment we foresee enveloping us.

Phase one of human enterprise, '*strong fish eating weak fish*', was the prevailing norm during the Hunter-Gatherer Economy and the Agricultural Economy. This period was characterized by the dominance of tribal chiefs, warlords, kingdoms and strong rulers. Cheops (King Khufu) of Egypt who made the tallest pyramid around 3000 BCE, Hyksos (the Arab ruler of shepherds) who ruled the Valley of the Nile for 500 years till about 1700 BCE, the Assyrians who conquered West Asia around 1000 BCE, the Persian King Cambyses II (6th century BCE) and Alexander the Great (4th century BCE) of Macedonia are stark symbols of this way of life, until the birth of Christianity. The Greeks, the Romans, the Turks, the Vikings, the British, the French, the Spanish, the Portuguese and the Japanese continued the era of brutal domination. The majority of the human race helplessly accepted the rule of the mighty, as the privilege of living.

The key leadership traits displayed during this phase were ruthlessness and frequent foolhardiness.

Phase two of human enterprise, '*big fish eating small fish*', started with the beginning of the Industrial Economy, and the concept of the 'joint stock company'. The British East India Company was set up in 1600, and the Virginia Tobacco Company in 1606, creating an ingenious financing model while lowering risk. In Europe and, later, in the US, the trading and industrial enterprises became the 'big fish'. The states acquired their revenues primarily through these 'big fish'; in return the state gave them protection, thus institutionalizing crony capitalism. Industrial enterprises kept getting bigger, giving birth to multinational corporations. Collusion between industry and government became the norm.

The leadership during this phase primarily exhibited the traits of opportunism and pragmatic cunningness.

Phase three of human enterprise, '*fast fish eating slow fish*', began with the emergence of the Information Economy, characterized by the death of distance and the birth of the internet, unleashing a new spirit of entrepreneurship. Microsoft was incorporated in 1981, Dell in 1984, Amazon in 1995, HTC (Taiwan) in 1997 and Google in 1998.

Though prompted by youthfulness and risk-appetite, the leadership that evolved during this phase stuck to the age-old penchant for greed and monopolistic tendencies.

Phase four of human enterprise, '*intelligent fish eating dim fish*', took shape in the early 21st century, creating new amalgams of innovative technologies and even newer corporate entities. Infosys, TCS and Wipro in India; Embraer and Sadia in Brazil; Lenovo, Haier and Alibaba in China; Samsung and Hyundai in South Korea; Hon Hai and Acer in Taiwan; Koc and Sabanci in Turkey; and hundreds more in several other countries—all of them carved their own distinctive niches.

The leadership in this phase started with intellectual idealism but also fell prey to erstwhile established norms of indifference and disregard for both society and the environment.

As I have analysed all along, all the four transitions consistently failed to meet the aspirations of the vast majorities in each nation. Collectively, the leaders could not summon the resilience and the resolve necessary to seek long-term sustainability over short-term gains. It is not surprising, therefore, that in each of these phases, while political and business elites amassed wealth, only a handful have left behind an admirable legacy. Another transition is therefore inevitable; in fact, it is already perceptible.

Typically, a watershed moment is discernible long after it has been around. We are perhaps the first-ever generation in the human race to be able to observe one as soon as it arises. This is a rare occasion that confers on us a collective opportunity to deliberately choose the type of future we should let in. It is a choice that comes once in several lifetimes. If we summon and collate our collective courage and resolve, we should be able to mould the fifth watershed moment in human history—the transition from the Knowledge Economy to the Wisdom Economy—into a shape that is consistent with our aspirations for equity, justice and sustainability. This is entirely compatible with the fifth phase of human enterprise unfolding before us.

Phase five of human enterprise, '*realistic fish eating unrealistic fish*'[10] represents the momentous transition from the Knowledge Economy to the Wisdom Economy, a new era driven by increased demand for social consciousness and the need to function in sync with society and the environment. This is redefining the criteria of success as well as recontouring the routes to success. Even the skills required to stay successful are undergoing reconfiguration.

The foundation of this phase lies in a gradually increasing awareness that corporate leaders and political leaders can no longer ignore the direct and indirect impact of their actions on society and the environment. This is the new grassroots reality. One has to take cognizance of it and reinvent one's faculties and traits of leadership to continue to be relevant.

The New Realism

The new mindset and the new heart-set required to cope with this reality will become the new dividing line between nations and corporations that succeed in the short-term and fail soon after, and those who succeed with new paradigms now and prevail thereafter. Those who are 'realistic' enough to acknowledge the new 'realism' will emerge as winners in this new phase.

A company that only makes money shall hereafter be considered a poor company. A nation that enriches only the elite shall hereafter not be able to protect the elite.

This, in brief, is the essence of the Wisdom Economy, which we will explore in the next chapter.

Chapter 6

The Advent of the Wisdom Economy

Ushering in a New Planetary Civilization

Wisdom cannot be imparted. Wisdom that a wise man attempts to impart always sounds like foolishness to someone else... Knowledge can be communicated, but not wisdom.
One can find it, live it, be fortified by it, do wonders through it, but one cannot communicate and teach it.

—Hermann Hesse (1877–1962)[1]

Differentiating Knowledge and Wisdom

Knowledge has become a commodity. It is accessible everywhere, only a few clicks away. We are awash in an ocean of knowledge. The old saying, 'Water, water everywhere, but not a drop to drink' is quite pertinent in this situation: there is an abundance of knowledge but a conspicuous paucity of wisdom to analyse, understand and apply it.

The old Guinean proverb says it even better: 'Knowledge without wisdom is like water in the sand.' Devoid of wisdom, knowledge seeps through grains of sand; soon enough, even traces of knowledge do not survive.

Knowledge in its entirety is infinite and complex. Wisdom alone can help us 'de-complex' knowledge and identify those elements of knowledge that are relevant to the context in which knowledge is sought to be applied. *Apart from making knowledge relevant, wisdom also humanizes knowledge; it connects the individual with society and aligns individual aspirations with collective goals.*

A focus on 'only knowledge' tends to lean towards a culture of ownership, proprietorship and competitiveness at any cost—traits that prioritize private greed over public good. This often degenerates into private greed even at the cost of public good. Knowledge with wisdom softens greed, brings out the conviction that you cannot be a stand-alone island in the world; your well-being and your progress are intrinsically co-dependent on the well-being and progress of everyone around you.

Knowledge has neither space nor a provision for ethics. Wisdom, on the other hand, is anchored in certain non-negotiable ethics. Wisdom and ethics cannot be separated.

Knowledge-based leadership tends to be good at slogans and creating hype about what needs to be done even when there is no compatible plan or tangible commitment, or even a faint intention of doing what is said. Wisdom-based leadership, in contrast, is seriously concerned in its quest for finding solutions that foster inclusive growth.

Knowledge is certainly an essential component of the Wisdom Economy, but it is only a component. Knowledge by itself does not seek wisdom, but wisdom, by nature, continually seeks knowledge that is relevant to enable one to discharge one's duties as a responsible leader.

Wisdom in Practice

Knowledge is the accumulation of information; it is based on facts. It is usually linear as it is relevant only for the situations where it is specifically applicable. Wisdom is different; it has multiple dimensions. It not only knows, it also understands. It provides fluidity to your knowledge and helps you see beyond the facts. It provides the core substance of knowledge which enables you to relate it to other situations as well.

The difference is subtle but potent. While knowledge gives you a specific edge in specific situations, wisdom provides versatility and agility. It provides a multi-focal lens for interacting with reality, virtually transforming how you respond and how you think.

A fable illustrates this well:

> An old Arab man had seventeen camels. Just before he died, he left instructions that one-half of the camels should go to his first son, one-third to his second son and one-ninth to his third son.
>
> The sons were astonished. They had a good knowledge of arithmetic as well as camels, and they knew that his will could not be implemented without dismembering one camel. They consulted a priest, a scholar of scriptures, as well as the head of the tribe who was the most knowledgeable person they knew, but no one could offer a solution. Finally, they were advised to consult a Sufi saint.
>
> The saint had one camel of his own; he loaned it to them to help them carry out their father's wishes. Now they had eighteen camels. The eldest son took half: nine camels. The second son took six camels: one-third. And the third son took two camels: equivalent to one-ninth. Everyone was satisfied. One camel was left. As that was on loan from the saint, he took it back.

Knowledge is focused on theory and a narrow agenda. Wisdom is focused on practice and a holistic agenda. Wisdom tends to be naturally creative. While one can be knowledgeable with others' knowledge, one cannot be wise with others' wisdom.

Wisdom is the core of what a person is; it clearly reflects in a person's insights and understanding, and in his words and actions. While formal education helps in the cultivation of wisdom, it is not an essential prerequisite for wisdom; neither is age.

One often comes across wise people: among homemakers, shopkeepers, taxi-drivers, hairdressers and workers; in fact, in all professions. They are easily acknowledged and recognized because they tend to take a more holistic view while displaying a sense of greater tolerance and fairness.

Evolution from a Person of Knowledge to a Person of Wisdom

> *When a stone is thrown at a glass window and the glass breaks, what is the cause of the breakage? The obvious*

response is: 'the throwing of the stone'. One could also say, the brittleness or weakness of glass. If the glass was strong, it would not have shattered. One always has the opportunity and potential to strengthen one's 'glass' and reduce its vulnerability.

Looking outwards, one immediately blames the stone. Looking inwards or 'looking within oneself', one explores how to be strong on one's own. This 'exploration deep within' is the only way to discover one's dormant strengths and unravel one's full potential. It helps one advance to new frontiers. There is nothing mysterious about this; it merely enables everyone to challenge one's personal status quo in the serene silence of one's heart. Gradually, and unobtrusively, the process cleanses one's mind of irrational beliefs and biases, and one emerges wiser and stronger to face any challenge.

In this quest, you yourself are your best friend and you can uplift yourself, by yourself, from wherever you are. The discovery of your wisdom and inherent potential is the greatest discovery a human being can aspire to, and it is yours for the asking. You alone stand in the way of realizing this, and if you let yourself be the obstacle to your own growth, you are your own worst enemy.[2]

The resistance to the discovery of the inner wealth of wisdom which resides in your own heart can come only from within you. You face the 'paradox of change' syndrome. At one level, you want change. At the same time, at another level, you resist it. You fear the loss of what you have so assiduously built within you—a set of beliefs and assumptions—something that has given you security and comfort. You have to think of 'change' as not a loss but as an 'exchange' for something better. If you are ready to give up 'what you are' for 'what you can be', no power on earth can stop you from accessing the eternal wisdom within.

This progress hinges only on one question: how genuine is your longing for this evolution from knowledge to wisdom? If your longing for wisdom is committed and irreversible, and pursued with humility, then it is very easy, as easy as moving from a shaded space to a sunny space next to it. To move or not is the choice you have to make, and you alone can make it.

The Infinite Space of Choice

One has to make many choices every day. An individual's role and progress in life is determined by the choices an individual exercises. Wisdom creates, fine tunes and enhances one's ability to make the right choices.

Typically, if we have only one available option in a situation, we would have a mechanical response like a robot. If we have two available choices, we have a dilemma. When we have three possible alternatives to choose from, it becomes confusing. In practice, life offers infinite choices.

Wisdom is the ability to comprehend the '*space*' in which choice is exercised and its potential impact on that '*space*'. Choice is the creative power of life; it is also the destructive power of life. It can lead to an existence that is meaningful and purposeful or we can muddle it up by making it awful and miserable.

My Seven Laws of the Space of Choice

1) *Options for choice arise from the space in which you live* which is a confluence of your own wisdom and the wisdom of all the others who inhabit this space.
2) *Every choice you make will merge in that space,* which means your choice will have an impact on you as well as the space around you.
3) *While our choices impact the space and all its inhabitants, in the same way, we are also impacted by the choices made by everyone else in this space.* The impact of choice is not a one-way, unidirectional process; all choices have an impact on the entire space.
4) In most situations, one is usually not aware that one has *several options to choose from*, including a conscious decision not to exercise choice at that particular time in space.
5) *Everyone does not have the privilege of choosing from a multitude of choices and everyone does not have this privilege all the time.* Some of us are fortunate to have that privilege most of the time. This privilege does not come free; it is

accompanied by a sense of responsibility towards the space we live in. *We are accountable for the choices we make, in the space we live in.*

6) *If you set yourself up in a default-choice mode, which means you let your choices be made unconsciously,* you immediately surrender the trajectory of your future to forces outside your control. You believe you have enough past experience and knowledge to make immediate decisions. It does not often occur to you that one can never face the same situation twice—like one can never step into the same river twice. The water is different, the rate of flow is different, the composition of water may be different, and the environment upstream from where water is coming may also be different. Even you, as a decision-maker, are not the same person as before; that particular persona has already disappeared, along with everything else from the past.
7) *For many centuries, this space of choice was confined to our tribe, our community, or our nation. Today, the entire planet is virtually one space. The choice made by someone far away is as likely to affect us as is ours to affect them.* It is obligatory upon each of us to exercise every choice we make consciously, diligently, and with full awareness of its intentional and unintentional impact on everyone else in this space. This is possible only if we make our choices wisely.

Every choice we exercise follows one of the two paths: the path that tempts or the path that ennobles. Choosing the path that ennobles comes naturally to the wise.

> The purpose of wisdom is not to pursue perfection or idealism, nor an attempt to pretend to be better than we are. One does not become good by trying to be good. One becomes good and great when one has discovered the inherent goodness and wisdom that is already within oneself.

It helps to know that the sum total of goodness in the world far exceeds the sum total of meanness; that is why I believe it is far easier to be good than 'not good'. All one has to do is to not halt or disrupt the natural flow of the goodness you have discovered within yourself to the world outside. Wisdom helps in both—first in discovering the goodness within you, and then in facilitating the flow of natural goodness from within to the world outside.

Wisdom Is Singular—It Is the Eternal Truth

> *If I look into a mirror and do not see my face in it, it is not necessarily because the mirror is not reflecting the object in front of it; it could be because the reflected image is not perceptible due to a layer of dust on the mirror. When I clean the mirror, the act of cleaning does not create the reflection of the face; it merely unveils the reflection that was already there.*[3]
>
> *Similarly, most of us are not aware of our innermost potential because the 'subjective mind' reflecting it is thickly coated with past tendencies and experiences, generated by personal priorities led by the ego. If we clean up our mind and empty it of all our past notions and beliefs, the wisdom within is readily revealed.*

Wisdom, like truth, is singular. In fact, wisdom is truth. Wisdom cannot be acquired simply by reading books. It only reveals itself in the richness of your observations and experiences, provided you diligently follow the four precepts I outlined in my Invitation.

- Completely empty your mind of all past biases, beliefs and assumptions.
- Pay attention not just to what you are looking at but equally to where you are looking from.
- Become a child once again: brimming with love, seeing no barriers and believing everything is possible.
- Collaborate with a diverse group of people to ensure that the answers you are looking for will meet the aspirations of all people, and do so with the utmost *humility*.

Humility is the operative word. Without humility, wisdom is unattainable, in spite of all the endeavours the aspirant may make and the highest intellectual equipment he may possess.

Humility is the virtue of all virtues. Without humility, no virtue is possible. Humility neutralizes the 'ego', the person you think you are, so that you can become the person you really are, with an inherent resource of wisdom. EGO is that which 'edges the goodness out'. You deactivate the ego, and your innate goodness stays with you all the time.

Arrogance or pride is born of ignorance;
it clouds the vision and leads to darker outcomes.
Humility is born of understanding;
it imparts wisdom and leads to brighter outcomes.

As we start living the path of wisdom, we no longer see ourselves as separate from one another, or separate from nature. We see all of us together, with unity among us, and in unity with nature.

Survival of the Wisest

Charles Darwin formulated the theory of evolution by natural selection in 1859 in his book *On the Origin of Species*.[4] His theory is often pithily summed up as 'survival of the fittest'. The term 'fitness' referred not to an organism's physical strength or agility but its ability to survive and reproduce. As resources are limited in nature, organisms with heritable traits that favour survival and reproduction tend to leave more offsprings than their peers, resulting in an increase in the numbers of that species over generations. It appears this paradigm created a somewhat narrow view of why and how some of the species survived longer than others.

Some species do have competitive streaks but, more often, nature is a highly collaborative ecosystem in which the 'fittest' are not the strongest and the most aggressive but the ones who are most collaborative—such as ants, bees, elephants and dolphins. I would extend this rationale by adding that the survival criteria of the past can no longer ensure our survival in the future. Hereafter, the survival of our species, or even a part of our species, will be contingent on our ability to demonstrate a more collaborative ethos in every domain.

That is where wisdom will play a dominant role, and that is why I believe we are entering an era of the 'survival of the wisest'.

If we accept the new realities, we will find it easier to imbibe new traits and acquire a new understanding to cope with the new risks to society and the planet. The unprecedented access to new scientific knowledge and technological developments will ensure that more of us are cognizant of not only the grave risks that confront us but also the means to resolve them. We will have a clear-cut passage to ensure a transition to a Safe New World for the continued existence of the human species.

Attributes of the Wisdom Economy

The Wisdom Economy has been a subject of interest for over a decade. Julian Dobson,[5] a British author and social change expert, and Gregory Stebbins,[6] an American authority on leadership wisdom and founder of PeopleSavvy, have both done pioneering work in this field. Based on their thoughtful contributions, I have derived four key attributes of the Wisdom Economy:

One: The Knowledge Economy is innovative but restrictive; Wisdom Economy is reflective and transformational. Reflection doesn't displace innovation: it interrogates the purpose of the innovation and considers the consequences. The Knowledge Economy tends to be solely technological; Wisdom Economy is both technological and human. The Knowledge Economy views technology as the pot of gold at the end of the rainbow. The Wisdom Economy views technology as a tool and is more interested in how it is deployed. It tests technology for its contribution to human well-being.

Two: The Knowledge Economy wants more. The Wisdom Economy understands the concept of 'enough'. Wisdom knows that a person doesn't need an abundance of possessions for a good life. Wisdom understands prosperity as a state of sufficiency; knowledge without wisdom values only accumulation.

Three: The Knowledge Economy is competitive. It believes in zero-sum games. The Wisdom Economy is collaborative. Wisdom recognizes that abundance is only possible when we all grow together.

Four: The Knowledge Economy demands qualifications. The Wisdom Economy prioritizes qualities. Qualifications can be excellent but they don't make you a better worker or even a better thinker. The Wisdom Economy will recruit for attitude as well as for aptitude. A wisdom worker has a more balanced inward/outward perspective, and better understands her obligations to herself and others.

Fundamentally, the Wisdom Economy regards all activity as either socially responsible and worth doing, or not socially responsible and therefore to be avoided.

The term 'Wisdom Economy' is believed to have been first used in 1982 by Earl Cook, an American author and futurist, to describe a new economic paradigm that emphasizes the importance of knowledge, innovation and wisdom in driving economic growth. He also outlined nine characteristics of the Wisdom Economy, which he called the nine 'Neo-Malthusian Beliefs'. The first three of these are worthy of recall:

- Materials and energy balances constrain production.
- Affluence has been a much more fecund mother of invention than has necessity. That is, science and technology require an economic surplus to support them.
- Real wealth is by technology out of nature or, as English economist William Petty would have said, 'technology may be the father of wealth, but nature is the mother'.[7]

A Big Leap Towards a New Planetary Civilization

The Wisdom Economy isn't just another 'new economy'. It is a wisdom-led economy that emanates from restructured thought processes and wisdom-anchored principles, to help make better choices—focused on improving governance by completely transforming democracy as it is today to democracy as it should be.

The Wisdom Economy is not about ignoring knowledge; it is about taking cognizance of how that knowledge is deployed. It is about ensuring that knowledge is used for the benefit of all, not a few. It is about firmly believing that knowledge without values can be a disaster; only knowledge with values can lead us to a future that sustains, a future in which everyone will play a significant role for the benefit of all.

The four transitions till now were all consequences of the human race decisively breaking the barriers and frontiers in the external world. The advent of the Wisdom Economy breaks the barriers to the last new frontier humankind needs to cross over to enter our inner world and discover the enormous potential and dormant strengths and resources lying untapped within us. It is a grand leap inward that will take human progress to an altogether new level of civilization on a planetary scale.

Leadership with Wisdom Is Synonymous with Responsible Leadership

Economic growth in the world since the Industrial Revolution has been strikingly significant. But it has led to our being entwined in a mindset that lacks soul and is at odds with the aspirations of young people starting their economic journeys. In our quest for productivity, we have completely forgotten that the fundamental purpose of the economy is to serve society. *The blind belief that 'more is always better', has proven to be a fallacious conjecture, not just for the individuals busy gathering wealth, but also for the society in which they operate.* It is incumbent upon us all to completely overhaul the entire structure of policy frameworks and governance structures.

The Wisdom Economy will completely recreate the entire governance system and root it in a set of universal values and holistic principles that will be equally applicable to all individuals, corporations, and government and non-government institutions. The Wisdom-led economy will naturally pay more attention to what Sir Ronald Cohen[8] called the 'invisible heart' of our economic system (as opposed to Adam Smith's 'invisible hand').

The Annual Meetings of the World Economic Forum in Davos, Switzerland, are ostensibly dialogues among the world's most powerful people. Each Annual Meeting focuses on a specific theme. The Summit themes over the last five years have been as follows:

- 2024: Rebuilding Trust in a Fractured World
- 2023: Cooperation in a Fragmented World

- 2022: Working Together; Restoring Trust
- 2021: The Great Reset
- 2020: Stakeholders for a Cohesive and Sustainable World

These are excellent ideas and noble intentions, yet the problems linger on while world leaders move on to other themes. No one can argue that there is a lack of knowledge or lack of awareness about the issues and problems being discussed by the participants. The question is why the political powers and business elites do not reach a consensus for action. Why does their professed call to make the world better not lead to initiating the changes the world needs?

Is it lack of wisdom? Surely there are many very wise people at Davos every year. Or is it that individual wisdom does not carry much weight in the face of collective 'un-wisdom'? Or is it that collective knowledge is only geared to focus on narrow agendas and short-term goals while the wisdom to pursue holistic, sustainable growth does not effectively surface?

Many people appreciate the efforts of the World Economic Forum to bring these issues to global attention. Many wise voices and learned opinions are shared at these summits that point to the future we could have but have somehow failed to bring about any change.

The book titled *The Great Re-set*, by Klaus Schwab and Thierry Malleret, written just before the 2021 Davos Summit, made a compelling case to pursue a 'path that will take us to a better world: more inclusive, more equitable, and more respectful of Mother Nature,'—but leaving no doubt that this will be possible only if we 'summon up the better nature of our angels and make the right moral choices'.[9] It would be wonderful if the World Economic Forum Summits could sincerely attempt to rise to this simple expectation.

Can Individual Wisdom Transcend to Institutional Wisdom?

Peter Senge, senior lecturer at the MIT Sloan School of Management, expressed concern that while we have extraordinary powers to influence the world in incredible ways, both on large and on micro scales, we continue to evolve in an unbalanced way because there is no wisdom accompanying this power. In particular, institutionally, there is no evidence that we collectively possess any wisdom at all.

> The reason I emphasize *institutionally* is because most power is exercised institutionally. It's not just you and me as individuals driving our automobiles producing carbon dioxide. It's the whole infrastructure of production and consumption and gasoline production. These are all multi-institutional or inter-institutional processes, so consequently the development of knowledge, understanding, and wisdom needs to be at the institutional and inter-institutional level.[10]

It is my irrevocable belief that a wise leader can truly transform an organization and instil a culture that wields institutional power for good, in a spirit of love, peace and harmony. It is the only way to keep institutions alive and relevant or else the power and the resources that they have nurtured can be rapidly depleted through misuse.

Wisdom is a unique virtue. Most other virtues typically permit, even provide a licence, to misuse your attribute for unworthy purposes. For example, as scholar Michael Prinzing says: '[An] intellectually gifted person may use his intelligence to commit fraud, and a witty person may use his wit to ridicule others...But one cannot, it seems, be too wise or put one's wisdom to bad use. When it comes to wisdom, good use is part of the very notion of wisdom.'[11]

As the wisdom of the leader percolates down to others in the organization, we may observe the revival of some wonderful traditions of bygone years, still prevalent in some indigenous cultures, such as spontaneous feelings of shared joys and laughter, peace and goodwill. That is an intrinsic human trait but it is no longer the norm.

The normal we have been living with in the 21st century is rather odd. We claim the highest-ever GDP and yet we feel more fear and anxiety, more antipathy and hatred than ever. We do not feel safe; we are worried all the time. Rich or poor, we are all concerned about our future and are scheming all the time.

All of us need a Safe New World. If we think nothing can be done because this is a fait accompli, nothing will really change. If we think we can change ourselves by discovering our inherent wisdom, then we most certainly shall usher in the Safe New World.

The key attributes of Wisdom Leadership are portrayed in the next chapter. They will create the foundational framework for reviving responsible leadership and responsible entrepreneurship.

Chapter 7

Three Traits of Wisdom Economy Leaders

Awareness, Bridge-Building and Compassion

What lies behind us and what lies before us
are tiny matters compared to what lies within us.

—Ralph Waldo Emerson (1803–1882)[1]

The Dawn of an Epic Evolution

Just as the people living in the Hunter-Gatherer Economy would never have imagined that they would one day witness a changeover to the Agricultural Economy, people in each subsequent phase also never foresaw society graduating to the next phase. It is, therefore, quite understandable that all of us, the inhabitants of the Knowledge Economy, find it difficult to accept that wisdom could replace knowledge as the prime driver to determine the trajectory of our future.

Invariably, there is resistance to change but this will be one change welcomed by all—except obviously by the small minority that has disrupted the forward march of the entire human civilization, believing it is their right to do so because they are in power. The irony is that they do not think they are doing anything wrong;

perhaps nobody ever thinks so. An even greater irony is that so many political and business leaders take pride in outdoing others in their quest for absolute hegemony and utmost wealth. The last four years have magnified this reality and what was hidden is now wide open and what was considered a draw of fate has now been exposed as a deliberate manoeuvre by those in power. Nothing else can explain how there has been a multifold increase in the wealth of the billionaires, while billions in most countries have become poorer.

It is a distressing thought that while the entire world is awash with a surplus of knowledge, most of it cannot be gainfully deployed as it is devoid of wisdom. At the same time, it is most heartening that the stage is set for an epic evolution of wisdom in our governance systems.

Homo Sapiens—The Wise among the Primates

Our species, the human race, was given a new name in 1758, the '*Homo sapiens*'.[2] This Latin-origin word literally means 'wise man': homō (*hominis*) means 'human being', while sapiens means 'discerning, wise, sensible'. The question is whether we, the *Homo sapiens*, are really wise in the true sense of the word.

Man is indeed a unique creature. Unlike other species, man is not merely a form in the landscape, he is also a purveyor and shaper of the landscape. He is an explorer; he does not merely look for habitats but makes his own habitats wherever he goes. His powers of observation, his inventiveness, his imagination, and his perseverance make it possible for him not to accept the world as it is but to change it.

All living creatures, humans and animals, possess a mind. As they come in contact with the world, impulses and feelings are generated in their minds that are manifested in their actions. Human beings alone have the capacity to discriminate and analyse feelings as and when they arise, and allow their actions to be guided and directed by this power of discrimination, instead of being carried away by momentary impulses.

This faculty of discrimination, the power of judgment, the capacity to distinguish between right and wrong, what should be done and what should not, is the function of the intellect. The culture and progress of humankind lies in the exercise of this faculty and when this wondrous equipment is left neglected, humans are bound to deteriorate to the status of other species and suffer the consequences.

Four Types of Leadership Mindsets

Over the millennia, there have been four alternative leadership mindsets, with distinct characteristics. As we look at these broad classifications, we may find a certain component of each mindset in every leader.[3]

1) *Stone-like Leaders*

Once upon a time, and this is still not uncommon today, human awareness of the world was generally vague or indistinct. In such circumstances, the responses of the leaders tend to be preordained, with little concern for their impact then or later. Such a pattern of behaviour is akin to 'stone-like conduct', as it closely resembles the mode of inert objects, just existing because they are there, with neither consciousness nor stimulus.

Such leadership conduct manifests itself as *ruthlessness* to pursue a single-point agenda—such as continuing to retain command—at any cost for as long as possible with neither awareness nor concern for the consequences. Such stone-like leaders are unable to discriminate. They have no plans, and no pangs of guilt. The likes of Pol Pot (1925–1998) of Cambodia and Idi Amin (1952–2003) of Uganda represent this category.

2) *Plant-like Leaders*

Plants are a little more evolved than inert objects. They are predominantly stationary; they remain where they are and their reaction to the world is confined to securing the basic necessities for their existence. The rudiments of discrimination seem to emerge in the plant kingdom, but just barely. They are steeped in inertia. They can never exert or do anything innovative. Such persons fall under the category of 'plant-like leaders'.

They are able to distinguish between sunlight and darkness (prosperity versus poverty), growth-nourishers versus growth-inhibitors, and they endeavour to obtain whatever they need (living entirely for themselves). Emotion (or concern for community) is conspicuous by its absence; a mother-tree does not allow even its seedlings to grow under it when the latter come in the way of its quest for food and water.

In his poem 'The Hollow Men', Thomas Stearns Eliot[4] described how such people live broken lives, somewhere between life and death, in a world in which they have no stakes, just a limited survival instinct. North Korea's Kim Jong-Il (1942–2011) and Rafael Trujillo (1891–1961) of the Dominican Republic would come under this classification.

3) *Animal-like Leaders*

Animals are more evolved than plants and have a better awareness of the world. Traces of the faculty of intellectual discrimination are also discernible. While they tend to respond to opportunities and threats in the environment, their reactions are all desire-ridden, passionate and ego-centric. Their intellectual discrimination is limited and being extroverts, they constantly engage themselves in fighting, procuring and aggrandizing to support themselves and their kith and kin. They have no concept of future, neither for themselves, nor for anyone else. Their activities are mainly guided by impulses rather than by discrimination and understanding. Adolf Hitler (1889–1945) stands out as the most representative example of this mindset.

The species of the animal kingdom do not normally, willfully harm or kill other members of their own species. Even the most dangerous animals are usually not afraid of their own kind.

Sadly, we *Homo sapiens* have lost the capacity to live harmoniously with each other. We build imaginary walls between ourselves and nurture the right to fight and kill in the name of nationality, religion, caste, race and for a multitude of other reasons. We have never lived up to our moniker of 'wise being'. We might as well be rated as the most destructive and vicious species that ever inhabited this planet.

Four Types of Leadership Mind-sets

Reflecting the Process of Evolution

Stone-like Leaders	Plant-like Leaders	Animal-like Leaders	Humane Leaders
No consciousness	Limited self-centred consciousness	Ego-centric, greed-led consciousness	Fully developed consciousness
Ruthless exercise of brute power	Lethargic exercise of power	Aggressive, self-aggrandizing exercise of power	Balanced, holistic exercise of power
No ability to discriminate	Very limited ability to discriminate	Developed discrimination skills for self-preservation only	Fully developed intellect and ability to discriminate

4) *Humane Leaders*

The fourth variety, the 'human being' is the most evolved form in creation. They have the maximum capacity for emotion and their feelings can embrace the entire universe. Human faculties of intellectual discrimination know no bounds; one can discriminate extrovertly in the gross world and can also delve into the subjective layers of one's own personality to access the spiritual core within oneself.

Leaders who are unable to make use of this great inherent capacity, for whatever reason, belong to one or more of the aforesaid three categories. But the leaders who develop universal love and constantly engage themselves in activities under the guidance of their superior intellect can be called 'humane leaders'. They alone can lay claim to the prestige, dignity and glory of human life.

These women and men truly and literally represent the species, unencumbered by any residues of stone-like, plant-like or animal-like leadership mindsets. These are the ones our planet needs today—the likes of Mahatma Gandhi, Nelson Mandela and millions of others we come across, all over the world, in our daily lives. Such are the potential wise leaders who possess the capability to usher us into the Wisdom Economy.

Three Precepts of Wisdom Leadership

Wisdom Leaders are easily noticeable. They reach the summit of leadership not because they love power but because they engage the power of love to serve others—the institution, the community, the nation and the world at large. They live and lead with three sacrosanct precepts as their intrinsic guide in all that they think, say or do. Pursued in unison, the precepts enable them to evolve a cohesive thought process which becomes their first nature. I call these precepts the ABC of Wisdom Leadership.

A. Awareness
B. Bridge Building
C. Compassion

A) Awareness: 1st Precept of Wisdom Leadership

Awareness is a multi-faceted trait. It has three dimensions

- *Awareness of one's own 'True Self',*
- *Awareness of the Ground Realities—Encompassing all Externalities, and*
- *Awareness of the Collective Human Capabilities—Including the Potential of Technologies*

First Dimension of Awareness: Awareness of One's Own True Self

Awareness of the self is the source and substance of everything we observe, perceive and know. Being aware is our natural state. But somehow, in real life, most of us live in a default mode and spend an inordinate proportion of our time and energy on limiting our faculty of awareness. We tangle ourselves in a plethora of unwanted and irrelevant data masquerading as experience and deprive ourselves of realizing the infinite potential within that is ours and ours alone. The immensity of this dormant energy is nearer to us than anything else and yet most of us are unaware that it is so readily accessible.

Awareness is neither active nor passive, it is inevitable; it just happens if you let it. You do not become aware by concentration, it happens naturally. Awareness cannot be contrived, it is transparent. It is the only true source of clarity. The fact of being aware is the most satisfying, natural experience. If you are not aware, it is you alone who are withholding it. It is the pure state of 'being' which inevitably leads to a feeling of sustained joy and peace, and wisdom that matters.

> To be aware is not 'knowledge'. It is a discovery. It is not an achievement. It is not a possession, either. It is just 'you'—the real 'you'—that you are not aware of.

There is only one way to be aware of one's true self: take a pause from the usual routine and spend a few moments to look inwards. Looking inwards means 'looking heart-ward'. Each of us has the inward-looking eyes to do so and make this discovery. Even a blind person has this God-given ability to look inwards. This inward sight provides access to the most significant discovery in the human kingdom—access to one's conscience, the deep-within power that nourishes and sustains life.

The conscience is the moral compass endowed by wisdom that is present within each of us. The word is derived directly from the Latin word *conscientia*, which means 'knowledge within oneself, a sense of right and wrong'. The online Etymology Dictionary defines conscience as the 'faculty of knowing what is right', originally (c.1200) in the context of Christian ethics, and later as 'awareness whether the acts for which one feels responsible do or do not conform to one's ideal of right'.[5] In the late 14th century it implied, more generally, the 'sense of fairness or justice, the moral sense'.

'Conscience is the ever-present inner light that illumines the truth, helping one do the right thing even when no one is looking. One's conscience isn't swayed by greed of pleasure or fear of pain. Conscience isn't selfish. It is objective, true, pure, and dependable.'[6]

The conscience is a human being's most treasured asset. It comes with life. It is an intrinsic part of life. A life that fails to take cognizance of the presence of one's conscience and prides itself in ignoring its calling is not a life well lived, it is mere existence. A wise person is not only able to discover the conscience within but also develop the sixth sense to listen to her conscience. It is the pure voice of reason that constantly highlights the difference between right and wrong. Whether you listen to it or not, whether you accept it or not, is entirely your call. But it is worth remembering that, 'The voice of conscience is so delicate that it is easy to stifle it; but it is also so clear that it is impossible to mistake it.'[7]

A life that acknowledges the constant presence of a conscience within, and uses this inherent and infinite strength as a vigilant guide and mentor, will forever be at peace within, and at peace with the world. That is true living.

> A life lived without a conscience is a disgrace.
> A life lived with a conscience is full of grace.

The conscience opens your heart to 'truth', one that inspires you to go beyond the inhibited personal self and its projections, misconceptions and false beliefs. It helps you to unleash your highest potential. It brings cognizance of the reality that one's own true self is aligned and synonymous with the true self of every human being. You feel empowered by the simultaneous development of harmony between inner power and outer action, with constant guidance of the 'truth', the conscience, or the heart—whatever you call it. For the wise, this continuous self-awareness of conscience, listening to it, and acting upon it, naturally becomes first nature. This is the metamorphosis that makes a difference in how you lead and how you live.

Second Dimension of Awareness:
Awareness of the Ground Realities—Encompassing All Externalities

This component of awareness pertains to our being fully alive to what is happening all around us in the world, and refers to our ability to take an unprejudiced, unrestricted view, embracing both human-created situations as well as those created by nature.

We all live under the same sky but see different horizons. Awareness implies taking the entire view—beyond even the known horizons—with an unbiased mindset and an unencumbered heart-set. That happens when one is willing to go beyond the familiar and tries to genuinely learn what one does not already know. You remove self-imposed barriers that blind your faculties and start perceiving what you did not, or could not, perceive. You develop new insights, leading to a connection with what was previously unconnected. Perspectives and decisions based on such awareness tend to be more sustainable because they are always more equitable.

Embracing 720-degree Leadership

Usually, such a view is taken from the perceiver's vantage, with reference to her mind, and processed in her intellect—a complete 360-degree view. It is not easy, and yet it is only half the job. Each of our decisions and actions has an impact on others, directly or indirectly. The 'complete awareness' comes when we take an additional 360-degree view, as perceived by others, with reference to their minds and as processed in their thoughts. Awareness is a 720-degree view.

A 360-degree view excludes; a 720-degree view includes those who are excluded. A 720-view is the most significant criterion for the 'inclusive growth' that global leaders routinely talk about.

Plainly, awareness means opening your hearts and widening your minds. It is possible only when you sincerely acknowledge that your decisions may have an unintended and irrevocable adverse impact on some whose views *may* have been excluded. For taking the right decisions, you need a holistic overview of the entirety of issues, a detached observation of all perceptions. This realization can only emanate from a keenness to be cognizant of the views of all others, particularly those who were not part of your decision-making process. The motivation to do so comes from a genuine interest in seeking truth, justice and goodness. The obstacles to tuning antennae to seek complete awareness lie not in the techniques or resources, but in closed hearts and narrow minds.

The enlarged multi-scopic vision makes it easier to focus attention on interrelationships rather than objects, on processes rather than on structures, and on networks rather than on hierarchies. In my earlier book, I referred to this trait as the trait of wholeness.[8]

Awareness is a 720 Degree View

With commitment to 720-Vision or wholeness, one discovers new insights that cannot be deduced by studying components. One begins to capture the meaning of the oft-repeated phrase: 'the whole is more than the sum of its parts'. Wholeness enables one to acknowledge that one's own domain of work or influence is not and cannot be a stand-alone, independent system, which can be in equilibrium by itself. It is neither possible to negate its impact on the externalities, nor can it be isolated from the impact of the externalities.

Wholeness connects us to one another and to nature. We start realizing that our individual actions, even our thoughts and intentions, affect other people around us, and are affected in turn by other people. This makes us a part of a network of connections. With this realization, we become a part of the solution rather than remaining a part of the problem.

In essence, wholeness, or total awareness, emphatically empowers one to comprehend multiple perspectives from different points of view and realize that there is no 'one answer'. This is the beginning of finding the right answers—innovative, sustainable and 'win-win-win' answers.

In practice, awareness helps us strike a 'balance', a balance between diverse, conflicting demands; a 'balance' leading to a seamless integration of opposing views. You acknowledge the existence of seemingly irreconcilable extreme positions yet you succeed in discovering an acceptable posture which is an integrated solution to meet the triple bottom line criteria of institutional goals, economic and community justice and ecological sustainability.

As a leader, wholeness gives you an incisive understanding of all geo-economic, geo-social and geopolitical issues and perspectives. 'Balance' in the decision-making process also acts as an 'organizational energizer'. It heals the conflicts of the mind and collates inner and outer considerations, as well as individual and community interests. It manifests itself as integration within the self, integration with community and nature, and a synthesis of diverse views and traditions. This awareness of the unity and interconnectedness of all beings leads to a reverence for life, an acceptance of the kinship of humanity, and a commitment to heal our wounded planet and its people.

Third Dimension of Awareness: Awareness of Collective Human Capabilities, Including the Potential and Power of Technology

A profound comprehension of the current status and potential of all natural and man-made resources, including the power and prospects of science and technology, are an essential constituent of awareness. Only then can a wise leader generate the best possible solutions for the multifarious problems facing humanity. In a world where it is not easy to keep pace with technological progress and innovation, a wise leader will ensure that he has other equally wise leaders, well versed in these disciplines, to guide him and mentor him on all relevant innovations, as also on the possibilities to steer technology inventions towards equitable growth and progress.

New technologies have improved our lives in many ways, yet they can lead to significant, unintended (or maliciously intended) consequences for individuals, organizations, societies and even nations. The technology outcomes are neither universally positive nor universally negative. They could be beneficial for some and, at the same time, harmful for others. Negating the detrimental impacts of technology, naturally, becomes a vital component of every mission.

We have been through four industrial revolutions. The first Industrial Revolution started in 1769 with the steam engine, water power and mechanization. The second Industrial Revolution was anchored by electricity and mass production. The third Industrial Revolution was shaped by electronics, IT systems and automation; and the fourth Industrial Revolution took flight with AI, robotics, augmented reality and the convergence of digital and biological innovations. The onset of the fourth Industrial Revolution has led to widespread concerns that the development of AI will tend to have a dehumanizing impact on society.

Authors William Davidow and Michael Malone take the view that instead of generating productivity improvements that increase GDP and prosperity—as previous industrial advances have—AI may lead to boosting productivity while driving down GDP. Among the potential results are: 'an abundance of innovative products, yes, but also declining wages, growing economic inequality, less work all around, and the emergence of millions of "ZEVs"—people of Zero Economic Value, individuals you would not hire even if they worked for free.'[9]

Where Is Technology Steering Us Today?

We are now on the cusp of the fifth Industrial Revolution, an accelerated AI revolution reinforced with quantum computing, and aiming at machine intelligence working together with human intelligence. Often without it.

Mustafa Suleyman, AI pioneer and the founder of DeepMind cogently explains:

> The coming wave of AI is characterized by a set of four intrinsic features. *First*, its hugely *asymmetric* impact can create unthinkable vulnerabilities and pressure points against seemingly dominant powers. *Second*, it is developing fast, a kind of *hyper-evolution,* iterating, improving, and branching into new areas at incredible speed. *Third*, they are often *omni-use;* they can be used for many different purposes. And *fourth*, they increasingly have a degree of *autonomy* beyond any previous technology.
>
> While omni-use and asymmetric impacts have been inherent in several technologies, that isn't the case for *autonomy*. Technology has always been about allowing us to do more, but crucially with humans still doing the doing. Not anymore. With AI, there is no need for a human to laboriously define the manner in which a task should take place. Instead, we just specify a high-level goal and rely on a machine to figure out the optimal way of getting there. Paradoxically, these technologies are largely beyond our ability to comprehend at a granular level—yet still within our ability to create and use.[10]

So far, machines have never been able to make suggestions or take decisions on what to do. Today, AI-empowered machines can create new ideas as well as implement them. This power—which includes the power to be destructive—is well within the realms of possibility, particularly if super-intelligent AI systems are not aligned with ethics and values. For example, AI-empowered hackers can launch random cyberattacks and security breaches; AI systems can even be set up to automatically choose targets and subject them to surveillance, oppression or warfare.

There is nothing to suggest, up to now, that this machine power, like an alien power, could have the ability to acquire human faculties to be compassionate or just.

Meanwhile, deepfakes powered by AI are already making it extremely difficult to verify if audio, video or even text communications are coming from a real person or a manufactured entity. Naturally, such identity manipulation would significantly distort the credibility of public discourse, as well as seriously undermine the trust in digital interactions and information sources.

Security expert Audrey Kurth Cronin is deeply apprehensive that:[11]

> The worldwide dispersal of emerging technologies, such as commercial drones, cyber weapons, 3D printing, military robotics and autonomous systems, is generating gaping fissures in the ability of conventional armed forces to combat lethal capabilities of non-state actors, most notably terrorists, but also rogue lone actors, insurgent groups, and private armies. Never before have so many had access to such advanced technologies capable of inflicting death and mayhem. Unless we better understand the rapidly developing threats, governments, especially democracies, will be increasingly unable to combat them.

Yet, global safety and accountability norms are still elusive. Regulation alone will not contain AI. Regulation must be paired with adequate systematic research on AI safety, of which there is relatively little. Many experts fear that containing AI may be all but impossible.

Notwithstanding the above, AI also has the potential to play a tangible positive role in addressing some of the most persistent challenges we face, particularly in disease detection and drug discovery, improving access to quality education, optimizing crop yields, developing eco-friendly technologies, predicting and mitigating the impact of natural disasters, and public safety and security, to name a few.

I believe technology is morally neutral. Whether we steer it to serve society and foster inclusive growth and development depends on us, the leaders of business and society. If we take the wrong call, we will all perish. With wisdom, we can take the right call and we will all advance.

'The Future of Jobs Report 2023' compiled by the World Economic Forum estimates that '44 per cent of workers' skills will be disrupted in the next five years. Six out of ten workers will require training before 2027, but only half of them are seen to have access to adequate training opportunities.'[12] As a society, we are still not prepared to meet the challenges ahead. The Wisdom Economy leaders will need to have a good grip of the new confluence of technologies presently advancing the Fifth Industrial Revolution. It is vitally important to keep asking at every stage: Is it benefitting the entire human race or just the elite? What has it made us—morally superior, or greedier?

B) Bridge Building: Bridges of Understanding and Connectedness—Second Precept of Wisdom Leadership

An individual invariably has limitations. It has therefore been an established human practice to build teams and groups to achieve more. That is how organizations were formed. Organizations facilitate a group of humans to work together to plan and accomplish tasks that could not otherwise have been done individually. This is applicable at the family level, the community level, the national level and, equally, at the international level. Those who have succeeded have effectively demonstrated that there is strength in collaboration and unity, and even greater strength in diversity and unity.

By the same rationale, every organization also has its own limiting constraints, as also every community and every nation. That is how the culture of commerce and collaboration evolved. The greater the collaboration and commerce, the greater the prevalence of peace and goodwill in the world. Today, our national and community leaders have to ready themselves to cross the last frontier to propel collaboration to a new level, and aim at removing the increasing vestiges of distrust and fear which keep arising because of either misunderstanding or the absence of understanding. The absence of understanding is a consequence of the lack of efforts to understand the other viewpoint.

Building bridges that narrow the distance between minds and hearts has a magical impact on eliminating suspicions and strife. Impelled by wholeness, you start discovering infinite bridges of understanding all around; you start seeing the bridges that were always there but were not seen because you tended to ignore the things that fell in the broad domain of 'otherness'. *Now there will no longer be a chasm between us and others; there is only us—one big community living on one small planet.* When you do not readily find a bridge, the impulse to build a new one comes naturally.

Wise leaders work with a strong conviction that there is more that unites the world than what divides it. Connectedness is in their DNA, and they are inspired by the vision of collective growth and progress.

There is a famous African proverb, 'A person is a person through other persons.' In short, it means that everything we learn and experience in the world is through our relationships with other people. We are therefore called upon to explore all options to enter into a purposeful dialogue with all those we come in contact with. We do so by building bridges of understanding with them. If there has been a conflict, the bridges of understanding create a more congenial environment for a mutually acceptable resolution of the conflict. If there is no conflict, then the bridges of understanding prevent a conflict from arising.

Archbishop Desmond Tutu taught the world 'to embrace the concepts of "human invaluableness" and interdependence because we all derive our humanity by virtue of being members of the human tribe'.[13] This notion of connectedness is an intrinsic part of African culture, expressed through the word 'Ubuntu' which fundamentally signifies: 'I am because we all are.' We think of ourselves far too frequently as just individuals separated from one another while we are all connected through our common humanity. The practice of Ubuntu is a constant stimulant to look at each human interaction as an opportunity to foster a more positive environment by building bridges to connect, to relate to, and understand each other.

Nelson Mandela, the first black and democratically elected president of South Africa in 1994, set for himself the goal of peacefully transitioning the apartheid state to a democracy. Desmond Tutu christened it the 'Rainbow Nation'. Together, they pioneered the notion of restorative justice by setting up the Truth and Reconciliation Commission, a forum where all South Africans could tell their own story of living under apartheid, blacks and whites alike. As a nation, they chose to see the wider perspective. To move forward, they had to allow everyone to share their stories, good and bad, so that they all felt a part of the new nation that was being built. They had to see other people's experiences as part of their own. This was a platform to let them choose to see the wider perspective.

Mandela was acutely conscious of the difficulties but he knew that the task had to be done. There was no other way. He and Desmond Tutu identified and practiced two significant pre-requisites to build bridges of sustainable collaboration: 'forgiveness' and 'free debate and dialogue'.

Forgiveness

Forgiveness is a potent strength every individual possesses; it has the power to create miracles in one's life. Forgiveness is the only way to bury the past and make you totally free to create the future you want. Unconditional forgiveness empties you of all the pent-up anger and hatred stored within you, and frees your mind to think creatively with nothing holding you back. The past becomes irrelevant; you feel you are 'present' in every moment, and your entire focus shifts to opening up new vistas.

Genuine forgiveness immediately creates inner peace, as you completely and perpetually banish the pain and suffering that has been constantly occupying your mindspace. You begin with forgiving yourself first, and then everyone else who has ever been a part of your life. You lose nothing; you only receive an instantaneous gift: complete dissolution of the artificial self-created barriers within you. You experience a rebirth of an energizing freedom to live and to love.

For many people, forgiveness is difficult as they wrongly associate it with weakness and victimhood. That is not true. It may appear to be an act of kindness to someone who has wronged you; in reality, forgiveness is more an act of kindness and compassion for yourself. The phenomenal power of forgiveness transforms your life by setting you free. Forgiveness does not alter the past but it certainly paves the way for a better future.

Free Debate and Dialogue

Real life is far too complex to be controlled by those at the top. As Tolstoy puts it, 'they could not be expected to understand it at all, because they were not part of it or close enough to witness it'.[14] Those who claimed such understanding were either naïve or were claiming knowledge for some other purpose—to wield power, for instance. As his novel *War and Peace* shows, it is those at the base of the pyramid who make history, even if they do not know it.

It is ironic that in the professed pursuit of the 'Golden Rule', leaders assume that they know what others want or need. Actually, there is a much better way to decide what to do if you really want to help others: Ask people what they want, they will be more than willing to tell you.

To permit free debate and dialogue, create neutral platforms for people to express their opinions freely and fearlessly. Giving dignity to others, and listening to them with patience, tolerance and respect creates an amiable environment for amicable solutions.

Wise leaders in the Wisdom Economy will also bring about another makeover, a transformation not merely limited to dominance of soft power over hard power, but way beyond that to the domain of '*shared power*'. It shall be based not on what type of power to wield, but on how to share the power one wields. When leaders empower others in a manner that they together use that power to achieve shared goals, the entire world will perceive the stunning transformation that connectedness can bring about.

Inspiring Bridge-Builders in Society and Business

There are many examples of global leaders who displayed prodigious skills in building bridges of understanding and connecting with adversaries while fostering positive outcomes for all parties. The former Secretary-General of the United Nations, Kofi Annan, did that admirably in negotiating peace in the Bosnia and Kosovo conflicts. Former Chancellor of Germany, Angela Merkel, navigated complex negotiations with her pragmatic and inclusive approach to build consensus among EU member states. George Mitchell, the businessman diplomat, created strong bridges of trust during pivotal peace negotiations in Northern Ireland, bringing an end to violent sectarian conflict in 1998.

In the business sphere, Paul Polman of Unilever, Indra Nooyi of Pepsi, Zhou Qunfei of Lens Technology, and Ajay Banga of Mastercard are exemplary role models who consider people with different worldviews not as adversaries but as potential partners. They demonstrated how a humanistic vision can build lasting bridges of collaboration while fostering sustainable operations, inclusive workplaces, and innovative growth-ways for marginalized communities. Their leadership approach is anchored on the belief that business progress and societal good can be mutually reinforcing, not antagonistic. They have proven, beyond doubt, that with understanding and compassion, every constraint can be a gateway to new frontiers of progress that benefit all stakeholders.

Polman, the former CEO of Unilever, launched the 'Unilever Sustainable Living Plan', aimed at nurturing diversity, equity and inclusion across the organization to build collaborative teams at all levels of leadership. Nooyi closed gender and racial pay gaps within the company, created employee resource groups to develop a sense of belonging for under-represented communities, and nurtured an all-inclusive environment for innovation. Qunfei was the first CEO in China to provide equal opportunities for learning and advancement to every employee, including those from humble origins like hers, a process which helped build a committed workforce. Banga set up the Centre for Inclusive Growth to support economic development with focus on income inequality, gender inequality, education of girls, and barriers to entrepreneurship.

Banga, on taking over as the World Bank president in 2023, shared his vision for his new role: to create a world free of poverty on a liveable planet. 'We are writing a new playbook. It sets us on a journey that will require reimagined partnerships, and a new way of working and thinking. We need the scale, resources, and ingenuity of the private sector. If done right, we could draw in institutional investors to put their $70 trillion to work in developing countries. This has been the thing of fantasy for years. There is nothing that gives me more hope than our capacity to work together in common purpose.'[15]

Time will tell how the new partnerships will take shape to deliver impactful results. But on the yardsticks of sincerity of effort and honesty of purpose, the envisioned alliances—built on bridges of shared goals—could well become global game-changers in a short time.

C) Compassion—Third Precept of Wisdom Leadership

As you experience awareness and build bridges of understanding all around, you simultaneously acquire a complementary trait, the trait of compassion which endows you with the spontaneous wisdom of the heart.

Compassion is a blend of fairness, kindness and gentleness, with a sprinkling of generosity and humility. It represents a feeling of unconditional love and concern for others, with a sense of responsibility. Most of all, it transforms your feelings of connectedness to 'connectedness with love'.

Very often, people talk of empathy in the same vein as compassion. I think it is necessary to understand the subtle difference between the two.

> *Empathy* means: I see you. I relate to you. I understand your need.
>
> *Compassion* means: I see you. I relate to you. I understand your need. And I am going to do something about it.

- Empathy is a noble intent. Compassion is a noble action.
- Empathy is a feel-good sentiment for the empathetic person,

while compassion is a feel-better consequence of the actions of the compassionate person.
- Empathy is an emotion. Compassion is a force for action to deal with it.

Compassion Is a Verb

Thich Nhat Hanh says with crystal clarity that 'Compassion is a verb.' Not just a noun, or an abstract idea or feeling.

> Compassion is a mind that removes the suffering that is present in the other. The essence of compassion is understanding, the ability to recognize the physical, material and psychological suffering of others. Shallow observation as an outsider is not enough to see their suffering. We must become one with the object of our observation. When we are in contact with another's suffering, a feeling of compassion is born in us.[16]

The prefix 'com' means 'with'. Compassion literally means, 'to suffer with'. Acts of compassion not only benefit the giver and the receiver, they also inspire others who simply observe the compassionate act.

Buddhist scholar Thupten Jinpa speaks of compassion as:

> [A] response to the inevitable reality of our human condition, our experiences of pain and sorrow, and offers the possibility of responding with understanding, patience, and kindness, rather than, say, fear and repulsion. Compassion lets us open ourselves to the reality of suffering and seek its alleviation. Compassion is what connects the feeling of empathy to acts of generosity, and other expressions of our altruistic tendencies.[17]

For those who care, compassion is not just a fleeting feeling; it becomes a way of seeing and being in the world. For them, being compassionate is the norm and it arises effortlessly. Compassion is an innate trait of the wise leader and readily opens new vistas of understanding and awareness. It substantively enhances the perceived competencies of a leader and enables her to perform even the toughest of actions in a humane way.

Compassion is perceived at two levels—at the individual level in one-to-one or one-to-many interactions, and at a societal level when the exemplary actions of many compassionate persons become a catalyst for generating widespread societal compassion. This is the potential macro impact of wisdom in practice.

Profiles in Compassion

His Holiness Dalai Lama writes that there are three styles of compassionate leadership in the Buddhist tradition: *the trailblazer*, who leads from the front, takes risks and sets an example; *the ferryman*, who accompanies those in his care and shapes the ups and downs of the crossing; and *the shepherd*, who sees every one of his flock to safety before himself. Three styles, three approaches, but what they have in common is an all-encompassing concern for the welfare of those they lead.[18]

Mary Robinson, Ireland's first female president (1990–1997) prioritized social justice and education investment across Irish society. Later, as the UN High Commissioner for Human Rights and a sustainability foundation leader, her compassion helped give voice to marginalized communities globally.

Dr James Orbinski, the president of 'Doctors Without Borders' in the 1990s, displayed admirable leadership, emanating from courage and compassion, while providing medical relief during humanitarian emergencies.

Oprah Winfrey, media celebrity and philanthropist, is widely known for her compassion and generosity which she has commendably demonstrated in her talk shows and through her multiple social initiatives.

Rahul Bajaj, former Chairman of Bajaj Auto India, the voice of compassion and care long before others, was the leading pioneer of comprehensive village development programmes in the areas around their plants, with focus on education, health, water and infrastructure.

Hamdi Ulukaya, the Turkish immigrant founder of Chobani Greek Yogurt, built his company while paying his employees well above minimum wage and giving them significant shares options, even for hourly workers, thereby creating a model of compassionate capitalism.

Rosabeth Moss Kanter, Harvard Business School professor, has been a powerful emissary of humane and inclusive workplaces for over three decades. She has provided the moral and business case for leading with compassion and continuously prodded business and societal leaders to do so; not as an obligation to society but more for their own preservation.

All these leaders, and a multitude of others, reinforce the belief that compassion is a source of impregnable strength and positive change for human dignity and justice.

The Journey of a Wise Leader

The seeds of these traits of wisdom already exist in all human beings. It is the nature of seeds to grow. If we become aware of these seeds and let the seeds within us blossom, the path to wise leadership is smooth.

When wise leaders pursue this journey, they feel genuinely connected to everyone around them and continuously discover or build bridges of understanding. They find the balance and display compassion in all that they think, say and do. Their innermost feelings are deeply aligned with the feelings of others in the world outside.

> Wisdom is knowledge enlivened by awareness, committed to bridge building and infused with compassion.

Wisdom is all-encompassing and alive. It is knowingness beyond knowledge. In practice, leaders with wisdom apply self-analysis and self-regulation in the personal domain, feel genuine respect for the presence and needs of others, believe in interdependence as an essential feature of the life-system in which we exist, and seek proactive engagement to foster equity, sustainability, transparency and justice.

Each of us can pursue this path to the summit of Wise Leadership and be the architect of unity in diversity and a 'Master of Connectedness with Love'. That will be a celebration of the oneness and the interconnectedness of the world. This can happen as soon as more and more of us realize and start believing in the necessity of wisdom in the people who lead us.

Wisdom Economy Is Essentially a Human Economy

We are at a threshold moment in civilizational evolution. The transition to the Wisdom Economy has the propensity to become a truly human economy—a shift with profound implications for our future.

Dov Seidman, American author and founder chairman of the HOW Institute for Society, wrote that economies get labelled according to the work people predominately do in them. The Industrial Economy replaced the Agrarian Economy when people left farms for factories; then the Knowledge Economy pulled them from factories into office buildings. When that happened, the way workers added value changed, too. Instead of leveraging their brawn, companies capitalized on their brains. No longer 'hired hands', they were 'hired heads'. Seidman says, 'In the human economy, the most valuable workers will be "hired hearts". The know-how and analytic skills that made them indispensable in the Knowledge Economy would no longer give them an advantage over increasingly intelligent machines. But they will still bring to their work essential traits that can't be programmed into software, like creativity, passion, character, and collaborative spirit—their humanity, in other words.'[19]

The ability to leverage these strengths will be the prime source of any entity's superiority over another—be it an individual, an organization, a community, or a nation. With the momentum of the Wisdom Economy, the welfare of society becomes more paramount than the welfare of the individual, and in this simple transition lies the new trajectory of our future as a human race, which we will explore in Part Three.

PART THREE

Transition from Capitalism to Peopleism

Chapter 8

Peopleism

The Fundamental Precepts

The pessimist complains about the wind;
The optimist expects it to change;
The realist adjusts the sails.

—William Arthur Ward (1921–1994)[1]

The Anatomy of a Human Enterprise

A human thought is an exceedingly powerful resource. It has no barriers, no blockades, no boundaries, no limitations, no bondage. Each human being has complete freedom to think whatever she likes, whenever she wants to. One may be influenced by what one sees, reads, or hears in the world outside, but what one thinks is entirely one's exclusive prerogative.

Every thought a person ponders over, whether she expresses it or not, has either a positive or a negative impact on all her endeavours. Worthy thoughts lead to worthy outcomes with worthy impacts; unworthy thoughts naturally lead to unworthy outcomes with unworthy impacts. A thought by itself has no power. It is only when a person identifies and believes in the thought that she gives power to it.

A powerful thought is the source of every human enterprise. Its birth, its fruition, its growth—each stage is an outcome of the thought process of the entrepreneur. But no entrepreneur can accomplish anything significant by himself. Every entrepreneur requires three essential components in every endeavour: capital, people and nature. Small or big, every enterprise requires the engagement of other people, external inputs, usage of natural resources and support from several private organizations and government institutions. Intrinsically, an enterprise is a highly collaborative activity.

Worthy enterprises contribute to the pool of collective goodness in the world. In every period in history, the masses are generally more virtuous than the leaders. Most of the small and medium enterprises tend to be worthy. But even a few big unworthy enterprises, with partisan support from governments, have the ability to successfully hold a large number of people hostage to their entrenched self-interest. This exploitation of people sustains till such time as the unworthy enterprises or the governments themselves collapse under their own intrigues arising from the self-induced mix of complacency, arrogance and ignorance.

Notwithstanding the impenetrable cyber walls one can create, all of us now live in glass houses. Surveillance is not a one-way street. The going-ons and the doings of the elite that include unworthy entrepreneurs, referred to as 'unworthy capitalists' in Chapter 4, will, in fact, be subject to greater scrutiny. The protests and the remonstrations of ordinary people could be effectively controlled and suppressed till now because they could never gather a critical mass.

However, the masses are now awakened. Those wielding power cannot assume forever that the masses will not reach a critical mass. Look out for the big protests rising in disapproval, way beyond the critical mass. This happened in late 2022, in China (the blank paper protest); in Iran (the hijab protest); the widespread farmers' protests in India in 2021 and 2024 (on minimum support price) and in Europe in early 2024 (against EU green policies and supply-chain disruptions). Those in power cannot be sure that even the forces one normally relies upon to continue the status quo—the police or defence forces—will always be compliant in such circumstances hereafter.

There is a universal call to create an open, transparent and collaborative ethos in the world. The unworthy capitalists can perceive that they are unlikely to survive for long. This leaves them only one choice: accept the new reality and reform voluntarily to join the ranks of worthy enterprises at the earliest. This is one domain where there will be a decisive early-bird advantage. When they change, the impact of their actions will also change.

The persons who own 'capital' will continue to be capitalists. But they will soon discover that for continued success, market acceptance, and organizational alignment, they also need to be *Peopleists* and *Natureists*. As soon as that happens, the new future will have its dawn.

This is the narrative the book introduces, portraying the new thought-stream and work-ideology which will carry everybody, including the erstwhile unworthy capitalists, to new vistas of peace and harmony, acceptance and trust.

> In every human endeavour, you need all three components: capital, people and nature. To be a successful capitalist, you must also be a Peopleist and a Natureist.

The Essence of Peopleism

In the first two decades of this century there has been a profusion of ideas and books aimed at reforming capitalism, with titles such as conscious capitalism, creative capitalism, organic capitalism, saving capitalism, citizen capitalism, rebooting capitalism, fusion capitalism, reinventing capitalism, and many more. Many of these are brilliant books and I have learnt a lot from them. As have others, I am sure.

But I am concerned if the target audience tends to presuppose that capitalism per se is fine; it only requires a new adjective. While I know that this is not the narrative these books generate, an impression has somehow been created that capitalism is okay, it just needs some incremental reforms. Some even believe that if they allocate enough funds for social projects, business as usual can still continue and there need be no drop in profits or stock valuations.

I do not want to sound apologetic or defensive about Peopleism. Those who pursue this path may or may not have hefty profit increases; they may or may not have block-buster stock market appreciations. But one thing they will certainly perceive is an augmentation in the things that count: increased trust and respect of their employees and customers; and if they are good entrepreneurs, their organizations are very likely to have a longer life span with sustained, acceptable profitability. They may even end up with higher profits as well.

It is now widely acknowledged that the ills of capitalism emanate mostly from the impact of the unworthy actions of unworthy capitalists, assisted overtly or obliquely by the legislators and governments in power, explicitly as a quid pro quo by the media, and stealthily by pliable regulatory institutions. The current state of affairs cannot last indefinitely at this inflection point in the onward march of human destiny. Naturally, those who look only at the rear-view mirrors are finding it difficult to accept that past practices are no longer defensible.

Psychologist Abraham Maslow in his landmark book, *A Theory of Human Motivation*,[2] outlined a hierarchy of five needs that motivates people to achieve higher performance and goals. Starting from the bottom of the hierarchy, the needs are: physiological (food and clothing), safety (income security and health), love and belonging (family and friendship), esteem (status and recognition), and self-actualization (morality, meaning and a desire to become the best that one can be). Typically, individuals pursue higher needs after their lower-level needs have been satisfied.

Most leaders in business and society show remarkable alacrity and dedication to reach the fourth level of needs but they tend to stop there, seeking more and more of the same. This happens when greed, far beyond need, becomes the sole creed. This worldwide phenomenon, premised on self-focus and a relative disregard for the impact of their actions on people and nature, has been increasingly accepted as the default doctrine of capitalism. Since greed has infinite dimensions and no limitations, our leaders today are never satisfied.

As a result, most leaders are in a perpetual state of WUMA (worried, unhappy, miserable, and apprehensive). Behind the façade of outward confidence and power, they are actually scared and frightened all the time. They had never imagined that wealth and power could be accompanied by such misery. This need not be the case; in fact, this would not be the case provided they let themselves be open to enthusiastically embracing new contemporary thought streams. They would be surprised beyond imagination as they discover the enormous virtue of the transformed mindset and compassionate heart-set. Almost immediately, they will discern the inherent collateral advantage—a positive transformational shift in one's level of happiness, a sustained feeling of joy, peace and contentment, not only in their own lives, but also in the lives of everyone around them. A sort of a priceless miracle.

Just one subtle change can catalyse this momentous transformation. As an owner of capital and as a leader, one needs to respect people (all people, no exceptions), and also respect the entire realm of nature (no exclusions). This becomes the foundation for a new orbit of holistic, global governance.

A Global Agenda for Better Governance

If we were to discard all our past notions and beliefs and reflect with a completely open mind on the type of structure the world requires to bring about the transformations we need, the following would emerge as the dominant criteria:

- A system geared to frame policies and plans that aim *to uplift all citizens*, particularly the lower half of the population in each country, with a policy framework and an action agenda that is in sync with nature, and with adequate checks to ensure that the interests of no section of the lower half of society are ignored or sacrificed, even temporarily.
- A system committed to *humaneness, with respect for all humans.*
- *A system not based on incremental changes, but a transformational approach* that daringly carves and treads a new path.
- *A system that cleanses* democracy of all its prevailing ills.
- A system that would be potentially *applicable to all countries*—small and big.

It is envisaged that all capitalists will gradually see the benefits of this new system of governance, where the focus is primarily on the people. This chapter outlines the contours of Peopleism, and explores and addresses the ramifications of putting it in practice, in governments, business enterprises, civil society and all national and international institutions.

The Core Concept of Peopleism

Peopleism is a way of governance that restores citizenship to every citizen of the country by democratizing democracy. It does so by extending the same rights and privileges to 'all the people', by diligently practicing transparent equity in opportunity and genuine equality before the law.

The system demands exemplary integrity of its leaders and rigidly abides by the spirit and discipline of the sovereign constitutions which are sacred. It does not entitle the majority to do whatever it pleases; it focuses on all people, whether in the majority or in the minority.

Peopleism is based on the cardinal premise that good governance in a society emerges not by the acquisition of authority by a few, but by the acquisition of the capacity by all to resist authority when it is abused. This non-negotiable feature has to be embedded in a nation's DNA by educating the masses about their rights and their inherent capacity to regulate and control authority.

Differentiating Features of Peopleism

Peopleism is the operating system that demarcates the periphery and sets out the limits within which the government of a country can operate—limited not in accountability or responsibility, but limited by the rule of law, by the discipline of a constitution that has been accepted by all, and limited in its capacity to misuse, misinterpret or unwisely amend any aspect of the constitution.

Peopleism focuses on people, on their shared humanity and joint ownership of the nation's resources. It embraces the spirit of entrepreneurship from capitalism and the spirit of inclusivity from pluralism, and merges the two to generate a holistic model of responsible governance and responsible entrepreneurship.

A society is a cooperative venture for mutual advantage. As more and more people identify a commonality of interest, social cooperation can make possible a better life for all. But at the same time, there is also a conflict of interest, since persons are not indifferent to how the benefits produced by their collaboration are shared. They each want a larger share rather than a lesser. A set of principles is required for choosing the social arrangement to fairly determine this division of advantages. These are the principles of social justice.[3] This concept of social justice is a strong tenet of Peopleism and has to be firmly enshrined in all constitutions.

Peopleism is democracy without its cracks and faults. I see it traversing an open, untrodden path beyond the high-walled boundaries of capitalism that tend to exclude others. This would enable setting up a transparent system based on the predominance of public good over personal aspirations, and thus ensure a more equitable and sustainable development for every citizen.

Critics of capitalism often say that capitalism offered the great deception that everyone will be richer in the future, thus justifying gross inequality and humiliation today. Capitalism ostensibly offers liberty at the expense of social justice. Critics of socialism claim that socialism offered a spurious equality at the sacrifice of individual liberty.

Peopleism finds the balance by aligning the aspirations of the lower half of the population with those at the top, on a platform of shared meaning and marginal sacrifice by those who are well-off for those who are not so well-off.

It would be fair to say that while capitalism prevailed as the dominant economic idea of the 20th century, Peopleism will emerge as the viable new economic architecture for the 21st century.

For over two decades in this century, we have seen that many nominal democracies have slid towards monocracy. They maintain the notional appearance of democracy through elections but without the accompanying rights and institutions that are the more important aspects of a functioning democratic system. It is sad that democracy is so brittle in so many countries; it advances only for a short time and readily collapses in the face of political maneuvering.

The Role of the Legislature and the Legislators

The founding stalwarts of democracy clearly laid down that the three pillars of democracy, the legislature, the executive and the judiciary, must always play an independent role. Then alone can the fruits of democracy be equitably shared. The legislature is the prime pillar of this triad. Even though the executive and the legislature share governmental power, the legislature discharges the more dominant functions. Unfortunately, legislators across the world have virtually forgotten both their role as well as their responsibilities. It is necessary to emphasize that they must be unambiguously aware of both and scrupulously follow them.

The *prime* role of a legislature is to function in such a way that it is seen to be independent of the executive. It must insist on participating in the initiation of policy and not just become a second fiddle to rubber-stamp executive proposals. Otherwise, the fundamental purpose of representative democracy cannot be sustained.

The *second* major role of the legislature is to effectively represent both the various constituencies in each lawmaker's electoral district as well as the nation. John Stuart Mill, British philosopher, wrote in 1862 that:

> In a representative democracy, the legislature acts as the eyes, ears, and voice of the people. The proper office of a representative assembly is to watch and control the government, to throw the light of publicity on its acts, to compel a full exposition and justification of all of them which any one considers questionable; and to censure them if found condemnable. In addition, the Parliament has to be at once the nation's Committee of Grievances, and its Congress of Opinions.[4]

A legislator must also understand this dual role. On one hand, the legislature makes laws that affect the entire nation and are presumably intended to be for the good of the nation as a whole. On the other hand, its individual members, the legislators, have a duty to represent the interests of their individual constituencies. Political theorist Edmund Burke made it clear that:

> A representative must have an unreserved communication with his constituents. Their wishes ought to have great weight with him; their opinions high respect; and their business unremitted attention. But his unbiased opinion, his mature judgment, his enlightened conscience, he ought not to sacrifice to any man. Parliament is not a congress of ambassadors from different and hostile interests, which interests each must maintain as an agent and advocate, against other agents and advocates. Parliament is a deliberative assembly of one nation, with one interest, that of the whole, where not local purposes, nor local prejudices ought to guide, but the general good, resulting from the general reason of the whole. You choose a member, indeed; but when you have chosen him, he is not a member representing only you, he must represent the whole nation.[5]

The legislature's *third* role is its representational function, providing service to constituents by responding to their requests for information and taking care of their interests with respect to public expenditures and local projects.

Fourth, legislators also have a unique educational role. They must simplify complicated issues, define policy choices, and use resources and expertise to resolve conflicting ideological positions and present their constituents with clearly defined options.

And, *finally*, legislatures must display foresight by continuously looking ahead to develop policies to meet the future needs of the state.

In terms of law-making, all legislators are expected to operate under a system of collective decision-making. They adopt policies and make laws through the process of deliberation by welcoming diverse perspectives and positions on issues from both organized groups as well as individuals. However, over the last several decades, a major crack has been institutionalized in the democratic structure of governance, in many specious democratic countries. The majority party caucus has become a principal forum for deciding key issues, virtually shutting out minority members. Unrestrained partisanship has damaged civility, eroded public trust and confidence and undermined the legislature as a working institution.

Intrinsically, a parliament's main function is to facilitate the passage of laws through meaningful debate, intelligent bargaining and sincere compromise. Alan Rosenthal, professor at Rutgers University, makes the important point that:

> An essential core activity in this process is the *question period*, during which time members of the government must diligently answer pointed inquiries from members of parliament, mainly of the opposition. Equally important is the function of standing committees chaired by senior legislators, by virtue of their abilities and interests, in which the rank and file of both the majority and minority parties also play a proactive role.[6]

Ensuring the Integrity of the Elected Legislators

English writer William Somerset Maugham once said, 'It is a funny thing about life, if you refuse to accept anything but the best, you often get it.'[7] This is equally true of democracy. If people refuse to accept any but the best citizens as candidates, it will usher in the golden age of a nation. Democracy gives, as life gives, what you ask of it.

The cardinal requirement is to ensure that every electoral candidate is a person of impeccable credentials and unquestionable integrity. With altruistic leadership at the helm, people start believing that their dreams may actually be realized. On this issue, citizens have to take the initiative in their own hands. They can be supported by independent non-government institutions to undertake an unbiased and autonomous evaluation of the integrity and capability of each candidate. Citizens are also free to post their own views. The expenses of these organizations should be a part of the annual budget of the Election Commission.

The citizens should also demand that each legislator must represent the will of the people in his or her constituency. Whatever she does must be good for them, as well as equally good for the nation. If she senses a clash between regional and national interests, she has to study the entire matrix of options and find the sweet spot among the available choices. The legislator should take the decision in the larger national interest and not be bound by a party directive. The leaders of political parties must discontinue the practice of issuing whips on how they are to vote. Law-making is a serious business. It cannot be decided by a handful of party leaders.

Each law must be debated and discussed at great length, first in an open dialogue with the people at large and then among the legislators. This is an essential feature of democracy. The legislators represent the people; at no stage should people feel that the legislator they elected is neglecting the interests of any segment of the electorate.

Historian Niall Ferguson emphasizes the role of parliaments in another context:

> Civilization means a society based upon the opinion of civilians. It means violence and arbitrariness are replaced by parliaments where laws are made, and independent courts of justice in which those laws are maintained over long periods. That is civilization—and in such a soil, freedom, comfort and culture continually grow. When civilization reigns in any country, the masses of the people live without harassment.[8]

The Role of the Individual Leader in Peopleism

Peopleism demands resolute commitment from every elected legislator and every appointed office-bearer to adhere to an unequivocal standard of personal integrity in all public and private dealings. Apart from the statutory oath as specified in the constitution, the state should call upon each legislator and nominated officer in the state to voluntary sign this 28-word 'declaration of integrity':

Declaration of Integrity

> *I will observe integrity in all my personal and professional decisions and actions, and refrain from all acts to gain unfair advantage for myself or for anyone else.*

This is a part of a larger 126-word 'Code of Living'. Those who wish to express their total commitment and dedication also have the option of affixing their signature to the entire code.

Code of Living

As a responsible human being, I *commit* to abide by this Code of Living in all my personal and professional decisions and actions:

1. Principle of Integrity
I will observe integrity and refrain from all acts to gain undue advantage for myself or for anyone else.

2. Principle of Mutual Respect
I will take cognizance of the diverse views and concerns of all stakeholders, with love and respect.

3. Principle of Environmental Preservation
I will preserve the environment of our planet by ensuring zero carbon footprint, reducing consumption and waste, and conserving resources and eco-balance.

4. Principle of Spreading Happiness
I will make conscious endeavours to help those in need, to alleviate their suffering and make them happier by unconditional monetary, educational, physical or emotional support.

Sustaining the Sanctity of the Constitution

We have seen, how, in country after country, the democratic process has been hijacked by vested interests. No constitution is ever perfect. Loopholes can always be found within the constitution and exploited to pursue the interest of a minority at the cost of the majority, or even vice-versa. Even the best written constitutions can be misinterpreted, altered and amended to suit the whims and fancies of those in power. The constitution belongs to the people of the nation and it should never ever be allowed to become a plaything in the hands of those in power.

One effective way is to create a permanent Constituent Assembly of about twelve to twenty people with the sole task of ensuring that the spirit of the constitution is never tampered with. If at any time they discover a loophole or a lacuna or the absence of an important element in any of the clauses in the existing constitution, or they sense wrongful interpretation of the constitution in any judgment by the Supreme Court, or a departure from the constitutional principles in any new law passed, they would then initiate the process of corrective action including, if necessary, the amendment of the constitution.

Their proposals are subject to overwhelming consent in both the Parliament as well as a referendum thereafter.

Let us take the example of the US. The founding Constituent Assembly led by titans like John Adams, Alexander Hamilton and Thomas Jefferson gave the country a reasonably good Constitution. Over the years, the US Supreme Court's interpretation of the Constitution has not always been compatible with the spirit of the Constitution, particularly when the appointed judges tended to support the views of the political party that appointed them.

A series of US Supreme Court rulings has enabled 'corporations' to be classified as 'legal persons' ostensibly enjoying constitutional rights that were intended solely for citizens. Neither the Declaration of Independence nor the United States Constitution ever mentioned corporations. But thanks to these court rulings that moulded the law to favour the interests of the elite, corporations were granted 'citizen rights' that empowered them to even deny real citizens their prime fundamental rights. Over the years, this status of corporate personhood has corrupted the functioning of the government.

The rationale behind these rulings rested on a fundamentally flawed premise of 'freedom'. Corporations simply cannot have the same rights as citizens because they are not citizens. They are not allowed to vote in elections, nor can they be elected to public office. They are instruments of human action and if their actions, in any capacity, undercut the freedom of individuals or challenge the spirit of democracy, then it is justifiable that these powers be regulated. The late Justice Ruth Bader Ginsburg, in her dissenting note on the judgment upholding the rights of a corporation, rightly asked why incorporation seemed to allow proprietors to shed personal obligations while retaining personal rights.

The judgments of the US Supreme Court on this issue continue to prevail and remain unchallenged because the elected members are too elitist to let go of such derived privileges which give them unfettered rights at the cost of less well-off majorities. The political system has been usurped by the advocates and lobbyists representing the rich. The elected representatives do not really represent the interests of the majority of the people of the United States. There is no way that they will seek a review of Supreme Court judgments or amend the Constitution that overrules Supreme Court rulings on these issues.

Now imagine if you had in place a permanent structure of a Constituent Assembly comprising people of the mettle of George Washington, Benjamin Franklin and James Madison. They would surely have initiated an appropriate amendment in alignment with the principles enshrined in the Constitution in the larger, long-term interest of the nation.

Members of a permanent Constituent Assembly would function as custodians of the nation's interests at large. A Constituent Assembly cannot make laws. Its role is to be a permanent watchdog to ensure that neither new laws nor the interpretation of old laws in any way dilute the spirit of the constitution. These members represent the conscience of the nation and they will always be well tuned to the interests of all citizens. They would not have any past association or affiliation with any political or lobbying interests and they would not be eligible to hold any office of profit, or any position in government, even after they are no longer a member of the Constituent Assembly. They alone will have the right and the responsibility to fill the vacancies that arise in the Constituent Assembly from time to time.

Peopleism across the World

While democratic constitutions in several nations have created an effective platform to resolve their national issues, our collective capacity to deal with global issues such as economic turmoil, climate change, military aggressions, epidemics and a swarm of many other disruptions is totally inadequate. Our global institutions are simply not up to the task of governance today. There is no workable mechanism where rational decisions can be meaningfully discussed and the best solutions evolved.

If only a few countries adopt Peopleism, the confrontation between short-termism to benefit a few and the long-term approach to benefit global society will continue as before; the powerful nations will continue to drown the contrary voices. But if a critical mass of countries starts pursuing the tenets of Peopleism in real earnest, their voices will prevail and the holism in Peopleism will help resolve the stubborn global problems that have been humanity's curse for so long.

The next three chapters deal with some of the potential outcomes as the spirit of Peopleism embraces all of us.

Chapter 9

Peopleism in Practice

Infinite Potential and Boundless Possibilities

Over 2500 years ago, Gautama Buddha said,
'To see what few have seen, you must go where few have gone.'
For that, let us not follow the path.
Let us go where there is no path and begin the trail.

Conscience and Compassion in Flow

In the aftermath of the March 2019 shooting in two mosques in Christchurch, New Zealand, that left fifty dead and dozens injured, the entire world watched with great admiration the exemplary leadership displayed by Prime Minister Jacinta Ardern.[1] She went to console the victims and their families wearing a black scarf, like a hijab, as a mark of solidarity and respect for the Muslim community, and united the mourning nation with the rallying voice, 'They are us.' A few hours after the attack, she announced a clampdown on the country's lax gun laws and promised to 'weed out' racism both in New Zealand and globally. 'We cannot think about this in terms of boundaries,' she insisted. Addressing Parliament for the first time a few days later, she took a small but brave step forward by opening her remarks with the greeting 'As-Salaam Alaikum'. Ardern's compassion, cultural sensitivity and resolve earned her accolades across New Zealand and abroad. When she said, 'The world doesn't need a whole lot of massively thick-skinned politicians; they need people who care,' the world listened.

There is infinite power in the voice of compassion that comes straight from the conscience. This is Peopleism in practice.

Peopleism Is about Fairness, Not Leveling

Winston Churchill once spoke about the difference between the left and the right.[2] He said that while the left favours the line, the right favours the ladder. Leftists support policies that encourage voters to line up for entitlements, leading to the unintended consequence of keeping them trapped in poverty. Rightists, on the other hand, say people should be able to climb the ladder of opportunity and get out of the poverty trap.

'Peopleism' is neither a leftist nor a rightist ideology. It is a centrist approach that makes certain no citizen is deprived of the opportunity to climb the ladder. The economic system today makes it extremely difficult for billions to even get anywhere close to a ladder; there are few ladders and they are all possessively guarded. We need to create millions of new ladders.

The elites in every country like to be surrounded by urban cultures that are capable of only reproducing elites. In the process, those who were left out at the starting line are virtually confined to perpetual poverty. Perhaps it is the consequence of social mobility which is more often dependent on affordability. In any case, Peopleism is not aiming at levelling the results. It is more focused on making the starting line large enough for everyone to join and run, with the assurance that the referees are fair.

It is for governments to ensure that everyone, whether in urban areas or rural, irrespective of colour or creed, must have a liveable home, well equipped with potable water, electricity and hygienic surroundings. This is a paramount pre-requisite to ensure that everyone can get to the starting line without hassles. This mission can neither be postponed nor relegated to market forces. Governments alone can undertake this task.

The Real Wealth beyond Capital

Human nature is a mix of conflicting passions and possibilities. For centuries, a person who devoted his life to making money was not regarded as a good role model. Greed, avarice and envy were included among the deadly sins. Usury, making money from money, was an offense against God. It was only in the 18th century that greed became morally respectable. Gradually, money-making became a normal, acceptable way of life. Then onwards, money alone talked; only money mattered.

But money is available only to a few. It is easier for those with money to borrow more money and do so at the lowest rate of interest, while those without money or less money find it a nightmare to borrow money, even at the highest rates of interest. The entire financial system and the banking networks are geared primarily to cater to the rich. The change Peopleism seeks is to ask if the rich could stop wanting to be richer, sometime. If they could retain as much money as they need to lead good lives, would they be open to deliberate on what they may never be able to spend?

In the same vein, when developing countries borrow money from global multilateral institutions, they have to pay much higher interest rates compared to developed countries, even without considering the costs of exchange rate fluctuations. Countries in Africa borrow, on average, at rates that are four times higher than those of the United States and eight times higher than those of Germany.[3] High borrowing costs make it difficult for developing countries to fund important investments, which in turn further undermines debt sustainability and progress towards sustainable development.

Peopleism envisages a society of private wealth holders who would keep whatever wealth is required to lead good lives but, beyond that, not to turn their wealth into 'capital' but to deploy it, instead, to help more people lead good lives. It is a shift from the 'need to have' towards the 'need to share'—the transition that helps one discover the enormous wealth that lies 'beyond capital'. This is a key core component of the process of transition from 'Capitalism to Peopleism'. Bill and Melinda Gates, Warren Buffet and MacKenzie Scott from the USA, Azim Premji from India and Mo Ibrahim from

Africa have done precisely that. They have donated a substantial part of their personal fortunes to address global problems.

The Bill and Melinda Gates Foundation, the largest private-funded foundation in the world with an endowment of $75 billion, has been doing ground-breaking fundamental research in public health and has saved millions of lives through vaccination and nutrition programmes. Buffet has committed over 90 per cent of his wealth to the Bill and Melinda Gates Foundation. Scott's multi-billion-dollar donations to underfunded non-profits doing avant-garde work and empowering their leaders to make their own decisions has been transformative. Premji has bequeathed over $21 billion, including much of his stake in Wipro, to the Azim Premji Foundation that is focused on education. Ibrahim pledged half his fortune to the Mo Ibrahim Foundation to support good governance and responsible leadership across Africa. Overall, their collective efforts have perceptibly improved lives, advanced essential causes and made the world a better place.

There are many reports that repeatedly highlight how big business and the super-rich continue to fuel the inequality crisis by dodging taxes, driving down wages and using their power to influence politics. As more among those who are well-off start recognizing that they have enough, and that they should start enjoying what they have instead of always wanting more, Peopleism will make great strides.

Peopleism is a response to the repeated wake-up and shake-up calls for the elite, which have never worked. It is a mechanism to bring about a radical transformation in the way we govern our economies, principally to ensure that the policy frameworks are relevant for all people and not just a fortunate few.

Social Justice and a De-Corrupted Society

The anatomy of Peopleism has a unique feature. It tends to generate in most leaders a spirit of service towards society, a growing belief that they are not masters but servants of the country's citizens. As a result, the leaders take it upon themselves to make certain that the dream of justice for all can be no longer deferred. To guarantee social justice, the practice of Peopleism focuses on two sacrosanct aspects: equality in opportunity and fairness in outcome. Any perceived or real lack of equity or transparency has to be immediately remedied.

Peopleism knows that moral judgment and civic verdicts cannot be outsourced to market dynamics. Morality has no role in market forces; their only yardstick is potential return on investment. Peopleism assures that effective institutions are in place to ask the right questions and find the right answers. A strong 'Right to Information Act' is an effective catalyst in carrying the fruits of Peopleism to the grassroots level. Zero tolerance for corruption, especially among legislators and bureaucrats, sends an unequivocal message to the masses that corruption is neither accepted nor tolerated.

In a society, a majority would be dishonest and corrupt under any of these two conditions:

- The leadership is either unabashedly corrupt or blatantly indifferent to corruption; and,
- Nobody associated with the government in power is indicted or punished for being corrupt.

In such a scenario, you can be sure that corruption will be widespread. You could also come across a situation where the leaders of the government in power create a great hype about the need for integrity and honesty while simultaneously creating an opaque, impregnable wall behind which they can freely demand and access donations for themselves and their political party.

The corruption to be addressed is not just political or financial corruption but also moral corruption. The patriarchal culture based on male supremacy has for long festered unabashed abuse of women, virtually in every society. The MeToo movement, which began as a social phenomenon in October 2017 as a hashtag, became a worldwide movement overnight, forcing governments and corporations to institute immediate corrective laws and practices to guarantee respect for women. But the real change is still to seep into social consciousness. It may take time but eventually, it will.

Peopleism stipulates that the leadership team at the top has to be transparently committed to a high standard of integrity and rigorously practice zero-tolerance for corruption of any kind, small or big. They would ensure that any government official, irrespective of rank or seniority, will be suspended from service the moment there is a prima-facie case of corruption against him or her. They would institutionalize fast-track courts, led by impartial, honourable judges, to handle all cases of corruption against legislators and government employees and pronounce judgment within four months. The punishments must be exemplary. The convicted would not only face imprisonment, but also be required to return their ill-gotten wealth with penalties.

Miraculously, we would have a situation where most leaders are perceived to be impeccably upright, and honesty in public service becomes a new normal. This is not difficult at all as long as we elect honest leaders. This is what determines societal culture. Not talking ad-infinitum about one's old civilization. Not singing praises of one's ancestors while continuing to engage in one vicious deed after another. That is utter hypocrisy.

In the final analysis, from a common citizen's perspective, Peopleism will work because it abandons all antiquated rigidities and moral laxities of the past and enforces a culture of respect for every human being and integrity in day-to-day dealings.

Re-imagining the Indices of Development

Typically, governments have focused on GDP growth as the index of progress. Peopleism challenges that basis and seeks to differentiate between mere growth and real development. Economic growth is an essential component of development but, in itself, does not ensure development; it requires active public policies to ensure that the fruits of economic growth are widely shared. Growth tends to cater to a select minority while development encompasses all citizens. Economists Jean Dreze and Amartya Sen coined the term 'unaimed opulence', referring to the indiscriminate pursuit of economic expansion without paying much attention to how it is shared or how it affects people's lives.[4] They believe development must lead to total freedom for people, removing all obstacles and empowering them to choose their own destiny.

Nobody asks the tough questions. People are so fixated with empirical indices like per capita income, kilometres of new roads built, number of mobile phone users, that we forget to look at the whole picture. Unless we radically reinvent the institutions that create and sustain inequality such as an elitist education system, a biased media controlled by the elite and the financial markets, it is virtually impossible to transform society at the grassroots.

Peopleism is about ensuring that all institutions that can potentially abet inequality must be reformed in such a transformational manner that their propensity to encourage or feign indifference to inequality is permanently neutralized.

As long as a country's policies are transparent and aligned with the aspirations of all sections of society, growth leads to development. But if the governance model is opaque and the growth is perceptibly skewed in favour of the very few, overall development is the first victim. Not only that, each such phase of selective enrichment of the elite radically weakens and damages the institutions that are ostensibly meant to foster development.

The United Nations Development Programme created a Human Development Index (HDI) in 1990 to emphasize that people and their capabilities should be the determining criteria for assessing a country's development, not economic growth alone.[5] The HDI is a summary measure of achievement in three key dimensions: health, education and quality of life. The health dimension is assessed by life expectancy at birth, the education dimension is measured by mean of years of schooling for adults aged twenty-five years and above, and expected years of schooling for children of school-entering age. The standard of living dimension is measured by the logarithm of per capita gross national income (GNI) to reflect the diminishing importance of income with increasing GNI. The HDI is too simplistic and too ad hoc a measure of what human development entails. It does not reflect inequalities, poverty, empowerment, pollution, gender disparity and many other significant features.

Till we evolve a good index of development, I would suggest computations of annual per capita income growth rates for the less well-off 80 per cent of the population in each nation. I believe that would be a more relevant criterion for the effectiveness of the implementation of many of the 2030 Sustainable Development Goals in every country.

Foster an Environmentally Conscious Culture

Today's capitalist system generally ignores the welfare of the unborn generations. Till now, this did not matter so much. However, with the world population at 8 billion plus, and aggravating resource constraints relating to energy, water and food, our peril is unparalleled and our collective global response has been bizarre. Unlimited growth is no longer possible. A balanced, holistic approach as propounded by Peopleism alone can tackle these issues because Peopleism is anchored on creating a balance between short-term imperatives and long-term sustainability. Peopleism is about being mindful of the future and accepting full responsibility for the long-term consequences of our actions.

Free markets are often touted as a source of stable prosperity but this is a misplaced assumption if externalities such as environmental pollution and carbon footprints are not properly priced, and if the rules of the game thwart free and fair competition. The 'invisible hand' is a fallacy. Markets do not police themselves, only governments can hold players accountable.

Firms feel free to dump greenhouse gases into the atmosphere while spending hundreds of millions of dollars to lobby against carbon regulation. The world can no longer delay levying a punitive tax on carbon pollution to spur everyone to reduce climate-damaging emissions, invest in efficient energy systems and develop low-carbon energy sources. This single policy change—explicitly using prices within existing markets to shift investments and alter behaviours—offers a greater potential to combat global warming than any other policy, with minimal regulatory and enforcement costs.

The framework referring to these issues is covered by Article 6 of the 2015 Paris Agreement on climate change. Unfortunately, negotiators have been unable to agree on the rules for Article 6. Peopleism would expect that this impasse be immediately resolved in a manner that encapsulates the four cardinal principles recommended by a group of thirty-two eminent leaders, including four Nobel laureates.[6]

- Carbon emissions should be taxed across fossil fuels in proportion to carbon content, with the tax imposed 'upstream' in the distribution chain.

- Carbon taxes should start low so that individuals and institutions have time to adjust, but then rise substantially and briskly on a pre-set trajectory that imparts stable expectations to investors, consumers and governments.
- Some revenue from the carbon tax should be used to offset unfair burdens upon lower-income households.
- Subsidies that reward the extraction and use of carbon-intensive energy sources should be eliminated.

A New Economic Structure of Surge-up Economy

Inequality has trapped hundreds of millions in poverty. It has fractured our societies and undermined democracy. Across the world, people are being left behind. Their wages are stagnating yet corporate bosses take home million-dollar bonuses; their health and education services are cut while corporations and the super-rich dodge taxes. We saw a similar dynamic in the US government's response to the pandemic in 2020; an uncomfortably large share of the benefits from the stimulus ended up with very large firms and wealthy individuals.[7]

Peopleism contends that this is not a sustainable situation. One cannot allow practices that lead to such unfair outcomes to continue. One has to negate the laws that perpetuate unequal outcomes. Peopleism will achieve that by an approach that focuses on 'surge-up' economic growth models as distinct from the 'trickle-down growth' models that have been the flavour of policy-makers for over a century. The new approach is designed to have a salutary, positive impact on equitable development.

In the first phase, a policy revamp with the following six parameters would be a good starting point to initiate the transition to a surge-up economy. The figures shown are only indicative and would vary from country to country.

- Levy a uniform corporate tax rate (20 per cent to 25 per cent) and remove all locational, sectoral or ad-hoc exemptions of all kinds. The only permissible incentives could be a 200 per cent weighted reduction on wages for new jobs created for a minimum of three years, and expenditure spent on research and development in designated new technologies with the potential to create a positive impact on the majority of the global population. On the flip side, for tax purposes, disallow 50 per cent to 60 per cent of certain expenses for industries that pollute, leave carbon footprints and use excessive natural resources.

- Maximum individual tax should be capped at the same rate as corporate tax, with no exemption on dividends, capital gains, agricultural income or any other source. Increase the taxable threshold income by two to four times, which will put enormous buying power in the hands of over 75 per cent of tax-payers. The resultant mass consumption will generate a ripple effect in new employment opportunities across all spectrums.
- Substantively increase minimum wage over a five-year time-frame and legislate that women and men are paid the same wages at all levels, in all positions.
- Create a favourable Value Added Tax (VAT) structure for basic goods and services—such as 2 per cent for education, health and staple food products, 10 per cent for all commonly used essential goods, and 18 per cent for luxury goods. Goods primarily consumed by the top 15 per cent of the population should be classified as luxury goods.
- Tax evasion by individuals and corporations should be made a criminal offence, with the chief executive officer and the chief financial officer of corporations being held personally accountable. To ensure tax transparency, companies must declare beneficial ownership associations with all related holding companies and subsidiary companies, in the nation in which they operate, as well as overseas.
- Create a framework to end financial exclusion. Money lies at the heart of a market-driven world. To be excluded from it is to be left out of the many things one needs. Money, as Adam Smith wrote, is easy to make when you already have some of it. No one extends credit to you otherwise. Financial exclusion is presently the norm in an economy driven overwhelmingly by market principles. We must decisively put an end to it and

> bring about an entrepreneurial revolution through multiple micro-financing mechanisms.[8]

In the capitalist version of democratic functioning, elected leaders believe they can do what they like. That is unethical. Peopleism unambiguously lays down that winning an election does not entitle the leadership to do what it pleases.

> Democracy permits majoritarianism.
> Peopleism denounces it; it focuses on all people,
> whether they are in the majority or in the minority.

Democracy as it exists—'democracy of the elite and for the elite' breeds capitalistic excesses; democracy as it should be—'democracy of the people and for the people', will give shape to Peopleism.

Peopleism Is Governance from the Heart

Peopleism is not about words to describe a concept, it is more about the conviction of distinguishing between what is right or not, what is fair or unfair, and being able to do so from the perspective of virtually all citizens. You may call it by whatever name you like but, when it comes to feelings, they are straight from your heart, guided by your sense of values and best judged by your own conscience. Of course, we need laws to facilitate this process and an environment which makes it easier to pursue this path while making it more difficult to not pursue it.

But there is also a serious concern; nothing must be taken for granted as far as the future is concerned. Shoshana Zuboff, professor emerita at Harvard University, has cautioned us about the perils of 'surveillance capitalism'—a quiet assault on democracy that subverts the very idea of what it means to be a free individual.[9]

> Unscrupulously, powerful global corporations are claiming ownership of private human experience, and unilaterally positioning it as something to be bought and sold in the marketplace. This could shift the threat from a totalitarian Big Brother state, to a ubiquitous digital architecture: a 'Big Other' operating free from democratic oversight—endangering democracy, freedom, and our human future.

Peopleism will find it is well equipped to take cognizance of such unsolicited impacts of 'technocracy' and evolve credible ways to deal with them. It is a clear case of prioritizing people over capital and the supremacy of citizen rights over corporate rights.

Peopleism is a viable and tangible alternative to replace the present version of democracy that survives only with capitalist support. Peopleism will pervade the earth not by dispossessing the rich of their property but by providing a rationale for behaviour that focuses not on accumulating wealth but on creating an equitable, sustainable world. Nothing in the world can stop Peopleism from re-inventing democracy. It is just a matter of time.

Meanwhile, Peopleism will also be the driver to evolve a receptive environment of approval to initiate a relentless focus on worthy new themes for the 21st century.

Democratizing Science and Technology

In itself, technology is never morally flawed. Its impact on humanity is determined by whether we can steer the trajectory of technologies towards the collective good of all people. That can happen only when human progress, rather than profit, is the key driver. That is what brings out the nobility in science and the compassion in technology.

Scientists and technologists are basically discoverers of new knowledge, but when entrepreneurs and investors come in, they build the things that they want. For example, faster photo-sharing apps, the luxury of instantaneous 3D-communication anywhere on the planet, fast access to big data, powerful algorithms for stock trading, targeted surveillance, and the like. Somehow, they are unable to imagine and actualize the potential of technology from the perspective of the marginalized, the unemployed, the homeless, factory workers, unskilled labour and those living in rural areas.

Fortunately, it is not as difficult to democratize science and technology and make it an asset for all people, provided the state gives it the utmost priority. We need a concerted effort to break the invisible walls that preclude the poor from being the beneficiaries of the enormous latent potential of scientific and technological advances.

Technology has not only changed society; it is even changing what it means to be human. While AI has the potential to transform virtually every industry by providing innovative solutions to complex problems, it has also displayed potentially apocalyptic implications. Natural Language Processing (NLP) may facilitate translation services and human-computer communications and Large Language Models (LLMs) may enhance capabilities in content generation and code generation but they both will also make it easier to generate fake news and deepfakes.

Genetic engineering technologies like CRISPR[10] could lead to human beings being tailored to particular purposes, either by themselves over time or by other human beings. There are apprehensions that humans may become products or commodities, subject to remote manipulation.

It is for us to ensure that AI and biotechnology, while creating new capabilities, will enhance what it is to be human and not threaten it. Technology can and should be a natural accelerant for human progress rather than a retardant.

It is too big a collective responsibility for industry leaders, researchers and scientists, software designers and writers, industry regulators and governments to make certain that these technologies are not steered for malicious use. It all depends on the personal ethical standards of these men and women, less than a million of them worldwide.

They must also ensure that all technologies pursue a completely green trajectory of development, and follow all environment-conscious policies. Serious concerns are being raised that generative artificial intelligence and semi-conductor manufacturing use massive amounts of energy for computation and data storage and billions of gallons of water to cool the equipment. The International Energy Agency (IEA) projects that electricity consumption by data centres in 2026 will be double that of 2022—1,000 terawatt hours, which is equivalent to Japan's current total consumption.[11] Google's data centres consumed about 5 billion gallons of fresh water in 2022—20 per cent more than in 2021.[12] Microsoft's water usage rose by 34 per cent in the same period.[13]

Peopleism can be an effective enabler to mandate an integrative approach to technology advancements, in sync with the holistic development of society. This means respect for privacy and human rights over pure profit motives, judicious assessment of potential risks and unintended consequences, generation of in-built features to bridge digital divides, and creating more inclusive technological ecosystems across social, economic, environmental and political spheres. We would then have crossed over to a new convergent culture of humane technology, sustainable economy and biosphere consciousness.

Women as Growth Catalysts

Gender prejudice continues to be a fault line that has become an enormous handicap in the realization of our aspirations for a humane society. The United Nations Agenda for Sustainable Development by 2030 has a specific goal on this: 'Achieve gender equality and empower all women and girls.' And yet, this is the goal in which least progress is always reported. Once again, the world has failed to make up for the centuries of inaction.

Globally, women have not seen their participation in the labour force improve since 1990. Even when they work, they aren't paid equally. A UN report says:

> For each dollar men earn in labour income globally, women earn only 51 cents. Only 61.4 per cent of prime working age women are in the labour force, compared to 90 per cent of prime working age men. At current rates, over 340 million women and girls—an estimated 8 per cent of the world's female population—will live in extreme poverty by 2030, and close to one in four will experience moderate or severe food insecurity.[14]

Gender equality cannot merely be looked upon as one of the SDG goals within the 2030 Agenda. It is the basic foundation of a fair society and a goal upon which all other goals must stand. We cannot defeat poverty or resolve any global problem with half the world's population neglected.

The World Economic Forum Gender Gap Report 2023 alerts that it may take another 131 years to close the global gender gap.[15] Meanwhile, the political gender gap closure is also stalling; women hold only 22.9 per cent of parliamentary seats and 16.1 per cent of ministerial positions worldwide.[16] No country has yet achieved full gender parity, although the top nine countries (Iceland, Norway, Finland, New Zealand, Sweden, Germany, Nicaragua, Namibia and Lithuania) have closed at least 80 per cent of their gap, setting excellent benchmarks for other nations to follow.[17]

His Holiness St. John Paul II has often emphasized that the advancement of women will mark the dawn of the 'civilization of love'—which represents a radical affirmation of the value of life and of the value of love.

> Women are especially qualified and privileged in both these areas. They are naturally responsible for affirming the intrinsic value of life, because they enjoy a unique capacity for doing so because of their intimate connection with the mystery of life's transmission. Women can bring to every aspect of life, including the highest levels of decision-making, that essential quality of femininity which consists in objectivity of judgment, tempered by the capacity to understand in depth the demands of interpersonal relationships.[18]

The fact that there have been women heads of states, chief executives, university presidents, and state governors, may imply that women and men have equal access to the highest positions in society. In reality, they do not. The impediments they face are so subtle that it is not easy for them to overcome. In reality, women are not only turned away as they reach the penultimate stage of a distinguished career; they fall out of contention at many points leading up to that stage.

Claudia Goldin, the winner of the 2023 Nobel Prize in Economics has done groundbreaking work in advancing our understanding of women's labour market outcomes.[19] Three of her insights deserve special attention.

- Integrating women into the labour force can result in substantial productivity and income gains for a country.
- Growth does not automatically bring about higher female labour-force participation and wage equality across genders. It explains the puzzling experience of India, where the female labour-force participation, one of the world's lowest (30 per cent), actually declined in the past two decades, despite fast growth.

- The pay gap between men and women, particularly in the US, is primarily explained by children. Men and women's earnings paths tend to be similar until a woman has her first child; then they start to diverge. This 'child penalty' weighs more heavily on pay and career outcomes than bias or discrimination. More flexible professional arrangements, such as working from home and convenient hours to accommodate family needs, would help close the pay gap.

Authors Alice Eagly and Linda L. Carli believe that an appropriate metaphor for what confronts women in their professional endeavours is the 'labyrinth'.

> As a symbol, it conveys the idea of a complex journey toward a goal worth striving for, but passage through a labyrinth is not simple or direct; it requires persistence, awareness of one's progress, and a careful analysis of the puzzles that lie ahead. For women who aspire to top leadership, routes exist but are full of twists and turns, both unexpected and expected. Because all labyrinths have a viable route to the center, it is understood that goals are attainable.[20]

Perceptible change will come about only when Peopleism becomes the prime mover of decision-making processes and when societal norms insist that women must be equal partners in every niche of every domain with no exceptions. No real change can come about without that unflinching recognition and commitment. On the ground, this would entail overcoming long-held prejudices and, like any significant social change, it could entail struggle and conflict. While many governments have enforced anti-discrimination legislation to eliminate inequitable practices, the implementation has been far from rigorous.

Apart from the specific themes mentioned above, Peopleism will forever be an effective stimulant as well as a catalyst to continuously discover and enliven a wide array of unfulfilled dreams and aspirations of the seven billion disenfranchised people on our planet.

Chapter 10

Peopleism Kindles Responsible Entrepreneurship

Simultaneous Pursuit of Wealth and Happiness

Responsible entrepreneurship is to Peopleism what entrepreneurship is to Capitalism.

Responsible Entrepreneurship: A Confluence of Commercial and Social Entrepreneurship

While probing the contours of responsible leadership in Chapter 1, we found that a leader's sense of responsibility is mirrored in her ability to undertake all tasks with sensitivity, understanding and commitment, with implicit acceptance of personal accountability for everything she does or does not do. This facility stems from the DNA of one's character which clearly displays three distinct personal traits: capability, service above self, and integrity. This is the base foundation of responsible entrepreneurship, which necessarily encompasses social entrepreneurship.

The concept of a 'social entrepreneur' is reported to have evolved in 1972. But it came into widespread usage after 1980, when Bill Drayton founded Ashoka,[1] a non-profit organization to promote social entrepreneurship worldwide, based on the idea that the most powerful force for good in the world is a social entrepreneur: a person driven by an innovative idea that can help correct an entrenched global problem. Ashoka was the first such entity to identify and support innovative individuals with a 'bold breakthrough idea' aimed at changing a system that was causing major social or environmental problem. Drayton pioneered the lofty mission that 'social entrepreneurs are not content just to give a fish or teach how to fish. They will not rest until they have revolutionized the fishing industry'. Ashoka's projects are driven by its core values of youth empowerment, grassroots community development, and innovative systemic change. Project Kiva, a microfinance platform to facilitate microloans, revolutionized micro-project entrepreneurship in developing countries. Million Villages Mission in India uplifted millions of rural households by providing them access to economic opportunities, education, and healthcare services. The Asian University for Women, in Bangladesh, provided high-quality education and leadership opportunities for women from underserved regions across Asia.

The world was fascinated by the stories of outstanding individuals who pursued this path. The corporate world was pretty much enamoured by their sense of social responsibility. Many governments also embraced 'social enterprise' as the 'third way'—income-generating charities that did not entirely depend on public funding while dealing with the increasing number of social problems that failed to receive requisite government attention.

All of a sudden, social entrepreneurs were in the limelight and everyone wanted to be one. But there is one question that keeps coming up repeatedly, ever since former American president Bill Clinton raised it: 'Nearly every problem has been solved by someone somewhere. The frustration is that we can't seem to replicate those solutions anywhere else.'[2]

In a serious endeavour to make it happen, David Wilcox set up 'ReachScale', an institution that began with two questions:[3]

- Why are there are no globally scaled social enterprises; and
- Can a network be built that identifies the social enterprises that should be scaled up and then assist them in scaling up globally?

More fundamentally, Pamela Hartigan, former CEO of Schwab Foundation for Social Entrepreneurship, provocatively asked 'if transformational systems change can ever be achieved on a massive scale by non-profit organizations or even by well-meaning "hybrids". Even decades after the launch of the concept, the impact on solving any of the major global problems is at best peripheral or marginal.'[4] The world of commercial entrepreneurship continues as before; investments in social entrepreneurship are a miniscule fraction of the total investment pie. The way business has been operating for over a century must be disrupted because we cannot survive as a society or a planet if we do not tear down the walls that compartmentalize economic, social and environmental activity.

We need to challenge the division between social and commercial entrepreneurship, on the basis that the sheer usage of the two terms tends to formalize them into separate, standalone compartments. For the corporate sector, it has created a false separation between 'this is where we make money, and this is where we do good'. That is exactly what led capitalism astray, and that is precisely what needs to be corrected.

Every Entrepreneur Can Be a Responsible Entrepreneur

Responsible entrepreneurship is still a concept in its infancy. Entrepreneurship born of traditional capitalism is still the norm. The more money you make, a better entrepreneur you are considered. It does not matter how you make it. But this is likely to rapidly change as the key tenets of responsible entrepreneurship gain widespread momentum.

> Responsible Entrepreneurship is not about making less money. It is about feeling responsible and fully accountable that the money being made is neither at the cost of nature, nor at the cost of any part of the society in which we live.

Award-winning author, Carol Sanford, puts it crisply:

> Responsible entrepreneurs are a special breed of people. Their mission is not just to build a better company, but to build a better

> world. They not only seek to transform the industry they enter, but the society as well. They grow their business into a powerful platform that can leverage change, and even change the foundations that cause our most pressing problems and issues. They challenge and refine cultural assumptions, laws, regulations, and even the processes of governance; they think far beyond what is usually required of business leaders. In the process, they end up creating companies that are truly holistic and humane, in all that they do.[5]

Professor Muhammad Yunus, recipient of the Nobel Peace Prize in 2006, is an exemplary practitioner of responsible entrepreneurship. The pioneering founder of the Grameen Bank in Bangladesh in 1983, he revolutionized the traditional concepts of microfinance and microcredit. Typically, 90 per cent of the approximately 9 million borrowers from Grameen Bank are women, who pay their loans back at a remarkable rate of 97 per cent—a recovery rate higher than any traditional banking system.[6] It has since been a benchmark of how trust and solidarity can open up hitherto unthinkable avenues and opportunities.

The principles of Peopleism, in the normal course, would nurture a novel business ethos where every entrepreneur would be eager to be a 'social entrepreneur'. A widespread prevalence of 'responsible entrepreneurship' is the only realistic way to pave the path for sustainable livelihoods in sustainable societies.

Being an entrepreneur is a challenge in any field. Trying to change the world through your business is an even more demanding challenge. By simultaneously working on both these challenges, responsible entrepreneurs end up creating pioneering new business models. They are focused on ensuring that everything they do makes an effective contribution to the making of a more sustainable and equitable economy. As the share of responsible entrepreneurship in a nation continues to increase, even the traditional entrepreneurs will tend to become more responsible.

Profiles in Responsible Entrepreneurship

It is heartening that there have been quite a few companies worldwide that displayed an exceptional sense of responsibility in showing care and compassion during the most difficult period of the Covid pandemic. MAIF, a French insurance firm, demonstrated what I consider a role-model approach in 2020.[7] All its 8,000 employees received salaries even when they were on partial employment. The company did not accept the €20 million grant from the French government's employment support scheme. 'These funds should go to companies that would have to lay off workers without such assistance,' said Pascal Demurger, the company CEO. During the lockdown, car accidents fell by 80 per cent. MAIF decided to refund its €100 million savings to its 2.8 million policyholders. 'By giving back this money, we want to do our part in the collective effort [to rebuild our society]. It was inconceivable for us to derive any benefit from the crisis,' explained Demurger.

MAIF adopted the legal status of 'Entreprise à Mission' in 2019, the first French company to do so, defining its 'raison d'être' as the following: 'Convinced that only a genuine attention paid to others and to the world can improve the common good, we embed it at the heart of every one of our commitments and each of our actions. This is our reason for being.' Demurger is an admirer of Gandhi and of his adage 'Be the change'.

Indian conglomerate Tata Group has several companies in the airlines, hotels, financial services and automotive sectors that were severely hit by Covid, but the group did not lay off any employees. It only cut the salaries of its top management by up to 20 per cent. The group patriarch, Ratan Tata, had this to say when he learnt about rampant layoffs by many Indian companies, 'These are the people that have worked for you. These are the people who have served you all their careers. You send them out to live in the rain. Is that your definition of ethics when you treat your labour force that way? It is impossible to survive as a company if one is not sensitive to its people. Whatever your reasons may be, you have to change in terms of what you consider fair or good or necessary in order to survive.'[8]

MassMutual, an insurance company based in Massachusetts, doesn't have shareholders and is governed by its policyholders. In the midst of the Covid pandemic, CEO Roger Crandall wrote to employees: 'If 2020 taught us anything, it's that society works best when it works for everyone. We supported our employees by offering

80 extra hours of time off for Covid-related needs, and we helped our communities cope with the virus by creating HealthBridge, a free life insurance programme to provide up to a total of $3 billion in protection to eligible healthcare workers on the frontlines of Covid-19.'[9]

Kyocera, an electronics and ceramics manufacturer from Japan, founded by the legendary Kazuo Inamori in 1959, has a non-negotiable tradition of leading by the 'Kyocera Philosophy' of life and management, based on the cardinal principle: 'Do the right thing as a human being.' Employee welfare and care is an intrinsic part of their DNA. Chairman Goro Yamaguchi reiterates this unequivocally: 'We have always valued the idea of "Living Together" and working not only for ourselves but for the world. There are three types of co-existence—with society, with the world, and with nature—which we have been maintaining since the 1970s. A company cannot continue to exist without co-existing with society and with nature.'[10]

Wide-ranging programmes such as Patagonia's 'We're in Business to Save the Planet', IKEA's 'People and Planet Positive Strategy', Ørsted's 'A World that Runs Entirely on Green Energy', Warby Parker's 'Buy a Pair Give a Pair' and Natura's 'Well-Being and Being-Well', are some of the most commendable initiatives that deserve to be celebrated and applauded.[11]

There is another commendable project by Business as an Agent of World Benefit (BAWB), 'Change the story about business from best IN the world, to best FOR the world' which is run by students to chronicle inspirational business stories from all over the world.[12] These are wonderful, motivational examples. Yet, such companies still comprise a very small minority. The task before us is to deploy the compelling rationale of Peopleism to get a large majority of companies to embrace this mode of thinking.

The Family Business Network (FBN)[13]—the world's leading organization of business families—is a group of 4,000 families with 17,000 individual members. Generally, they tend to be more socially conscious than the big global corporations that have a wide ownership structure spanning a large number of shareholders. And yet, their organizational motto continues to be quite self-focused: 'By families, for families, together across generations.'

As they embrace Peopleism, their motto should change to: *By families, with families, for the One Big Global Family*. Simple directional changes like these tend to alter the perceptions of leaders across generations to think ahead and go beyond the comfort zone of relatively narrow life missions.

Education to Sow the Seeds of Responsible Entrepreneurship

While our immediate focus is naturally to create an ethos of societal responsibility in every entrepreneur today, we must also launch an impetus to educate the next generation of leaders so that they look at responsible entrepreneurship as the preferred mode of entrepreneurship and the only format that can generate sustained customer loyalty and employee commitment. For that, we have to sow the appropriate seeds in our education curriculum today.

Education is not about information; it is also not about knowledge. Education is the only way to transmit civilizational values from one generation to the next. It can do so if it fulfills two essential criteria: it must build character and it must create a love for knowledge and wisdom. For that, we must acknowledge the critical need for competent teachers, particularly at the primary-school level; teachers who can build the foundations for a new culture and a new character, and guide every citizen, without exception, to proudly belong to a 'Nation that Cares'. If we can do that, the path from pre-school to the bachelor's degree will become a luminous gradient that will uplift the entire society.

The first step in this task is to create the right school infrastructure in every village and every municipality in every nation, and evolve the right educational content. Fortunately, enough online resources provide the basic content which one can adapt to one's needs. The critical part is skilling the right type of teachers in every school. That could be done by every nation creating a National Program of teacher-trainers, one of whom must visit every school at least once a month, to give on-the spot instruction to teachers on values, ethics and good citizenship.

Many nations have compulsory military training for all able-bodied men. We should consider creating a similar programme for all young women and men with a flair for teaching and a passion to promote ethics in society. The corporate sector, supported by chambers of commerce, may wish to lead this initiative by seconding 1 per cent of their employees every year to be a part of this pioneering initiative. As social thinker Garry Jacobs points out:

> A values-based paradigm in education would shift the focus from the subject to the student, from passive indoctrination to active learning, from memorization of information to independent thinking, and from competition to collaborative, peer-to-peer forms of learning. This would establish a culture of liberalism that places emphasis on thinking rather than facts, questioning rather than learning all the right answers, and perceiving reality in its rich, many-sided complexity.[14]

The educationists today should look upon their new role as creators of hundreds of eminent institutions of learning that will produce a new incorruptible class as leaders of tomorrow.

In this context, the Centre for Contemplative Science and Compassion-based Ethics, Emory University, USA, with inspiration from His Holiness the Dalai Lama, has designed a Social, Emotional and Ethical (SEE) Learning Curriculum for educating the heart and the mind.[15] The programme calls for a higher level of emotional literacy—'intelligence with a heart—which can be learned through specific focus on the awareness of emotion in ourselves and others, the capacities to love others and ourselves, while developing honesty and the ability to take responsibility for our actions'.[16]

Fortune for the Bottom of the Pyramid

C.K. Prahalad's book, *The Fortune at the Bottom of the Pyramid*, published in 2005, received global acclaim for steering corporations to cater to the needs of those who are at the bottom of the pyramid.[17] But in the whole discourse, the fortune referred to the fortune *for* corporations. Peopleism envisions a world where the focus must shift to creating a fortune for the *people* at the bottom of the pyramid.

Responsible entrepreneurship is an attempt to combine the best of the not-for-profit, philanthropic approach with the best of for-profit, business approach. This innovative hybrid is not a charity, it does not rely on donors; it aims to generate a profit that is sufficient to sustain its ongoing operations and provide a reasonable return to investors.

A Hundred Per Cent Green Nation

The governments pursuing Peopleism would be committed to the key assertion in the proposed Universal Declaration of the Rights of Mother Earth that 'we are all an interdependent part of Mother Earth, that Mother Earth is a living being with inalienable rights, and that all living beings share these rights equally.'[18]

Responsible entrepreneurs who launch ventures that accelerate efforts to become a hundred per cent green nation, in all activities, will be the new heroes of the coming decades. Their life purpose is premised on the commitment, as Jerry Mander, American author and activist, says, 'not to advance human-created economic systems that do not acknowledge the carrying capacities of the planet. Growth beyond carrying capacity is actually suicide. An ecocide. We humans are inseparable from our environment, and we cannot flourish if the health of the earth deteriorates.'[19]

Jeremy Rifkin, American economic and social theorist, called for an 'Empathic Civilization'[20] to set in motion a transition from the Age of Faith and the Age of Reason to the Age of Empathy while generating new perspectives about science. He also emphasizes the growing recognition that old science must be replaced with new science. Responsible entrepreneurs will enthusiastically adopt his depiction of new science.

- Old science views nature as an object; new science views nature as a relationship.
- Old science is characterized by detachment, expropriation, dissection and reduction; new science is characterized by engagement, replenishment, integration and holism.
- Old science is committed to making nature productive; new science is committed to making nature sustainable.
- Old science seeks power over nature; new science seeks partnership with nature.

- New science takes us from a colonial vision of nature as an entity to pillage and enslave, to a new vision of nature as a community to nurture.
- The right to exploit, harness, and own nature in the form of property is tempered by the obligation to steward nature and treat it with dignity and respect.

A Youth-led Movement: Be Responsibly Profitable

Human life is precious and short; the period of youth is even shorter and even more precious. The opportunities offered during this limited period of youthfulness are endless. A nation that can direct the energies of its youth to capture these opportunities will continuously unfold rosters of ever-new achievements.

There are so many young people today who are unhappy or uncomfortable about something in the world that they find unjust or inequitable or unnatural. Unlike the rest of the world, they take it upon themselves to go forward and accept the challenge of being the initiator of new movements of change and, in the process, discover the sweet intersection of their passion and the potential for positive impact of their work. A system that encourages, facilitates and rewards all such efforts can make a quantum difference to nourishing responsible youth entrepreneurship. It is akin to a youth-led movement focused on being 'responsibly profitable'.

Nazambi Matee quit her day job in Nairobi, also her social life, and invested all her savings in an experimental project in her mother's back garden. Today, she is the proud founder of Gjenge Makers, a company that uses discarded plastic to produce building materials. Lighter and more durable than cement, these materials are affordable and are used to pave walkways for homes and schools. Her business now produces 1,500 pavers per day. It is an excellent initiative to prove that it is possible to move from a linear economy toward a circular economy, in which products and materials remain in use for as long as possible.[21]

MBE: Masters in Business with Ethics

In my conversations with students and faculty at various business schools, I often ask the students whether they would be happy if the nomenclature of their coveted master's programme was changed from MBA (Masters in Business Administration) to MBE (Masters in Business with Ethics). Invariably, over half the students enthusiastically support the change. But the dean and the faculty are not enthused at all.

In the wake of Peopleism, I look forward to the day when the Fortune 500 Corporations and the Family Business Enterprises will insist that the management graduates they recruit should come only from the MBE stream. This transition from the 'MBA' to the 'MBE' culture would be more than a symbolic change. It would be an unmistakable clarion call from the business community that it is truly ready to embrace Peopleism.

Advertising to Uplift Human Spirit and Society

Hazel Henderson,[22] a visionary humanist with an exemplary passion to make the world a better place for every human being, launched a remarkable initiative in 2005, to catalyse an inspirational transformation in the global media and advertising industry. She introduced EthicMark Awards® to promote advertisement campaigns that uplift the human spirit and elevate it to such an extent that it becomes a powerful catalyst to transform the global advertising industry. The awards have already emerged as the Nobels for advertising, and provide an effective platform to transform the marketing ethos from promoting irresponsible consumerism to promoting human values and the Sustainable Development Goals.

The exemplary roster of winning advertisement campaigns over the years clearly indicate the direction in which the global advertising industry is moving voluntarily.[23] The winners effectively disseminate the importance of ethics and a higher level of consciousness focused on the common good. All short-listed finalists have displayed game-changing creativity in their message, based on the assertion that the most effective advertising message is the one that aligns with the values customers most dearly cherish. In the wake of Peopleism, these principles will become the norm for the entire advertising industry. Following Henderson's demise in 2022, the initiative needs a new home and new leadership to take the movement ahead.

It is time that all advertising associations as well as advertising agencies take a pro-active interest in this resurgence and sensitize their clients to the possibility that such themes create a far more positive image of the company than any plain marketing or social message. The companies that join and lead this initiative in their respective industries will be looked up to as the industry leaders and pioneers.

Future1000—A Roster of Responsibly Profitable Corporations

Fortune magazine publishes the Fortune500 lists of American corporations, ranked on sales turnover and profitability, and similar Fortune Global500 lists every year. Apart from that, it also publishes eight other rigorous annual ratings: 100 Best Companies to Work For, Change the World, Future 50, World's Most Admired Companies, Fastest-Growing Companies, Most Powerful Women, Most Powerful Women International and Businessperson of the Year.

In the framework of Peopleism, I envisage a far more significant annual ranking of what I call a list of the 'Future1000 Responsibly Profitable Companies'.[24] The purpose of this list is to recognize the fully transformed corporations that meet all the criteria of a responsibly profitable company. I expect that the leaders of Future1000 corporations will become the role models and the transparent lighthouses to steer our planet's corporate culture to the virtues and joys of Peopleism. It is not that only large companies will be considered for Future1000 rankings. Medium and small-scale enterprises, above a certain threshold, would be equally eligible to be included. The number 1,000 does not also signify a limit to the number of companies that can be a part. The nomenclature merely signifies a departure from the traditional 'Fortune 500' criteria of success—primarily size, profitability and rate of return.

> The corporations in the Future1000 are all profitable, but they are responsibly profitable.

The rankings will typically be based on the following eight criteria that would comprise the composite index:

- Integrity and diversity quotient of the corporate board
- Transparency in accounting
- Holistic employee policies
- Ethical marketing and advertising
- Insistence on ethical practices by all supply-chain associates
- Green component of existing practices, new investments and research and development projects
- Divestment of non-green components of business and
- Commitment to social values including gender parity and fair practices

Such companies will be the practitioners of Peopleism, and their business objectives will be fully aligned with the new societal expectations.

Responsible Entrepreneurship Catalyses Responsible Innovation

Given the right environment, responsible entrepreneurship also leads to 'responsible innovation'. Socially conscious entrepreneurs unconsciously integrate values into their goals, and their research and development plans invariably gravitate towards de-facto responsible innovations. Every responsible entrepreneur, by default, would necessarily be a 'responsible innovator'. This new approach to innovation will help develop unique, new practices, deliver more societal benefits and enable a better grasp of the impact and potential of technologies.[25]

The recent rapid advances in AI have generated multiple concerns in all sections of society, spawning fears that these developments have the potential to break the fabric of human society and culture. The leading companies in control of these technologies have a great obligation to ensure that the ongoing research is focused on responsible innovation.

A critical mass of responsible entrepreneurs would tend to motivate each other, as well as all others, to create a radiant spark of commitment to a relentless quest for the future the human race deserves. Those who acknowledge this new, contemporary role of business will inevitably emerge as the long-term winners in the next decade.

As many more leaders start pursuing this path, I would like to share a few words of prudence, based on my observations and interactions with corporate CEOs and boards:

- *Hope* alone will not work; it is a refuge for those who do not know what to do.
- *Determination* is necessary, but not until one knows what exactly it is that must be done.
- *Trends* are important, but it is time we take charge in generating the trends we need; not merely pursuing the trends others talk about.
- *Navigating* the path is vital, but not just for meeting the goals of your organization and yourself; navigation hereafter must equally focus on societal good.

Chapter 11

Peopleism Aligns Business and Civil Society

Collaboration is the New Norm

Never doubt that a small group of thoughtful, committed citizens can change the world; indeed, it is the only thing that ever has.

—Margaret Mead (1901–1978)[1]

Redefining the Roles of Civil Society and Business

There is a widespread perception that a large majority of business leaders have never really taken significant initiatives to advance the wider interests of society and planet. At best, other than a few notable exceptions, they have done the minimum required when subjected to scrutiny and pressure.

Civil Society Organizations (CSOs), a group of institutions outside the government and the business sector promoting social justice and addressing societal issues, have been presenting strong testimony to support the view that most business leaders have had a single-minded focus on augmenting their profitability and longevity, irrespective of the costs that present and future societies may have to bear. Very few corporate leaders have leveraged their enormous clout and influence to steer collective business efforts and organizational skills in a direction that would completely obliterate any adverse impact of their actions, within or outside the confines of their company. With the ever-widening chasm between the rich and the poor, and extensive degradation of natural habitats, business is often perceived as either the chief provoker or, at best, an unconcerned observer of the world around them.

Taking a historical perspective, business has been a prime mover in improving people's lives for centuries by creating jobs, driving innovation and fostering prosperity. But since the latter decades of the 20th century, warped government incentives to boost profitability and stock market indices have tended to exclude considerations that take cognizance of the concerns of the society in which the business functions. All this fortified the general impression that businesses are run for the sole purpose of maximizing profit and, in this pursuit, humans are merely considered as one of the resources to make money.

The heartening part is that despite such widespread apathy, quite a few civil society leaders acknowledge and applaud that there are enough businesses that have taken on the role of a driving force in social and community development. They have deployed their strengths and capabilities, as well as the spirit of enterprise and technological prowess in partnering with them and with governments to achieve the holistic goal of sustainable, inclusive prosperity.

To find a common ground and a mutually acceptable way forward, it would be necessary to de-link business from the imperative to make only money and de-link civil society from the imperative to be only critical of those who make money.

There is no lack of relevant ideas on any relevant issue. But there is a lack of understanding of the other viewpoint and the need to reconcile what have long been perceived as irreconcilable differences. Peopleism will help create an environment where decision-makers from business and civil society see each other as representing the same human race and create a new confluence where each respects the other and finds a way to align the differences and blend the perceptions.

Where Do Corporate CEOs Figure in This Debate?

These are some of the numerous questions often asked on this issue:

- How did the global economic system become so dominated with corporations having no social or environmental conscience?
- How did profit maximization become the default pattern in the global corporate culture?
- Were corporate leaders deliberately running away from such public concerns or was it that they did not consider them important enough?
- How many of them have consciously reached out to civil society leaders to openly discuss the societal perceptions on many issues with potential long-term impact on society? At best, some of them share a platform with them as panelists in a public discussion. But these generally tend to be cosmetic events where stated positions are repeated, but never really a deliberate attempt to break the logjam and bridge the opinion gap.

The blossoming of civil society is perhaps one of the most momentous social phenomena of the 21st century. The knowledge-based activism of these groups is radically reshaping the international agenda and has changed the way global issues are understood and dealt with. While UN organizations and a few governments have been actively engaging with civil society—a partnership generally acknowledged as benefiting society—the collaboration between business and civil society has not advanced in the same vein and with the same spirit.

Civil society claims that business looks upon this association as something 'nice' to have, not something which is a 'must have'. Business representatives claim that civil society has difficulty accepting that business also needs to make a profit. All this leads to the mutual denial of an inclusive partnership. There are two main causes that led to this chasm.

First, business leaders failed to realize that civil society was not prompted by anti-corporatism per se. It was the outcome of a societal perception about what is right and what is not. They did not acknowledge that this transformation was deep rooted and stemmed from a mass belief that a small fraction of the human race cannot continue to ignore the interests of the majority.

Second, since business leaders in most countries had a close nexus with the political elite, they genuinely believed they could effectively stem the influence of civil society activism. They thought they had nothing to fear and they continued to ignore the emerging influence of civil society.

However, the more enlightened business leaders saw the writing on the wall and willingly responded to the genuine concerns of civil society by forming new partnerships with them. This helped the businesses as well as the societies in which they functioned. But such collaborations between business and civil society happened only on the fringes.

Civil Society Needs to Be Totally Transparent

Civil society leaders know well that they are trying to alter a situation in which business has an established upper hand. It is therefore vital that CSOs earn the trust of their business compatriots by taking a posture that is not perceived as a threat. They cannot force businesses to change. They have to gently persuade them and prevail upon them to accept the need to change. To facilitate business and civil society working together, CSOs must also demonstrate non-negotiable standards of transparency and democracy in their own work culture, including how they determine their policies, how they are financed and how they spend their allocations.

CSOs must continuously reinforce the perception that though civil society stands apart from state and market forces, it is not in contradiction to them; it influences them as much as it is influenced by them. They have an important role in holding all stakeholders, including themselves, to the highest levels of accountability. I support the way the EU describes CSOs as, 'all non-State, not-for-profit structures, non-partisan and non–violent, through which people organize to pursue shared objectives and ideals, whether political, cultural, social or economic, that are membership-based, cause-based or service-oriented.'[2]

Civil society should position itself as the glue that binds business and society together in such a way that both are strengthened by each other. The greater onus is on civil society to make itself acceptable to business leaders and do so in such a manner that business considers civil society as an essential partner in its pursuit for survival as a responsible, profitable organization.

Two Paths for Industry Leaders

I have had several discussions with business leaders in many countries on the way forward and I am most encouraged by the tangible signs of a new business mindset emerging. One leader put it rather bluntly, 'I have nothing to say in defence of our inaction or indifference to the efforts of our civil society leaders, till now. In fact, if I was to choose one word to describe our collective response to their persistent call for a better world, that word is: "uncivil".'

Pursuit of profit can never be a sufficient reason to turn a blind eye or a deaf ear to legitimate cries for reform of our business models or operating systems. The true nature of the global economic system under which we have been living was not realized until it failed repeatedly, first during the global financial crisis of 2008, and then during the 2020 Covid epidemic, and the wars in Gaza and Ukraine, followed by runaway inflation. Imbued with the perennial feeling of supremacy, corporations just did not think it necessary to act with consideration for the societies that charter them and the planet that sustains them.

There are two paths big corporations can pursue hereafter. They can either voluntarily change course and transform their business models to include externalities related to society and the environment, or else they will face a slow but definite downfall. There does not seem to be a third option. They would do well to choose the civil society organizations they are comfortable with and seek their inputs and experience. In a voluntary, bi-partisan co-operation, CSOs can only be an asset to them, never a threat.

It is equally important to highlight the importance of resource efficiency, checks on material consumption, and certain built-in constraints on aggregate investment. As economist John Fullerton puts it, 'The planetary boundaries that dictate limits to growth also imply limits to investment, a constraint we have never contemplated before. How much the large economic actors invest and where, have critical implications for collective global security and needs to be a central concern of global governance.'[3]

It will not be enough simply to encourage so-called 'green investment' if we do not simultaneously curtail investments that have a negative impact. Our unquestioned belief in the unencumbered freedom of large corporations and other economic actors to invest indiscriminately needs to be challenged. Given the linkage between investment and throughput, how we choose to invest will determine to a significant degree whether we follow a path to the transition we seek or continue on the current passage to societal destabilization and environmental degradation.

The political elite is supported and financed by businessmen and rich professionals; most of them are well aware that they are losing societal trust. If the enlightened political parties and business leaders would take the initiative to invite civil society leaders to join them in a spirit of collaboration, they will be pleasantly surprised by the radical improvement in their ability to deliver better. In the wake of such a transformation, the businessmen may also be more willing to start talking to the erstwhile antagonists. Of course, genuine co-operation can never be mandated. The need for that has to be felt within, which happens naturally when one is guided by wisdom, or else when it is considered necessary for survival. Encouragingly, this feeling of 'collaboration for mutual interest' is now sprouting and this could foster the confluence we are seeking.

Reforms to Curb Business Greed and Political Collusion

There is another equally vital concern. Globally operating firms are not regulated globally. Their subsidiaries, spread all over the world, are subject to the laws of those nations. The national laws of countries are not aligned; they are often blatantly at variance with each other. In many countries, even when the laws clearly forbid certain conduct, states fail to implement them. It is open to question whether the states are scared of big corporations, or whether the private greed of a few political leaders brazenly overrides the public good.

Corporations' thirst for profit and the propensity of national leaders for greed have together made a mockery of both societal interest and the preservation of nature. In many resource-rich countries, the laws are either non-existent or purposely ambiguous, giving the rulers an unchallenged leeway to do as they please, sometimes openly, but more often surreptitiously. No wonder then that such countries dislike civil society players because they alone could embarrass the rulers by exposing their clandestine, nefarious deeds.

The weakest link in this process is the ease with which the rich can deposit their ill-gotten wealth in tax havens in so many countries. Apart from offering very low tax rates, tax havens also offer financial privacy and anonymity. It is outrageous that a few, otherwise civilized countries, are still willing accomplices in permitting banks and financial institutions within their jurisdictions to provide organized cover-up for crimes committed by citizens of other countries. All this in the name of the rights of private citizens of other countries, specifically their right to loot their own nations' wealth.

The world is losing $480 billion in taxes to global tax abuse every year. Of this, $311 billion is lost to cross-border corporate tax abuse by multinational corporations and $169 billion is lost to offshore tax abuse by wealthy individuals.[4] The 'axis of avoidance', comprising four UK protectorates (British Virgin Islands, Cayman Islands, Bermuda, and Jersey), Luxembourg, Switzerland and the Netherlands, account for 57 per cent of the global tax losses.[5] Together with the other Organisation for Economic Co-operation and Development (OECD) members, they represent 78 per cent. Another four territories, Singapore, Hong Kong, United Arab Emirates and the US, contribute to a large part of the rest. 'Moving money out of the usual offshore secrecy havens into the U.S. is now a brisk new trend.'[6] If this staggering amount of $480 billion in annual lost tax revenues were to be reclaimed by governments, it would have a salutary impact on growth in multiple ways. Increased allocation to spending on public services such as education, healthcare, infrastructure development, support for small businesses, and increase in threshold income for payment of income tax, would all contribute to increased employment at the grassroots and reduce inequality. Nations would be able to lower their net debt and balance their fiscal budgets, which would reduce inflationary pressures. The reclamation of lost taxes is a great opportunity to grab this low-hanging fruit and leverage it to show immediate results.

There are two questions of morality here:

- Who is more responsible for the malaise, the bribe-giver or the bribe-taker? Unmistakably, it is the bribe-giver; he has the option to walk out of such a situation. He does not have to accept a business transaction that demands unethical behaviour from him. And yet, many global leaders look upon it as a normal business practice.
- How can certain nations that imprison their own nationals for certain crimes encourage such crimes in the rest of the world without any inhibitions? How can the world continue to condone such irresponsible legislation in the countries that license the functioning of tax havens?

It is necessary to effectively plug these loopholes. One hopes this will be the prime domain for immediate industry-civil society cooperation. The G7 group of wealthy nations signed an agreement to tackle tax abuses by multinationals and online technology companies in June 2021, agreeing to a minimum global corporate tax rate of 'at least' 15 per cent, for the first time. This agreement is intended to cover only about 8,000 multinationals who are above certain threshold limits relating to profits and margins expressed as a percentage of revenue.[7] However, even after three years of discussions among nations, the operating rules pertaining to the two-pillar plan have still not been implemented.

In any case, this initiative is too little too late. Similar action for individuals and families who stash their wealth in these tax havens are nowhere near the anvil yet. Reprehensibly, it is noteworthy that the chambers of commerce around the world have been conspicuously silent on the G7 plans, reinforcing the commonly held belief that for the companies, 'stakeholder capitalism' comes into play only if their profits are not adversely impacted.

Market Regulators vis-à-vis Civil Society

Business is a primary source of investment and job creation, and markets are meant to be a highly efficient means for allocating scarce resources. Together, they wield great power to generate economic growth and reduce poverty. But markets and stock exchanges work optimally only if they are embedded within broader social and legal norms, closely monitored by regulatory institutions. Unfortunately, markets have become uncontrolled and unconcerned behemoths calling the shots on behalf of the corporations while regulatory institutions are completely ineffective in preventing fraud. They are called upon, primarily, to salvage the aftermath. Civil society, too, has not yet made much of a dent in this field.

The successive failures of two large global banks—Silicon Valley Bank (SVB) in USA and Credit Suisse Bank (CSB) in Switzerland, in March 2023, laid bare the virtual inability of the bank regulatory mechanisms in two of the supposedly most efficient financially managed nations in the world. The myth that the market knows best stands unmasked.

SVB was heavily exposed to start-ups in the technology sector and, as interest rates kept rising, the value of the bank's bond holdings declined, leading to significant book losses which led to a bank run, leaving SVB with little liquidity to meet withdrawal demands. Credit Suisse had long been a victim of its own scandals and compliance issues, high costs and a weak capital structure. Its share price plunged and a rival, UBS Group AG, acquired it in a deal brokered by the Swiss government to avoid a broader systemic crisis. Both bank failures were the result of inability to manage risks arising from a high-interest regime.

The stock exchanges need to take serious cognizance of this message, as it clearly means that it is perilous to continue business as usual. Implementing honest reforms in this sphere is not only a matter of social justice, it is also in the interest of the global stock exchanges. The CSOs' involvement in reviving the independence of regulatory institutions could ensure transparency in the entire process.

How Iconic Business Leaders Could Assist CSOs

It is worth exploring how former, holistic business leaders could help CSOs become more effective. To me, this appears to be in the realm of easy pickings. There are several iconic business leaders who have been widely acknowledged for their inclusive and balanced approach to the role of business in society. Such leaders should be persuaded to help guide the policies and plans of the CSOs. They would be perceived as insiders by business leaders and there would be a greater likelihood of better acceptance of their activism by the business community. Existing NGOs should also invite such people to join their advisory boards or otherwise play leadership or advocacy roles.

There are several former business leaders who have established exemplary organizations of their own to bring about transformational societal change. They include: Jeff Skoll (founder of the Skoll Foundation, supporting innovative solutions to global challenges), Pierre Omidyar, Founder Chairman of eBay, and Pamela Omidyar (founders of the Omidyar Network which supports initiatives that address social challenges, with focus on the social impact of technology), and Ajay Piramal, Chairman, Piramal Group (founder of the Piramal Foundation which improves the lives of marginalized communities by leveraging the power of youth and strengthening government systems). I have already mentioned Bill Gates, Mo Ibrahim and Azim Premji in another context in Chapter 9.

The Civil Society Needs Space and Support

The CIVICUS Monitor has consistently emphasized the importance of the quality of 'civic space' in a country for civil society to function in the larger public interest. They define civic space 'as a set of universally-accepted rules, which allow people to organize, participate and communicate with each other freely and without hindrance, and in doing so, influence the political, economic and social structures around them.'[8] On this criterion, they rate all nations in five classifications: *open, narrowed, obstructed, repressed* or *closed*. In March 2023, thirty-eight countries and territories (with 3.2 per cent of the world's population) were rated as *open*, forty-two as *narrowed*, forty as *obstructed*, fifty as *repressed*, and twenty-seven were rated as *closed*. And yet, there were over 12,500 protests in 2022, spread over at least 133 countries.[9]

The heartening part is that the CIVICUS 2023 State of Civil Society Report highlights that civil society is growing, diversifying and reinventing itself to adapt to a changing world.

> Much of civil society's radical energy is coming from outside the NGO universe: from small, informal grassroots groups, often formed and led by women, young people and indigenous people. In many of today's mass mobilizations, young people are at the forefront, taking action on issues that directly matter to them—such as the lack of economic opportunities, the climate crisis that threatens to rob them of their futures, and the denial of the rights of excluded groups to which they belong or stand as allies of. Many new groups organise horizontally, adopt participatory approaches and cultivate distributed leadership. They tend to rely on voluntary engagement and can achieve a lot with little.[10]

Even though governments and business leaders continue to view civil society as an adversary rather than a valuable partner, several multilateral and international organizations are willingly and enthusiastically collaborating with civil society groups in pursuance of their goals. The contributions of CSOs to promoting and achieving the implementation of the UN's SDGs have been widely applauded, and this has encouraged people in many countries to hold a very favourable opinion of their work and mission.

Governments and business leaders will find it exceedingly helpful to make them partners in nation-building and give them greater support and space to play a greater role.

Consumer Activism: The Ultimate Effective Weapon

The often-used argument in capitalist jargon is that collective labour rights are bad for economic growth because they drive up labour costs, whereas private property rights are good for growth, as they help protect wealth and promote its accumulation. This concept of economic efficiency basically stems from the flawed belief that protecting the wealth of the wealthy is far more important than letting the poor acquire even marginally more wealth.

There is no alternative to business leaders realizing that the not-so-well-off also have rights. So far, they have been demanding these rights, by and large, peacefully. Business leaders should not take their ineffectiveness in pursuing their rights for granted. More and more consumers are beginning to align with them. Consumer activism would be an effective nudge to alter business attitudes and we can see that happening.

Emerging Role of B-Corporations as New Benchmarks

Leaders of chambers of commerce and industry chambers are another important anchor in this process. They need to be convinced, beyond doubt, that all of us have to be serious about shared sacrifice. In this context, the B Corporation, also called, 'for benefit corporation', started in 2006, by B Lab in the US, has been a notable initiative. It is a non-profit network with the lofty goal of revolutionizing capitalism and remaking the global economy to 'benefit all people, communities, and the planet'. The first eighty-two B Corps were certified in 2007. As of December 2023, there were about 8,000 certified B Corporations around the world, across 162 industries in ninety-three countries. Over 95 per cent of B corps are small and medium-sized businesses, valued at under $100 million.[11] In order to receive B Corporation certification, a business must meet comprehensive and transparent social and environmental performance standards, comply with higher legal accountability standards, and build a business constituency for good business. The pool of B Corps includes a few major companies such as Ben & Jerry's ice cream (owned by Unilever), outerwear brand Patagonia, and Natura, the Brazilian cosmetics and fragrance maker.

The North American business of the French food giant Danone became the world's largest B Corp certified company in 2018, which made it legally committed to balancing the fiduciary interests of shareholders with a positive impact on people, communities and the planet. In June 2020, Danone shareholders voted unanimously to make it the first listed company to adopt the 'company with a mission' legal framework, which allows a for-profit company to embed specific social and environmental goals within its articles of association.[12] The company's then CEO, Emmanuel Faber, had an unambiguous message, 'We celebrated our 100th anniversary last year and the sequel needs to be written. The risk is that we fall asleep. We need to reinvent a model for a living enterprise, an economy that serves people, and an agriculture that renews the planet's resources.'[13]

But these actions by Faber did not go down well with the shareholders of the company. In the wake of the Covid pandemic, sales of the company's main products, Evian bottled water and yogurt, fell substantively due to closure of restaurants. Two of the company's shareholders, Artisan Partners and Bluebell Capital Partners, which together own less than 6 per cent of the stock, explicitly requested the board to sack Faber because they thought he cared more about people, the planet and social responsibility than its shareholders.[14] What belies understanding is that the company board caved in under these pressures and the major shareholders kept quiet. When will corporate boards summon the courage to challenge the views of shareholders not aligned with the new ethos rather than succumb to the Milton Friedman doctrine? That this could happen in March 2021 merely shows that for many shareholders, 'stakeholders' primacy' is just another empty slogan.

Harvard University, an educational institution, was the first chartered corporation in the US.[15] The corporate charters were granted for a limited time and could be revoked if conditions were not followed and laws were not abided by. In those early days, the privilege of incorporation was granted selectively and only to enable activities that 'benefited the public', such as the construction of public works like railways or roads. Enabling shareholders to make profits was seen as a means to achieve those ends. The conditions then imposed on corporations would be seen as quite radical and left-wing today.

We certainly need new structures of business enterprises that could reinvent the way we set up and run our businesses today. Many civil society representatives have put forward a balanced overview; businesses would do well to heed to their call and start adapting. It is heartening that increasing numbers of business leaders openly concede that it is also in their self-interest to do so.

Meanwhile, B Lab, the certifying authority for B Corp eligibility, must make sure it does not become some kind of a club. It should not become another 'greenwashing' opportunity. When Nestle subsidiary, Nespresso, was awarded B Corp status in May 2022, there was a widespread demand that the subsidiaries of large corporations should not be given this status if the parent company too was not certified. This, it was pointed out, would enable big companies to benefit from B Corp status without fully doing the work required to get there. This has set in motion a battle for the heart and soul of the movement. It is encouraging that a few more pioneering standard-setters such as the Social Enterprise World Forum, Employee Ownership Association and Co-operatives UK are endeavouring to fill the vacuum.[16]

The advance of Peopleism will get a sustainable boost if the industry chambers and the chambers of commerce work together with CSOs to bring about widespread awareness of the B Lab movement and create a favourable environment to accelerate the transition from corporations to B-Corps or similar structures with similar commitments.

A New Constellation of Coalitions

A more receptive business response is an essential prerequisite to make sure that business leaders and civil society leaders come together. There is also a strong feeling that business would in any case need to do so, for self-preservation. In this situation, the three nuggets in the World Economic Forum Report on the Future Role of Civil Society continue to be relevant.[17]

- *If you are a civil society leader*, embrace the roles of enabler, facilitator and constructive challenger, and help to broker solutions without losing sight of your core values. Civil society has the power to create the legitimacy, incentives and political space for business and government to make changes that otherwise would be difficult or impossible.
- *If you are a business leader,* put societal issues at the heart of business models. Corporations have the resources to drive solutions to societal challenges by embracing innovative approaches and collaborating with new networks across civil

society. Realize the progressive role business can play in local and global community-building, and 'step up' to create and enable a positive change agenda in policy-making, in coalition with other stakeholders.

- *If you are a government leader*, recognize the fundamental role that civil society plays in building confidence, promoting good governance and enhancing long-term stability. Invest in capacity-building, and build integrated consultation processes to crowd-source the expertise, innovation and energy of civil society and leading businesses in developing and designing social services.

Our times demand a new definition of 'collective leadership', a joint leadership concept that works for all constituents and relates equally to each of them. They demand a new constellation of international cooperation—governments, civil society and the private sector, working together for the collective global good. Therein lies the prescription for sustainable growth for all.

Freedom Is Less a Right, More a Responsibility

Businesses prosper because they enjoy certain freedoms, including freedoms to run their businesses. Industry leaders also need to acknowledge the responsibilities that come with freedom. They will soon discover that freedom is not fun; freedom is about making responsible choices. Freedom is less of a right; it is more of a responsibility. Freedom is a duty.

The starting point is whether the CEO of the company, irrespective of whether he is a professional or an owner, feels personally accountable for the social responsibilities of the company. If the CEO personally feels socially responsible, each individual in the organization also becomes socially responsible.

Such a grassroots feeling of social responsibility in the organization fundamentally emanates from the corporate character which, in turn, is defined by how personally answerable the CEO feels for the impact of her actions on society. Corporate Social Responsibility is not just a corporate cosmetic, nor merely a talking point. It is the decisive leap to make the company a 'socially responsible corporation' (SRC).

Rinaldo Brutoco, attorney and business executive,[18] co-founded the World Business Academy in 1987 with a prime focus to get business to adopt a tradition it has never had throughout the entire history of entrepreneurship: to share the responsibility for the whole. Every decision made, every action taken, must be viewed in the light of that kind of responsibility, a new role—not well understood or accepted. He explained the rationale that, 'Business is behind every major problem we have, and could uniquely provide the solutions to each of those problems and ones as yet unforeseen. The only way to get in front of the crises facing human society is to enroll business in creating those solutions. Business is the institution that is designed to deal with change itself and adapt rapidly to it.'[19]

Some of our brightest minds are in business today. I feel confident that the wise among them, and there are many of them, will respond to the call for transformation and play a decisive role in accelerating the transition from 'Capitalism to Peopleism and Natureism'.

PART FOUR

The Safe New World

Where Every Person Matters

Chapter 12

Life Is Beautiful

When Wisdom Leads and Peopleism Prevails

The fragrance of flowers spreads only in the direction of the wind. But the goodness of a person spreads in all directions.

—Chanakya (370–283 BCE)[1]

The Principle of Life and the Principle of Interdependence

The Principle of Life—the essence that unites all philosophies, cultures and religions—asks each of us to respect every human being on our planet, remembering that we all live under the same sky, we all breathe the same air, we all seek a happy home, we all aspire to live a life of dignity and peace, and none of us can do so by ourselves. All of us are one planetary family; we need each other and we have to live together with unconditional love and goodwill for each other.

The Principle of Interdependence—the recognition that our destiny as the human race is incredibly inter-linked—is all-pervading. We live in one world; we will all grow or we will all perish. This is such a powerful truism that any individual that does not accept this, will stand precluded from a life of happiness. That individual may have all luxuries, but a life of joy, peace and contentment will continue to be a mirage.

> There is a story about an anthropologist studying the habits and culture of a remote African tribe. One day, he placed a gift basket filled with delicious fruits under a tree and told a group of children that whoever got there first would win the entire basket. When he gave them the signal to run, nobody pushed one another; they all took each other's hands and ran together, and then sat together in a circle enjoying the delicious treats. When he asked them why they chose to run as a group, a little girl spoke up, 'How can one of us be happy if all others are sad?'[2]

Interdependence is an inherent feature of human reality. We find our value in a community and discover our humanity in belonging. This is Peopleism in action—as also espoused by 'Ubuntu', the essence of African wisdom. Life is beautiful for everyone who realizes this.

In an interdependent world, not only are problems interwoven, but the solutions are also interconnected. Philosopher David Spangler says, 'This means whatever we do to help ourselves and the world, we must do it together. And it is more than simply a kind of group togetherness, like a committee. It is a togetherness that is synergic, honouring of the differences we bring to the table—and the chaos as well—one that enhances us, both as individuals and as a co-creative team or group.'[3]

I have covered many of the key facets of these two principles in the last eleven chapters. I now propose to dwell on the practical aspects of bringing these two principles into the mainstream thought process, so that we can evolve sustainable solutions to the multiple economic and social issues that confront us, individually or collectively, at the local level, the national level and at the planetary level.

This is not an occasion to undertake a post-mortem of what went wrong, and who did what and why. Virtually every human being has brought something positive to life on this planet. Our focus is to strengthen all the positivities.

We have also identified the various negativities that have caused enormous grief and anguish among billions of our planet-citizens. Our mission is to completely uproot these deeply entrenched negativities. The following two principles could be a good guide for this important mission.

The Principle of Gratitude and the Principle of Awakening

The Principle of Gratitude—the appreciation that we will not be able to survive without the multitudes of daily essentials of life provided to us not merely by the few we know, but also by the many whom we do not know—is undeniable. We may have the money but we still owe our existence on this planet to the billions who toil to give us food, clothing, health services and infinite other necessities for day-to-day living. It is not only the eight billion fellow human beings we have to thank, but also the eight million plus species that sustain eco-balance and life on Earth, and the unique gifts of nature that nurture us all the time. *Gratitude helps us treasure what we have rather than crave what we lack.*

The Principle of Awakening—the recognition that the essential gifts of nature do not come to us as a birthright is unquestionable. We cannot take them for granted.

It is about reflecting on what we can do to pay off at least a part of the massive debt we owe by now. At this watershed moment in human history, the least we can do is to set right all the past transgressions and make certain that we will, hereafter, live with respect for every human being and in complete synchronicity with nature. It is up to each of us to become worthy of the multitudes of freebies bestowed on us at every moment of our life.

Former US Vice President Al Gore posed some sharp questions in his Nobel Lecture in Oslo:

> Will the next generation ask us why we didn't act? Or will they ask us how we found the moral courage to rise and successfully resolve a crisis that so many said was impossible to solve? We have everything we need to get started, save perhaps political will, but political will is a renewable resource. So let us renew it, and say together: We have a purpose. We are many. For this purpose we will rise, and we will act.[4]

Perhaps, 'we' are what is wrong, and 'we' must make it right. The time for a wake-up call is long past; it is now time to wake every one up. We have had glimpses of the wisdom that can show us the path—the wisdom that comes with a new pair of eyes, to see what we could never see before, and a new pair of ears, to hear what we could not hear before.

When Wisdom Leads

Sometime, somewhere, each of us meets someone in whose presence one is always energized, motivated and inspired to do better. She or he effortlessly and unconsciously radiates love and compassion, goodness and integrity, and enthusiasm and energy. Even if she does not speak, she displays an aura of fairness and equity and transmits thoughts that bring out the best in us. That is what one experiences when one is face to face with a wise person. I have known people who have shared similar experiences, even on video calls. When such a wise person takes over the leadership of a nation, or any institution, her benign sense of balance and equanimity becomes a strong anchor to guide the evolution and implementation of all plans and priorities.

One can readily discern the peace and tranquility that resides within the mind of such a wise person. Desmond Tutu explained it beautifully:

> The world is in crisis. It needs people who have the skill to combine inner power with outer action. Inner power comes from self-mastery, observing and controlling the ego, and deepening integrity through a regular practice of reflection or meditation. This generates not only the ability to transform conflicts, listen to others, communicate clearly and develop trust, but also the creative innovation and energy to resolve local and global problems.[5]

When such people are at the helm of affairs, we will begin to witness the realization of our vision for a 'Safe New World'. This is not wishful thinking. It's actually happening. I have sensed the longing for this 'peace within' in increasing numbers—particularly among millennials and Generation Z (as mentioned in Chapter 2). A global movement for 'humanity to be humane' is already underway.

Wisdom Is Silently Selfless but Its Echo Is Heard Everywhere

When a wise person with passion rises to achieve her vision, the work is done quietly, often unobtrusively, with selflessness, in a just and transparent manner, with no hidden motive for any personal gain today or tomorrow.

The generally believed meaning of selflessness is caring more about what others need and less about what you need. If you turn around the two words in selfless, it becomes 'less self', which makes it amply clear. It is a genuine attempt to serve others without seeking a favour for that service or soliciting anything in return. You are only driven by a desire to help others.

Selflessness does not imply that you do not take care of yourself; in fact, you need to be sound in body and mind, and financially stable and content so that you are not looking for gains on the side. Selflessness is not a virtue for the weak; it can only be implemented by the strong so that you do not let anyone take advantage of your selflessness in any way. A selfless person is habitually committed to doing the right things and this is what makes it easy for him to naturally connect with all humans.

A leader so dedicated to serve, and serve well, does not have to propagate or advertise her achievements; the word about her great deeds and noble efforts spreads far and wide through word of mouth, even without social media. When such leaders take over the destiny of a nation, or any institution, sustained and sustainable progress is inevitable. People often ask how such a leader would react to any acts of external aggression. The same way as any other great leader: without compromising the freedom and safety of citizens. Selflessness makes no concession for ignoring or showing weakness in face of overt or covert aggression; these acts must be firmly dealt with—aiming at a fair outcome of peace.

Wisdom Begets More Wisdom

If wisdom is so good, why aren't more people wise? George Bernard Shaw observed in a lighter vein that 'while people love to talk to beautiful people, they only like to look at the wise people.' Perhaps because they feel they are more at home with outside beauty than the beauty within the individual.

Wisdom is also defined 'as a combination of cognitive, reflective and compassionate qualities'.[6] You may spot one or two qualities in different persons but finding all the attributes in one person may not be as common. Yet, wisdom is something that can be easily cultivated. The primary source is the natural instinct to learn from every experience, and to look for meaning behind everything you observe and hear. Wisdom is about being watchful, vigilant and compassionate—while being constantly mindful of these four principles: the Principle of Life, the Principle of Interdependence, the Principle of Gratitude and the Principle of Awakening.

The most important factor that influences who we become is determined by who we see and what we see, hear and read. Wisdom leaders are easy to spot. You can readily sense their innate ability to 'see things clearly, as they are'. Once citizens in more countries start realizing the sustained virtues of wisdom leadership and the fallacy of populist measures that tend more to deceive rather than deliver—the shift to wisdom-led Peopleism will accelerate faster than one can imagine today. Wisdom begets more wisdom.

Guiding Principles for This Decade

A year before the world confronted Covid, Alan Murray and Katherine Dunn of *Fortune* magazine shared their worldview that, 'Inequality within nations grew, but inequality across nations declined. The result is a complex stew of internal and external challenges that will grow over the new decade. There is a crisis of confidence in the Western world, with the most fundamental tenets of democracy and capitalism being called into question.' As guiding principles, they identified three ideas:[7]

- Capitalism is the best system known for organizing an economy. It should be improved, not replaced.
- Globalization is both an inevitable and a desirable result of economic and technological progress. We should shape it, not fight it.
- Leadership matters. The decade ahead will put leaders to the test. They will need wisdom and courage, and must build a reservoir of moral authority to guide us through.

I have proposed three significant variations in their guiding principles:

- The capitalist will stay; the world needs him as much as he needs the world, but he will not function in a system that, by

default, gives primacy to 'capital', he will operate in a system that prioritizes 'people' and 'nature', over 'capital'. This is the most fundamental transformation required.
- Globalization will be more beneficial, mutually and multilaterally, if it is shaped on fair principles of equity and not on the erstwhile antiquated regulations of colonial principles of 'money is power' and 'might is right'.
- Leadership will matter more than anything else, more than ever before; and only those leaders will make headway who lead transparently with the three essential traits of wisdom: awareness, bridge building and compassion (Chapter 7).

Peopleism Generates a New Worldview

It is widely accepted that in most endeavours, an individual needs an organization to achieve his full potential. The organization also needs individuals to achieve its goals. Society needs clusters of organizations to attain a rising quality of life. These organizations then become the foundations for sustained human progress, with consistent inclusivity.

The long-prevalent mechanistic view of life has been based on the notion that 'if you cannot get the whole view—take the best view you can; it is not necessary to understand the parts that comprise the whole'. In practice, this led to leadership agendas derived from one's rather limited spectrum of understanding the world and its constituents. Generations of leaders have become so immune and impervious to what is happening in the world that they do not have the slightest response even when they see vivid photographs of disasters all around. While most people feel shocked or pained, many of these leaders appear to be least concerned about the misfortune of others. Such incapacitation of 'emotional awareness' tends to disrupt their decision-making ability; they struggle to distinguish between the right or wrong course of action. As a result, blatant disregard for public empathy and welfare gets institutionalized.

The holistic view of life that has been manifesting for some time maintains that 'to understand the whole, you must also understand the parts—each and every part.' Failure to do so will perpetually stand in the way of your providing the right kind of leadership. Lack of awareness stemming from ignorance or indifference is no longer an option.

With wisdom in action, a new interconnected holism is beginning to emerge, based on the premise that:

> The part is as important as the whole.
> Every part is an indivisible part of the whole.
> The part is as much in the whole, as the whole is in the part.
> Neither functions without the other.

This is the new worldview generated when Peopleism prevails.

Principle of Interconnected Holism

The Principle of Interconnected Holism is the key theme of Vedanta, the most ancient wisdom philosophy of India.[8] Fundamentally, it conveys that nothing is insignificant; nothing is smaller than anything else. The part represents the whole, just as the seed contains the whole. In effect, the part and the whole are both complete in themselves. There is a hidden wholeness that pervades the entire wholeness, and ultimately it is this invisible wholeness that matters the most. It is this recognition that catalyses a change in human attitude: you accept the necessity of resonating with all parts and stop ignoring some of the parts. You realize that all parts—big or small, here or elsewhere, are all interrelated in some way or another, even if one may not be able to comprehend that readily.

There is a nuclear affinity—like the electrons revolving around the nucleus—between Peopleism and the Principle of Interconnected Holism in that each is attracted to the other, and each is strengthened by the other in a virtuous cycle.

Practitioners of Peopleism work silently and peacefully; they are free of anger and fear. They are constantly in a state of vigilant awareness and tend to be more innovative and creative. They do not subscribe to incompatible objectives or contradictory goals; this makes it easier to coordinate all plans and actions.

In summation, they fully understand and observe the ten tenets that follow.

The Ten Tenets of Peopleism

1) Peopleism is a way of governance that restores citizenship to every citizen of the country by democratizing democracy. It does so by extending the same rights and privileges to 'all the people', by diligently practicing transparent equity in opportunity and genuine equality before the law.
2) Peopleism is based on the cardinal premise that good governance in a society emerges not by the acquisition of authority by a few but by the acquisition of the capacity by all to resist authority when it is abused. This non-negotiable feature is embedded in a nation's DNA by educating the masses about their rights and their inherent capacity to regulate and control authority.
3) Peopleism demarcates the limits within which the government of a country can operate—limited not in accountability or responsibility, but limited by the rule of law, by the discipline of the national constitution, and limited in its capacity to misuse, misinterpret or unwisely amend any aspect of the constitution. Peopleism denounces majoritarianism; it focuses on all people, whether in the majority or in the minority.
4) Peopleism upholds the sanctity of the constitution by creating the institution of a Permanent Constituent Assembly which functions as the prime custodian to continually review the relevance of each clause of the constitution, and to ensure that the Supreme Court judgments neither dilute nor temper the spirit of the constitution. The members of the Constituent Assembly cannot hold any office of profit or engage in any business or political activity directly or indirectly, during their tenure or any time thereafter.
5) Peopleism aims at creating a fortune *for* the bottom of the pyramid by radically altering the policy framework of the traditional trickle-down economy to a new configuration of a surge-up economy. It does so not by dispossessing the rich of their wealth, but by instituting policies that focus less on accumulating wealth and more on creating an equitable, sustainable world.
6) Peopleism has a relentless focus on institutionalizing gender equality, promoting a fair and unbiased media, encouraging

civil society to speak for unheard voices, challenging long-established unfair laws and conventions through social and societal innovation, and establishing zero tolerance on individual or institutional corruption of any kind.

7) Peopleism demands exemplary integrity of all its leaders. All candidates who seek election to legislatures or appointed to senior autonomous positions, are thoroughly scrutinized and approved by two separate, independent non-government institutions, to ensure each elected or nominated person has impeccable credentials and unquestionable integrity.
8) Peopleism ensures that all institutions that can potentially abet inequality are reformed in such a transformational manner that their propensity to encourage or feign indifference to inequality is permanently neutralized. This particularly encompasses the education and healthcare systems, the financial sector and wage differentials.
9) Peopleism is anchored on creating a balance between short-term imperatives and long-term sustainability. It is mindful of the future and accepts full responsibility for the long-term consequences of leaders' actions.
10) Peopleism believes in the universality of human values in all religions, and aims at achieving sustained harmony among adherents of all faiths, all over the world.

A New Eon of Love and Compassion

With Peopleism in practice, we will move on to a new eon. An eon of love and compassion; an eon of caring, sharing and serving. As that happens across the world, we will have kindled a new faith in humanity. All interactions will then be a dialogue of humaneness; among humans, for humans.

With love for all, with resolve to exclude no one, with commitment to do right, as guided by our conscience, we dedicate ourselves to the most pressing tasks that have been long neglected, and do all we can, individually and collectively, with purposeful unity, to ensure a just and enduring peace, within each of us, with each other, and among all of us, for all time to come. Life will then be beautiful for all.

Chapter 13

The Inevitable Ascent of Peopleism

Voices of Corroboration

We will either find a way, or make one.

—Hannibal Barca (247–183 BCE)[1]

We Are a Product of the Stories We Learn

Young people all over the world are deeply apprehensive about their future. The world they thought they knew has turned upside down. Whatever they believed in till now is no longer valid. They feel they are the collateral victims of a new emerging amalgam of indifferent politicians and technology monoliths. They grew up with certain notions and irrefutable convictions, a product of the stories that inevitably became a part of their lives. However, those stories do not work anymore. Honesty does not always pay. Hard work is no guarantee to success. Good education no longer ensures a job and a secure life. You can no longer progress by following the laws; you have to know the lawmakers.

We Need New Stories

Systems thinker Phoebe Tickell has analysed that stories 'situate us in the world in a way that gives a fundamental meaning and an orientation and direction. Storytelling is sense-making—a sense of connection, meaning, purpose, self-worth, justice, community, belonging, and a sense of love for this planet.'[2] She argues that we are in a period of story-breakdown. We're in a chasm between a story that used to function, and before a new story has gathered enough coherence to be credible.

We need new stories, ones that will combine the wisdom of the past and the possibilities for the future and directly address the concerns of the youth. With phenomenal access to information and the glaring apathy they see among decision-makers, it is unlikely that the youth will have infinite patience. How do we catalyse the process of generating new stories that are fundamentally holistic and humane?

It is human nature to be tribal, but the nature and the boundaries of tribalism have undergone an unprecedented metamorphosis. Jonathan Rawson, author, alerts us that:

> In an ecologically imperilled, technologically imperious, economically volatile, politically fractured and culturally charged world, you can feel it: we need our tribes. We need our bonds, our alliances, our security, our missions, our rituals, even our traditions; we need to belong. And yet, we also know that tribalism is part of the problem, part of the narrow mindedness, dysfunctional competition and collective action failure at the root of the world's problems. We need our tribes to be less like self-serving interest groups and more like nourishing eco-systems learning how to help each other in a regenerative, awakening world.[3]

'Team Human'—Can We Make It Work?

American writer Douglas Rushkoff[4] coined the term 'team human' to explore if a world of over eight billion people is ever likely to feel or act like a single tribe. Rushkoff believes that this 'kind of homogenization of worldview and harmonization of action is not only politically naïve, but also potentially scary; we humans are much too impish and subversive and transgressive to ever be corralled in that way'.[5] Most people agree with this view.

I immensely value human diversity. It must never be the intention to seek a uniform single platform to resolve all global issues. My modest goal is to identify the common denominators to create a structure that unites humans rather than divides us—a process that could generate an unfailing configuration of hope in every heart across all of humanity. When hope replaces fear, it will be a tipping point towards universal progress.

Peopleism is the ideology, the platform, as well as the vehicle to generate new stories for the decades ahead; it will become the fulcrum of an irreversible tide of equitable and sustainable progress. Anchored on the three pillars of the Wisdom Economy (awareness, bridge-building and compassion), coupled with an uncompromising focus on inclusivity for the excluded, and unconditionally embracing the marginalized, we will be pretty close to making 'team human' work for the common good.

The author Seth Godin writes that 'a group needs only two things to be a tribe: a shared interest and a way to communicate'.[6] My conviction about the inevitable ascent of Peopleism stems from the overwhelming ground reality that over 80 per cent of the global population has a discernible, cognizant shared interest in seeking a better future for themselves as well as for all of us. This is a powerful incentive to unite them, in spite of their diversity, and a strong force to keep them united as their lives start improving perceptibly.

As regards a way to communicate, the internet now makes it possible. The irony is that the forces of status quo, represented by big government and big business have so far used the social media more effectively than the disenfranchised masses. The former either own the communication channels or control them, and they have little interest in encouraging anything that could tamper or dilute their existing hegemony in these domains. The technology leaders know better than anyone else that nothing lasts forever, least of all industry leadership. The technology which made them technological monoliths has also the propensity to lead them to their descent.

There is a window of opportunity for them to reset their priorities, reinvent their business models, and start subscribing to a set of sacrosanct values that will govern their business. Else, new technology pioneers, firm believers in principles of responsible entrepreneurship, may make them irrelevant sooner than they can imagine.

Peter Georgescu, a refugee who eventually became a business executive and is currently the chairman emeritus of advertising firm Young and Rubicam, feels deeply grateful to his adopted country, USA. He also feels afraid for its future. He is afraid, he says, because the American economy no longer functions well for most citizens. For the past four decades, he says, 'capitalism has been slowly committing suicide'.[7] These are strong words, but it is no longer possible to ignore them.

Martin Wolf, chief economics commentator at the *Financial Times*, is concerned that the long-prevalent symbiotic relationship in which capitalism provided the prosperity while democracy set the rules and created a shared interest in the outcome, is now broken. He feels that:

> [It] is impossible to sustain a universal suffrage democracy with a market economy if the former does not appear open to the influence—and the latter does not serve the interests—of the people at large. This, in turn, demands a political response rooted not in the destructive politics of identity, but of welfare for all citizens—that is, a commitment to economic opportunity and basic security for all.[8]

Ruchir Sharma, economist, has given a new name to the present consensus of governance: 'Socialism for the rich, and capitalism for the rest.'[9] He argues that this is evident in the way the government stimuli in most countries, in every calamity, are skewed in favour of generous bailouts for the corporations to keep them alive while the less well-off have to do with minimal handouts, and struggle to survive. The absurdity of this approach was vividly highlighted again during the Covid pandemic. One should not be surprised if the young and the perpetually ignored refuse to accept this anymore.

Katherine Trebeck, economics researcher, also echoes the principles of Peopleism as she asserts that the only way to address today's vast inequalities and avert ecological collapse is to start consciously designing what she describes as 'wellbeing' economies.

> The current system is forced to invest a lot of resources in fixing and cleaning up and trying to heal the damage that it does—whether it's in an environmental sense, or a social sense. A wellbeing economy wouldn't demand so much fixing and healing. It would see the

> economy doing much more of the heavy-lifting in delivering good lives first time around.—The goal is to give up the pursuit of growth for growth's sake, and explore kinder forms of capitalism.—At its heart it's about an economy that works for people and planet, rather than the other way round.[10]

The practice of Peopleism has the inherent potential and edifice to evolve a path on which every member of 'team human' can grow and prosper.

A Systemic Shift in Human Thinking

Otto Scharmer, chair and co-founder of the Presencing Institute, has devoted his life to working on our transition to a new world. His words inimitably capture our concerns and our vision.

> We live in an age of disruption. Where something is ending and dying. And where something else is waiting to be born. What is ending and dying is a civilization that's built on a mindset of maximum me, of bigger is better and of special interest group-driven decision making that have led us to a world of organized irresponsibility. What's being born is less clear.
>
> It's a future that requires us to connect with a deeper level of our humanity. To discover who we really are and who we want to be as a society. The most significant disruptive change of our generation is yet to come. It has to do with the transformation of capitalism itself—which depends on our ability to reshape how we connect to each other, to the system and to ourselves.[11]

Tomas Bjorkman, a Swedish social entrepreneur,[12] makes the compelling case that in any complex system, when complexity increases, there comes a point where the present system will not hold any longer. And then the system—be it a society, or a natural system—has either to learn to organize in new, more complex, deeper ways, or it will break down. That's where we are right now. We need to change. We need to go from a paradigm of separation to connection and relationship. He cautions that, 'Many times throughout human history, civilizations have collapsed, but there were always other civilizations in other places. Right now, we don't have a backup civilization and we don't have a backup planet. We only have one chance, so we better try to make this transition work. We need to go from the world of things to the world of evolving processes.'[13]

We can no longer leave it to chance that, somehow, the human race will be able to 'manage' these deep transitions, as in the past, by trial and error. This time, we have to do so deliberately.

Evolutionary philosopher Daniel Schmachtenberger supports this viewpoint with a sense of urgency.

> We are on the threshold of a new transformation similar to the shift in biological evolution when we went from single-cell organisms to multiple cell organisms, right at the beginning of the history of the universe. We cannot plan or manage such a shift. But we may be able to facilitate it happening. It is up to us—the present generation, whether we have a breakthrough or a breakdown. Civilizations do tend to break down.[14]

Economist John Fullerton also says it unequivocally:

> This moment, forced upon us against our will, is the consequence of an extractive, exponential growth-driven economy as the source of our prosperity that has run to its natural unsustainable conclusion. Wisdom demands we see ourselves as one system, embedded in, not separate from, the sacred Blue Marble that is our only home. Wisdom demands we source our future prosperity by aligning our economy with the patterns and principles of a living system, that sustains itself over long periods of time—as a Regenerative Economy. Such wisdom is aligned not only with modern living systems science, but also with the teachings of Indigenous cultures around the world, the only cultures in human history that have not yet collapsed.[15]

All this means we need to completely change our worldview and totally rebuild our society. We need to develop new ways of knowing and generate new capacities for relating to ourselves, to others, to society, and to the planet. Such a change will not come by itself; it has to be consciously evolved, nursed, and led. Wisdom in action and Peopleism in practice are likely to first facilitate and then accelerate the process.

A Paradigm Change in How Organizations Function

There is also a discernible paradigm change in how organizations function. The old paradigm in the industrial economy was that organizations function as machines—an outcome of Frederick Taylor introducing scientific management in 1911, a breakthrough insight that optimized labour productivity and opened up an era of unprecedented effectiveness and efficiency. The 20th century was 'the management century'.

The Knowledge Economy brought forth the new paradigm that organizations are living organisms, substantively limiting our ability to control outcomes and calling for greater agility than ever before.

Tobias Rees, founding director of the Transformations of the Human Program at the Berggruen Institute, a think-tank in Los Angeles, puts forward the view that we are witnessing a transition from human-centred business to making business more in tune with nature, or even like nature. It is simply a new humility that no longer views us humans as the centre of the universe. This marks a radical shift in how we conceive of business and its design principles. As Rees points out:

> This means realizing that in the new tech enhanced biological age, the systems we are embedded in are not machines, they are streams. These streams can overwhelm and absorb us, propel us forward and carry us away. To thrive in them we need fluidity—of identities, ideologies, intelligences, senses, and emotions—and a symbiosis of technology and biology that helps us to be more attuned with life in its broadest, wildest sense.[16]

This is a very significant observation. National and organizational leaders need to acknowledge that our ability to manage the processes and the outcomes will reduce even more because a stream, by nature, is always in flow; the only way to keep pace with it is by continuous learning so as to be in sync with the whole—with people as well as with nature. If we can relate to and absorb these changes, we will naturally 'value resilience over efficiency, super-flexibility over rigid control, and a regenerative approach over extractive approach.'[17] Such important insights can only be meaningful for us if we continue to ask the relevant questions.

You Matter More Than You Think

Karen O'Brien, professor at the University of Oslo, is concerned that 'so many people today feel hopeless and despondent, because they feel they do not matter. We underestimate our collective capacity for rapid social transformation. Perhaps we are missing something. Every moment, we have the possibility to disrupt cultures and systems and generate new ones based on equity, integrity and oneness. To realize this potential, we have to make a quantum leap.'[18] And that is possible because we now live in a quantum world, and once we fully grasp that, nothing will ever be the same again.

Most of our understanding is based on a paradigm that sees humans as inherently separate from one another and the environment. Quantum Theory challenges 'separateness' and fragmentation, and invites us to rethink the relationship between subjects and objects. That calls for a fundamental change in our beliefs and metaphors. She asserts that, 'New metaphors have the power to create a new reality. Concepts such as quantum leaps, entanglement, and potentiality can serve as powerful metaphors that open up new ways of thinking about social change. Metaphors and stories do not exist only in our minds—we embody and live them, and can use them to generate new and more sustainable patterns.'[19]

'You Matter More Than You Think' is the theme of her splendid ongoing project. The values we believe in, individually and collectively, can steer systems and cultures—substantively and significantly—to create an equitable and thriving world. We need to open up and we will realize that the individual is indeed the collective. On its own, it can have no separate existence. So, if we think we do not matter, it is because we choose to think we do not matter.

I love the perspective, 'You matter. I matter. We matter.' It cognitively enhances human potential to shape our future before it shapes us.

It's Time to Unfold the Future

The rise of Peopleism as an idea has evolved after everything else failed to respond to the genuine survival needs of the entire human race. Like the evolution of new ideas in each age, every new ideology tends to be more inclusive in its worldview as compared to the ideology it replaces. Paradoxically, the ability to conceive new ideas and ideologies is at its zenith, only when it is absolutely necessary for our continued survival.

Susan Witt, executive director of the Schumacher Centre for a New Economics, based in Massachusetts, writes with conviction, 'A new economy, a next economy, a green economy, a responsible economy—a movement is building. Not by chance. Not by default. But informed by love of place and guided by wisdom that spans ages. Citizens are taking responsibility to put ideas into practical action. A new economy is emerging.'[20] She supports her contention by giving several examples of the places where it is happening: the Berkshire region of Massachusetts, Intervale in Burlington (Vermont), New Orleans in Albuquerque (New Mexico), and Westport (Connecticut), among others.[21]

Futurist Benjamin J. Butler echoes a similar view, 'Now is the time to look to the future and realize the promise it holds for those who wish to move forward into a world that is as magnificent as it is wondrous. The unfolding of the future is at hand for those ready to see beyond the past and the constraints imposed by our own narrow-mindedness and self-centredness. We stand at the threshold of a new beginning—a threshold beyond which there is peace and tranquility, justice and fairness, balance and humility.'[22]

Reinforce Your Hope with Action

My fourteen-year-old grandson, Arnav, asked me one day, 'Could you please tell me the purpose of the book you have been writing for the last few years?'

'You know the world is going through a very difficult time. The purpose of the book,' I explained, 'is to help create a better, safe new world for everyone on this planet. A world where everyone respects nature, as well as all people of every race and every religion. A world where all children, everywhere have a decent home, a good education, excellent health, and they all lead happy lives with their families, in peace, with no fear.' I paused. 'Do you think it is possible?

Are there any lessons from Star Wars stories and movies that could help make it happen?'

His eyes lit up as he said, 'I think it is possible. In *Star Wars Rebels* episodes, strangers from different backgrounds come together and become like a family, as soon as they sense that they face a common danger and may not survive. And they win. But defeating a powerful enemy is not easy. We should remember Yoda's advice: "Don't fall back on old habits and safe assumptions. If you are going to make a difference, you must fully commit to the new. Do or do not. There is no try."'

He added after a pause: 'The greatest weapon against an evil empire is the hope that good will always prevail. Rebellions are built on hope and faith that change is possible. You must, of course, reinforce your hope and faith with action.'[23]

I was truly awed by his response. If the millions of passionate fans of the Star Wars sagas all over the world also think the same way, that could kindle another source of inspiration for all. I was tempted to ask, 'Do you think George Lucas[24] could be persuaded to come down from his Galaxy to Earth and make a movie with this theme for our planet?'

He laughed. 'I could try. Or perhaps, it's easier to make one myself.'

My nine–year old granddaughter, Arunima, also chipped in gleefully, 'Wow, Dadaji! That would be a great book and a super movie. I would love to see all my hopes fulfilled.'

Her innocent reference to 'hope' kindled a new excitement in me. Hope can instill life into the present and has the potential to become an infinite source of strength against adversity. Maria Popova, creator of The Marginalian (earlier known as 'Brain Pickings'), adds a new dimension to hope in her beautiful piece:

> The capacity for hope is not merely a hallmark of human consciousness—it is the supreme umbilical cord between consciousnesses. To place our hope in another person is to instantly entwine destinies, linking self and other in a tender and tenacious recognition of interdependence. All love is a form of hope. All hope is the work of absolute sincerity, which is the emblem of being fully human. A cynic would hasten to retort that this

> openhearted expectancy is precisely what makes hope a portal to disappointment—but cynicism is, of course, the terror of sincerity, the cowardly attempt at self-protection from the heartache of unmet hope. If we are serious about the evolution of consciousness—and of our understanding of consciousness—we must place hope at the helm.[25]

It is necessary to bear in mind that hope is born of our aspirations and convictions that reflect our everyday vision, what we long for and what we firmly believe is possible. Hope is the seed we sow to realize our vision. To grow and fructify, it must continuously be nurtured by relentless efforts, persistent resolve, and resolute collaboration with all those who share that vision.

Noam Chomsky, a leading public intellectual of our times, sums it up best, 'If you assume that there is no hope, you guarantee that there will be no hope. If you assume that there is an instinct for freedom, that there are opportunities to change things, then there is a possibility that you can contribute to making a better world.'[26]

Voices of Concern

While reinforcing the voices of support for the thought process this book propagates, we must also take cognizance of the voices of concern.

Hedley Bull, in his book *The Anarchical Society*, made an important distinction between a 'system of states' and a 'society of states'.[27] An international *system* simply means that there are states which have contacts and dealings with each other. An international *society*, on the other hand, while presupposing an international system, shares a set of rules and institutions. He believes that the prevalent system of states has the propensity to be anarchical because there is no hierarchical level of sovereignty above that of each state.

Richard Haas, American diplomat, elaborates that the notion of 'society' in the international sphere is based on three principles:

- The principal 'citizens' of this society are countries.
- A founding principle of this society is that the governments and leaders who oversee the countries are essentially free

to act as they wish within their own borders. How the leaders come to occupy positions of authority, be it by birth, revolution, elections, or some other means, matters not.

- The members of this international society respect and accept this freedom of action on the part of others (in exchange for the others accepting similar freedom for them). It is not far off to describe this approach to international relations as a 'live and let live' cross-border understanding.[28]

There is no higher level of authority over states. There are certain expectations and conventions but no binding policies, principles or rules in the 'international system' that govern relationships between and among states. In such circumstances, the forces of sovereignty, nationalism, and dissension, invariably tend to prevail over the forces that tend to promote a peaceful and harmonious international society.

If we look at the rear-view mirror, one may say it is an incontestable hypothesis. But if we take the much larger windshield view, one can no longer ignore the glaring new emerging reality in the world today. The forces that unite the seven billion excluded and ignored people across all nations are getting stronger than ever before, generating an overwhelming conviction that the forces that unite the world are more sustainable than the forces which divide. States may also find it expedient to recognize some genuine common interests and common values that justify subordination of petty nationalism in order to achieve higher purposes.

Sean Cleary, executive vice chair, Future World Foundation, concurs that 'there is nothing in this construct that requires national entities to abandon their cultures, or that obliges states to desist from pursuit of the interests of their national populations. Effective application of the paradigm does however require that states recognize that the exclusive pursuit of their national interests, without reference to the interests of others, or indeed of humanity as a whole, is dangerous and potentially destructive of aggregate human welfare.'[29]

Yanis Varoufakis, Greek economist and politician, is more circumspect about the hardships people need to endure before we make headway in ending the sovereignty of capitalism. He believes that, 'Capitalism is dead; it became so dominant that it mutated into a variant so toxic that it killed off its host, capitalism, replacing it with something far, far worse—producing not machines that produce anything, but creating machines to modify human behaviour.'[30] He laments that, rather unknowingly, old-fashioned, terrestrial capitalists, and consumers at large, have not only funded these behemoths but have also been offering free voluntary labour, incessantly tweeting and posting, to train the new algorithms in real time to know us inside out. In the process, we have created a new breed of extremely powerful 'technofeudals'—a handful of owners of giant algorithm generating systems. He argues that Jeff Bezos, the owner of Amazon, doesn't produce capital, he charges rent. That isn't capitalism, it is feudalism. He concludes that 'these imagination-defying AI programs are not only asset-stripping our physical wealth, but also asset-stripping our brains. The only way we can turn these cloud-based artefacts from means of behavioural modification to means of human collaboration and emancipation—lies in reclaiming our minds.'[31]

This is a very thoughtful scrutiny but equally important is the inference that we collectively hold within us the ability to leapfrog from whatever morass we are in to a sane and safe new world. The path to reclaim 'our minds', and discover 'our hearts' clearly lies in consciously transitioning from knowledge to wisdom.

I mentioned in Chapter 1 that we are traversing a watershed moment in human history, a moment that provides enormous potential for a great transformation. Such dramatic potential is recognized not only by many thinkers and think-tanks, but also by billions of people all over the planet. That we can leverage this moment to make a giant leap ahead is an opportunity human race is unlikely to ignore. The inevitable rise of Peopleism is well on track.

Chapter 14

Collective Wisdom Outshines Collective Ignorance

An Irreversible New Dawn

How can we take advantage of this moment when there is an empty page for the co-writing of new futures?—In many moments we will not have answers to these questions. But this is not really a problem, as Daniel Wahl says: Questions are the way to collective wisdom.

—Futuro Possivel, Brazil[1]

Collective Ignorance Masquerades as Collective Wisdom

There is a fable about four monkeys left inside a large room-size cage, where a bunch of bananas was hung on top of a pole in the centre of the cage. Whenever a monkey climbed the pole and got near the bananas, photoelectric cells would activate strong water showers to drench him from all sides. The monkey would get scared and come down. Every other day, another monkey would make another attempt, encounter the same fate and give up. In due course, they stopped trying.

A few days later, one of the monkeys in the room was replaced by another one. When the new monkey started climbing the pole, the other three jointly pulled him down.

The new monkey tried again and again, but was always dragged back. Over a period, the four original monkeys were replaced, one by one, by four new monkeys. None of them had actually experienced the shower. In fact, it was no longer functioning, but no one was allowed by the others to even try to get close to the bananas.

This story illustrates that most of us, unconsciously, become unwitting victims of our environment, and creatures of social norms which are fostered upon us by widely, but not wisely, held perceptions in society.

This is a classic occurrence in most human lives. Unconsciously, and as a matter of course, we imbibe the beliefs of others and start defending them as if they were non-negotiable facts based on our own observations and experiences. We consider collective ignorance as conventional wisdom. We stop asking tough questions and absorb routinely formed views of others as personal convictions. We do not even realize that this diminishes our propensity to do what is best for us.

We end up doing things without really knowing what is right or wrong—often without any regard for whether it is good for us in the long run. For us to play a meaningful role in catalyzing change, either within us, or in the community around, or in the world at large, the starting point is to completely rid our minds of past beliefs and prejudices. It is not just thinking out-of-the-box, it is about throwing away all the boxes ossified in our cerebrums.

Many of us, particularly those who hold positions of leadership, tend to base our decisions and actions on whether they will make us wealthier or more powerful, forgetting all the time that wealth does not necessarily bring happiness. How you earn your wealth is a more important contributor to whether you can be happy as well as wealthy.

Being Wealthy and Happy

There is one thing common about every person in the universe, irrespective of whether one is a billionaire or one lives hand to mouth.

They all want to be happy in their lives, with peace all around. Aristotle called it the goal of all goals. Samuel Johnson corroborated it three centuries ago when he wrote, 'To be happy at home is the ultimate result of all ambition.'

And quite rightly so. This is the only life we have. What else can be more important than this? Unless of course, one loves being miserable. There are two elemental truths about happiness.

- Nothing in this world can ever stop you from being happy. If you are unhappy, it is usually by your choice. Happiness is not something you can find anywhere; it is located within you. It is quite normal to seek happiness. But you cannot look for it outside when it is inside. When you look inside, you find contentment with what you already have. When you look outside, you only generate bigger ambitions and more desires. There is nothing wrong in having lofty aspirations, but the efforts to achieve those must not be at the cost of harming any part of society or any component of nature.
- Making others happy invariably leads to genuine happiness, as expounded in this old saying:

  If you want happiness for an hour, take a nap.
  If you want happiness for a day, go fishing.
  If you want happiness for a year, inherit a fortune.
  If you want happiness for a lifetime, make others happy.

Lifting others' spirits and spreading cheer with noble actions, or being a source of happiness for others by contributing to their well-being brings real happiness which is clearly distinguishable from momentary pleasures one seeks all the time. Gradually, one begins to realize that being happy by making others happy is also the greatest service one can render the world.

The Focal Message of This Book

This is not meant to be just a feel-good book. It is more a pointer to shifting our attention to things that really matter. It is not merely meant to provide some take-aways to the reader; it is meant to enable every reader to embrace certain steadfast convictions. The book has articulated a vision and a path to reach the future we deserve—a sustainably happy life for all. It is about all of us. Collectively, we have to choose among us the producers and directors for our quest to realize this vision, and accept the role each of us need to play as an individual. We are also the audience, the critics and the benefactors. This book outlines a script but it is not binding, you are free to amend it and alter it as you proceed.

There is no reference here to what one did in the past. This is a vision that looks ahead. If one is already wealthy, following this path will make one wealthy and happy. All it asks is that, hereafter, we pursue the path of the Wisdom Economy and join the ranks of wise, responsible leaders. This is not about philanthropy; this is something the well-off need to do in their self-interest, to preserve, sustain and retain their status hereafter.

If you are not well off, seek and demand your rights and privileges that are legitimately yours by virtue of being residents of planet Earth. Natural resources in a nation are collectively owned by all the citizens of the nation. If a government licenses the exploitation of certain natural resources by a private entity, the fees and revenue generated from that transaction must be equally distributed among all citizens. This is a non-negotiable right of every citizen. A government by itself cannot claim ownership of national assets—be it mines, water, land, air, forests or any other part of nature's bounty. All these are a part of the 'commons'[2]—a term for shared resources in which each citizen has an equal interest. This can rightly be considered an inheritance of humanity and is therefore to be shared among those who inhabit those lands.

The income from the sale and licensing of these assets cannot be considered government income to be spent at the government's discretion. Government revenues should emanate only from taxes collected from individuals and corporations and from the sale of goods and services; this revenue should be adequate for meeting government expenses and spending on essential public services, infrastructure, law and order, defence and administration.

One may argue this is too drastic a departure from how governments are run. That is a fair point, but such drastic transformations are what the new millennium needs. This has nothing to do with the rigours of capitalism or socialism. This is a thought process which naturally emerges when 'People' are at the centrestage—not a preferred category of people who are born rich or the ones who can lobby, but all the people who inhabit the nation.

> People belong to a nation.
> The nation belongs to the people.
> This is the real meaning of Peopleism.

The End of the 'Divine Rights' of the Global Elite

In the Middle Ages, the idea prevailed that kings derived their authority from God and could not, therefore, be held accountable for their actions by any earthly authority such as a parliament or the people. Later, this began to be referred to as the 'divine right of kings',[3] justifying the king's absolute authority in both political and spiritual matters. King James I of England (1603–1625) was the foremost exponent of the divine right of kings and continuously faced revolts from his subjects. The doctrine virtually disappeared from English politics after the Glorious Revolution (1688–89). In the late 17th and the 18th centuries, kings such as Louis XIV (1643–1715) of France, continued to profit from the divine-rights theory, but not for long. The American Revolution (1775–83), the French Revolution (1789), and the Napoleonic wars stripped the doctrine of most of its remaining credibility.

Sadly, the collateral fault lines of capitalism have brought us to a similar situation today. So many elected leaders in so-called democracies, and the owners and nominated CEOs of large multinational corporations, pretty much assume they are not answerable to anyone but themselves. Shadows of the divine rights are resurfacing. A cozy relationship between companies, lawmakers and regulatory agencies has helped raise the incidence of corporate fraud to new heights. This is just not tenable, the perpetuity of the deemed 'divine rights' of the elite can continue no more. For sheer survival, the wise among them, and the wise among us, will have to start setting things right.

This will be a bold and persistent endeavour. Bold because something so drastic has not been attempted before, and persistent because we are bound to encounter obstacles. But we will have to stay the course with undimmed resolve. Let us continue to seek inputs from those who can contribute to speeding up the transitions, but let us give no quarter to those who try to hinder us.

For those who join this quest, I would like to assure them that we are not the pioneers on this path. Millions around the world have been looking at these issues for decades and have already laid markers and milestones on the road we will traverse.

Start Where You Are, Do What You Can

Aside from some rare exceptions, in every age in every part of the world, the masses have invariably been more virtuous than the rulers. The problem in the world today is not so much the wrongdoings of a few who rule but the silence of the majority who suffer. There are billions of outstanding human beings around the world who symbolize a tangible part of 'goodness in the world'. It is now time for them to break their silence and proclaim their goodness, not with pride but with humility, and be the anchors who encourage others to start pursuing the path to transform their destiny. Things will not change unless we ourselves take charge of the trajectory of our own future.

Never before has human society possessed so much power for good or for evil. Never before has power been so widely distributed among the people and nations across the world. The rapidly growing constituency for positive transformational change is gaining critical mass. The last few laps required to achieve global equity and justice may be much harder to cover, but the shoreline across is within sight provided we address these issues:

- Extreme economic inequality is out of control. The wealth of billionaires is rising. Since 2020, the richest five men in the world have doubled their fortunes. During the same period, 4.8 billion people globally have become poorer. Hardship and hunger are a daily reality for many people worldwide.[4]

We can no longer helplessly watch the miniscule elite using their gigantic wealth to bury even the last few remnants of democracy so as to completely disempower the majority of the human race.

- In Sub-Saharan Africa, the per capita income is the same as it was fourteen years ago. Development delayed is development denied. The World Bank estimates that in the next ten years, 1.1 billion young people across the Global South will become working age adults. Yet, in the same period and in the same countries, only 325 million jobs are expected to be created. The cost of inaction is unimaginable.[5] The nightmare of the demographic dividend becoming a demographic challenge is certainly avoidable—if only we pursue the discipline of Peopleism and implement surge-up economic policies in place of the trickle-down approach now in vogue.
- The IPCC 2023 report is much bleaker than previous assessments. Globally, households with incomes in the top 10 per cent emit upwards of 45 per cent of the world's greenhouse gases (GHG), while the families earning in the bottom 50 per cent account for 15 per cent at most. Yet the effects of climate change will hit poorer, marginalized communities the hardest. Between 3.3 billion and 3.6 billion people live in countries that are highly vulnerable to climate impacts.[6] The risks of inaction on climate are immense. Limiting global temperature rise to 1.5 degrees C (2.7 degrees F) is still possible, but only if we act immediately. The world needs to peak GHG emissions by 2025, nearly halve these by 2030, cut 60 per cent by 2035 and reach net-zero emissions around mid-century, while ensuring a just and equitable transition to non-fossil fuel alternatives. A narrow window of opportunity is still open, but there's not one second to waste.
- Many other catastrophic risks such as engineered pandemics, genetic engineering, nuclear risks in regional wars, terrorism, and financial meltdowns due to ballooning debts are all within the realm of possibility. Any one of these has the capability to seriously cripple human progress, or even destroy human civilization irretrievably.

It is not my intention to recap the action points and the direction-pointers that emerge from this book. It is only to emphasize that we have set for ourselves the onerous task of reinventing democracy. We have identified that the route to do so lies in graduating from Knowledge Economy to Wisdom Economy, and transitioning from Capitalism to Peopleism, not in incremental steps, but in big transformational leaps. We know it is an ambitious agenda, but as long as we have faith and confidence in our collective unity across the entire world, we know we can achieve it soon. We may take small steps but we must not settle for small victories. Our aim is to seek immediate and decisive changes—those that help accelerate progress towards our long-term vision. In Aldous Huxley's utopian novel *Island*, a visitor asks, 'Where do you start?' To which the islanders respond, 'We start everywhere at once.'[7]

As individuals—rich or poor, employees of corporations or civil society, working in either the government or the private sector, employed or unemployed—one can pick up any thread in the broad-spectrum narrative shared in this book and begin working on it. 'Start where you are. Use what you have. Do what you can.'[8] You will begin changing your life, and also every life you touch.

The 'Safe New World' Is Well Within Our Reach

My gratitude and love for all those who found time to go through the pages of this book. I have one favour to ask of you, the young and the young-at-heart. Please do not just believe that I or someone else or a group of us will propagate the messages of the book and, somehow, a better future will soon dawn. No, it does not happen that way.

We are not just seeking a change. We are seeking a transformation. A series of changes built on a rock-solid foundation, cemented with the immutable doctrines of equity, sustainability, transparency, and justice, to create a far better world, not only in the country we reside in but on the entire planet.

- I call upon you to *believe in yourself*. This arises from Awareness.

- I call upon you to *believe in all those whose lives you touch*—a reflection of their trust in you, and your trust in them.
- I call upon you to *believe in all of us, collectively*; this mirrors an alignment of our vision and our passion.

As all of you lend a hand, the Safe New World—in a Liveable Planet—is well within our reach.

A Message for the Well-Off

You are referred to as the crème-de-la-crème of the global elite, or the one-per cent club, or the millionaires of the world. You may be in business or in politics. You are considered the most successful human beings on the planet today; ostensibly you excelled way beyond others in whatever you chose to do. Some of you may be the beneficiaries of family heritage, or you may be entirely self-made. Today, you are in a significant leadership position and your decisions will determine not only the trajectory of your own future, but also the orbit of progress of all the lives that touch yours.

If the subject of this book attracted you and you found time to go through it, it is heartening. Your receptivity to new ideas and ideologies, and your apparent readiness to retune and reset your worldview is itself a great motivator for whosoever gets to know about it. Many of you would have participated in several initiatives, at various times, to join the chorus of what the world needs to do, to solve its perpetual problems. People appreciate that very much. But today we want to go beyond that. We want to start doing something about these problems, immediately.

No one needs to spell out what you should do and what you could do. Deep within, you know it already. There is no need to defend your past, or what you may have consciously or unconsciously done till today—something you may feel guilty about, or have remorse about. Let us only focus on the way forward. As you absorb the attributes of responsible leadership (Chapter 1), imbibe the tangible traits of wisdom (Chapter 7), and practice the precepts of Peopleism (Chapters 8 and 9), the DNA of the institutions you lead will be so transformed that you will be filled with joy beyond measure.

You will gradually generate a holistic purpose in life, which in turn will fill your life with meaning. While you move ahead on this path—you will be wealthy and happy, quite effortlessly. You will discover within you a feeling of universal love and peace, and start radiating that joyously to every life you touch. It is worth remembering all the time that:

He who sees a need and waits to be asked for help
is as unkind as if he had refused it.

—Dante Alighieri, 1265–1321[9]

A Message for Civil Society

You are the unofficial custodians of the planet's conscience, the catalysts to steer human progress in the right direction, and the guides and mentors for the multitudes who need support and inputs on how to escape the daily rigours of despondency, and transition to a better life. The best of you functions as role models for selfless service and courageous efforts to pursue these worthy goals. You are the thought leaders and collators of collective wisdom from all regions and cultures. You represent the Institutions to Promote Consciousness (IPCs), and you are the creators and implementers of realistic planet-encompassing programmes for transforming our world.

But there is a concern. People are surprised not by what you have achieved; they are surprised why so little has been achieved vis-à-vis the potential. My discussions with IPCs all over the world reveal that while preservers of the status quo appear to be more united in their pursuit of iniquity; the IPCs, the backbone of the global change-seekers, tend to be not as united in their pursuit of equity and justice.

There can be no doubt that the shared wisdom, the dedication and the commitment of proponents for transformation should make them much stronger than opponents of change. The latter may score small gains through violent acts, or with unjust policies, or with help from compromised judiciary and legislatures that have lost their conscience—I put them all in the same bracket—but their victories are short and reversible, and equally disastrous for them as individual perpetrators. On the other hand, the reformists, the

IPCs and the law-abiding silent citizenry are the emerging force of the future—potentially stronger than mighty armed forces and even nuclear arsenals, provided you can all unite, and also unite others around you, through the pursuit of awareness, bridge-building, and compassion (Chapter 7).

A united civil society, with one unified agenda, can achieve even herculean tasks. The rewards lie not in getting recognition from others, but in the fulfilment of the promises we have made to ourselves—to bring about a decisive change for the better, in the specific domains we choose. Nothing exemplifies this approach better than this couplet by Allama Iqbal:

Discard your ego and personhood,
If you want to reach the zenith of achievement.
Just like a seed merges with dust to become one with it,
So that it can sprout and blossom into a flower.

A Message for the Youth

There is a global youth bulge in the population of the world. Irrespective of where you live, all of you have a common trait—you are experiencing a qualitative change in how you view the world. You are the generation that has grown up in the internet age, with 24/7 access to live information, and have learnt with dismay how the many who seemed to be successful and invulnerable have fallen with disgrace, simply because they did not conform to norms of basic integrity. Social media carries so much fake news and hate content that some of you are justifiably frustrated and disappointed. There is a widely prevalent disgust that social media could become a big threat to society. Notwithstanding that, most of the youth movements and initiatives in recent years, referred to in this book, could not have taken off without social media.

You alone can be the saviours in resurrecting the potential of social media to make it a virtuous pillar of society, by helping to create 'The Age of Truth'. Create new platforms and set up new institutions and enterprises; boycott the organizations that cannot separate truth from fiction—do not helplessly accept what you do not like. Create a culture to rapidly expose unethical corporate practices, and do it ruthlessly so that organizations hereafter find it almost impossible to flout laws with impunity. If you do not support them, they cannot survive.

I know that young people all over the world today are more selfless, more caring, more creative, and certainly more altruistic than the youth of yesteryears. Soon, you will outnumber all other generations; the future of the world is in your hands. Work for success, but not success at any cost; success must be earned without compromising clearly identifiable human values. Prove that ethics and trust carry premium rewards, and that you do not have to be crooked and clever to succeed. This popular verse in Sanskrit literature could be a valuable guide:

Tasks can only be accomplished by sincere hard work,
not merely by setting lofty goals.
Despite the mighty power of a lion, deer do not voluntarily
enter his mouth as he sleeps; he has to strive hard.

A Message for Educators

It has been well acknowledged that the most precious assets of a country are invariably the people of integrity who gain stature by living the human values and principles they believe to be non-negotiable. As we have seen in various countries at various times, they energize the entire population, awakening them to realize the enormous power they can wield. Mahatma Gandhi in India, Nelson Mandela in South Africa, and Martin Luther King Jr in the US are luminous examples who galvanized their people and steered them to give shape to their aspirations and realize them. Whenever such men and women attain a higher vision, the lower visions of others disappear on their own. Their impact on a nation's progress is singularly momentous and all-pervasive.

One of the vital tasks is to get tomorrow's leaders to accept and espouse the traits of wise and responsible leadership, in word and deed, and be always ready to lead a transformation towards the world they envisage. For that, the entire educational system has to be values-driven, starting from schools and colleges, and carrying on beyond that in universities and business schools. Educators have a role to inculcate a reorientation of priorities and attitudes and evolve globally acceptable, pan-cultural concepts, leading to a trans-civilizational ethos of values. It is a task with maximum sustainable impact, and it is doable.

One can discern the beginning of a movement to reinvent education. There are numerous small fires all over the world, igniting the spark of values-based education in schools, colleges and universities. Many of you are doing wonderful work in ensuring that the majority, which has so far been on the right side of the moral fence, continues to stay that way. However, the net quality of leadership, in aggregate terms, has not yet tilted in favour of a values-based leadership. We have to meet the twin challenges of transforming today's leaders, as well as transforming today the leaders of tomorrow. This means de-corrupting the minds of today's leaders, as well as making the minds of coming generations incorruptible. The second challenge is more significant. We would require hands-on involvement of every educator in every educational institution, in every country, and urge each of them to create a new curriculum—which is aligned with the need to uplift the mindset and the heart-set of the future generations of leaders.

A Message for Consumers of All Products and Services

Five decades ago, Peter Drucker, widely considered to be the founder of modern management practices wrote that the purpose of any business is 'to create a customer', and then to retain him.[10] Gradually, business leaders evolved the notion that 'the customer is king'. That worked well for quite some time. The competition was real and monopolies existed only in domains owned by the state. Those were early days of capitalism. As the practice of capitalism started suffering from the widespread virus of lobbying to seek unwarranted and unmerited privileges from whichever organ of government they could influence (which essentially meant buying them out), monopolies and oligopolies became the norm. First, law-makers aligned with businessmen; in due course the independent regulators who were meant to protect the interests of consumers also succumbed to lobbying.

One comes across glaring examples of the alarming nexus between the industry regulators and the businesses they are supposed to regulate. Be it aviation, automobiles, pharmaceuticals, or food and agriculture, the complete disregard for gullible consumers, just to benefit certain corporations, can certainly be clubbed with acts of terrorism on innocent citizens.

I would urge consumers in all countries to remember that a 'consumer is still king' (or queen). You always have a choice. Exercise it. Let those who take advantage of your vulnerability receive an appropriate response. You, as consumer, have the enormous power to bring even corporate monoliths to their knees, provided your reason for resisting them or boycotting them, is based on a sound rationale.

Act as if you make a difference.
It does.[11]

—William James (1842–1910)

A Message for All Women

The messages above for the well off, civil society, the youth, educators, and consumers are meant for all genders, but this special message is specifically for women.

We all know that you have had to fight for your rights over many centuries. In the Western world, where the position of women is now nearing parity with men in several aspects (though much still remains to be done), we need to recall that the process to reach even this stage has been long and arduous. The US declared itself a constitutional democracy in 1776 but it was a limited democracy only for white males with landed property; women and slaves were excluded. You had to wait for 154 years before the U.S. Constitution granted American women the right to vote in 1920. The United Kingdom also delayed giving women the right to vote on the same terms as men (over the age of 21), till 1928, and the women in Switzerland gained the right to vote in federal elections, only in 1971. It is clear that the male prejudice against women, even in the so-called developed world, was so deeply ingrained that you have had to literally fight for every inch of progress.

It is sad, but quite likely that it may still take long in the Middle East, Africa, and Asia to change the equally entrenched attitudes of male domination. While India gave its women full voting rights in parity with men, right since the Constitution was adopted in 1950, the social status of women and how they are treated in society is still mired in centuries' old prejudices.

Women cannot indefinitely wait for men to voluntarily discard their irrational ideology. Women should not accept the present slow pace of change. The women of Iran have been showing exceptional courage in continuing their struggle to reverse the arbitrary status-quo. If women all over the world—over four billion of you—take a united, irrevocable stand, you will be surprised by what you can achieve. You comprise the biggest emerging market in the world; the countries that can leverage this vast untapped economic opportunity will become the next economic powers.

The Universal Declaration of Human Rights[12] adopted by the United Nations General Assembly in 1948, unambiguously reaffirms the dignity and worth of the human person and in the equal rights of men and women. In spite of that, global practices tend to accord a lower priority to human rights of women. It is time for a decisive paradigm shift. One more time—and now is the right time—you have to harness all the vigour and courage you can, individually and collectively.

I urge the top one thousand women leaders in every country, representing every profession, to take a united stand and demand new laws that will set right this most despicable inequity in the world. Of course, laws are just a deterrent; the real change will come about only when we instill this notion of equality in every home, at the pre-school age, in every boy and girl child. Every mother has to play this anchor role by ensuring there is no discrimination between boys and girls at home. This has to be followed up by continuously inculcating the principles of gender equality in every child's mind, by the teachers at primary and secondary school level.

This may seem to be a small step, but when two billion mothers[13] take the same step in unison, and with determined resolve, it is bound to have the desired results.

Peopleism Trumps Capitalism

The wide array of thoughts and processes outlined in this book bring Peopleism to life. This new system of governance with a singular focus and genuine concern for people, is bound to triumph and empower common people—each one of them. Capitalism (as we know it) will start receding till it totally disappears from the thought-streams of policy makers in all countries. Peopleism will decimate forever the potential to abuse democracy the way it has been done for decades. The political leaders will be more sensitive and conscious of their role; they will no longer be able to resort to manipulation in perpetuating lies and falsehoods.

Privileged elites and special interest groups will have no option but to align with people's expectations and become a party to devise effective policies and find efficient ways to help them advance and progress. It will not just be a government of the people, and by the people, but more importantly, it will be a government for the people—all the people.

The fears and concerns about the demise of democracy can be put to rest. Democracy will no longer be on sale. 'Unfracturable' democracy, till now just an elusive ideal to aspire for, is now well within our grasp—like never before. Peopleism will breed a new culture of liberalism, generate a fresh impetus for inclusiveness and tolerance, catalyse new levels of energy, and build the firm foundation for open and transparent governance—so that the institutions of democracy grow to heights where no one can ever bring them down again.

As people get convinced that their problems are being sincerely attended to; leaders with hyped populist slogans will have no role to play. Populism will then be buried. Divisive forces that create confusion will find there are no takers for them; issues will be debated based on truthful facts. Leaders in society and business will have a balanced sense of national identity and unity, in sync with one's global responsibilities for collaboration and cooperation. A new People's era is all set to begin.

As Wisdom Economy succeeds Knowledge Economy, as Peopleism takes deep roots in governance processes, as the shadows of crony capitalism begin to fade, and as love and compassion start dominating the public discourse, we the People, will together experience the joys of collective growth and progress.

The journey has already commenced. Let us all put our hands and heads together, and accelerate the process, remembering the sane advice of Patanjali that if you truly believe it can be done, then it will be done:

> *When you are inspired by some great purpose, some extraordinary project, all your thoughts break their bonds. Your mind transcends limitations, your consciousness expands in every direction, and you find yourself in a new, great, and wonderful world. Dormant forces, faculties and talents become alive, and you discover yourself to be a greater person by far than you ever dreamed yourself to be.*[14]

Notes

Invitation

1 Elbert Hubbard (1856–1915), an American writer, publisher, and philosopher, quoted in Chang, Laurence. 2006. *Wisdom for the Soul: Five Millennia of Prescriptions for Spiritual Healing*. Washington DC: Gnosophia Publisher.

2 This or a similar statement is attributed to Vladimir Ilyich Lenin.No citation is available, but it supposedly described the Russian Revolution.

3 This website indicates the Covid-19 cases and deaths reported to the World Health Organization; the actual numbers were estimated to be much higher. Accessed 5 November 2023. https://data.who. int/dashboards/covid19/deaths.

4 A similar thought process was also described in the book: Ramo, Joshua Cooper. 2016. *The Seventh Sense: Power, Fortune, and Survival in the Age of Network*. NY: Little Brown.

5 Mustich, James. 2019. 'The Past Is Never Dead. It's Not Even Past.On the American Tragedies of William Faulkner'. July 28, 2019. Accessed 5 November 2023 https://jamesmustich.medium.com/the-past-is-never-dead-its-not-even-past-a765d42cb8bc.

6 Hemingway, Ernest. 1926. *The Sun Also Rises*. US: Scribner.

7 This quote is attributed to Max Planck (1858–1947), the father of quantum physics, but there is no authentic record on this.

8 Huxley, Aldous. 1932. *Brave New World*. London: Chatto & Windus.

9 Orwell, George. 1949. *1984*. London: Secker & Warburg.

10 Lanchester, John. 2019. 'Orwell v Huxley: Whose Dystopia Are We Living in Today?' *The Financial Times*, January 18, 2019. Accessed 5 November 2023. https://www.ft.com/content/aa8ac620-1818-11e9-b93e-f4351a53f1c3.

11 Credit Suisse Bank. 2022. 'Global Wealth Report 2022.' https://www.credit-suisse.com/about-us-news/en/articles/news-and-expertise/

credit-suisse-global-wealth-report-2022-fast-wealth-growth-in-times-of-uncertainty-202209.html.

12 The seventeen Sustainable Development Goals (SDGs) were adopted by the United Nations in 2015 as a universal call to action to end poverty, protect the planet, and ensure that by 2030 all people enjoy peace and prosperity. UNDP. 2015. 'What are the Sustainable Development Goals?' Accessed 5 November 2023. https://www. undp.org/sustainable-development-goals.

13 Floyd, David. 2022. 'Measuring Inequality: Forget Gini, Go With the Palma Ratio Instead.' November 30, 2022. Accessed 5 November 2023. https://www.investopedia.com/news/measuring-inequality-forget-gini-go-palma/.

14 'Data Page: Palma ratio (Pretax) (Estimated)', part of the publication: Joe Hasell, Pablo Arriagada, Esteban Ortiz-Ospina and Max Roser (2023)—"Economic Inequality". Data adapted from World Inequality Database (WID.world). Retrieved from https://ourworldindata.org/grapher/palma-ratio-s90s40-ratio [online resource]

15 Edelman Trust Institute. 2024. 'Edelman Trust Barometer: Global Trust Report.' January 2024. https://www.edelman.com/trust/2024/trust-barometer.

16 Karam, Sami J. 2017. 'Capitalism Did Not Win the Cold War', *Foreign Affairs*, July 19, 2017. https://www.foreignaffairs.com/ articles/world/2017-07-19/capitalism-did-not-win-cold-war.

17 Antonio Gramsci (1891–1937), an Italian Marxist philosopher and a writer on political theory, wrote in a letter from prison in December 1929: 'I am a pessimist by dint of reason, but an optimist by force of will.' Accessed 5 November 2023. https://www.centreforoptimism. com/pessimism-of-the-intellect-optimism-of-the-will

PART ONE

Chapter 1: Paucity of Responsible Leadership

1 I heard Mother Teresa say these words in an address she delivered in Kolkata in 1979, just before she was awarded the Noble Peace Prize. She was canonized by Pope Francis I in 2016; thereafter she was called St. Teresa of Kolkata.

2 Machiavelli, Niccolo. 2015. *The Prince.* New Delhi: Fingerprint Publishing. The comment cited is adapted from this sentence from Chapter 6 of his book: 'There is nothing more difficult to take in hand, more perilous to conduct, or more uncertain in its success, than to take the lead in the introduction of a new order of things.'

3 Badaracco Jr., Joseph L. 2006. *Questions of Character: Illuminating*

the Heart of Leadership Through Literature. Boston: Harvard Business School Press.

4 Harari, Yuval Noah. 2018. *21 Lessons for the 21st Century*.London: Jonathan Cape.

5 Sloman, Steven and Philip Fernbach. 2017. *The Knowledge Illusion: Why We Never Think Alone*. London: Pan Books.

6 Taleb, Nassim Nicholas. 2008. *Black Swan: The Impact of the Highly Improbable*. London: Penguin. Nassim Taleb defined 'black swan' as a high-profile, hard-to-predict, and rare event that is beyond the realm of normal expectations.

7 Gillim-Ross, Laura et al. 'Compositions and Methods for Detecting Severe Acute Respiratory Syndrome Coronavirus.' US Patent 7,129,042, October 31, 2006. https://patents.google.com/patent/ US7129042B2/en.

8 Leitner, Brooks. 2024. 'What Is Long Covid? Understanding the Pandemic's Mysterious Fallout.' Yale Medicine. April 15, 2024. https://www.yalemedicine.org/news/what-is-long-covid.

9 Physicist James Hansen, the then director of the National Aeronautics and Space Administration's Goddard Institute for Space Studies, told a U.S. Senate committee in 1988 that 'global warming is now large enough that we can ascribe with a high degree of confidence a cause and effect relationship to the greenhouse effect. With 99% confidence, we can state that the warming during this time period is a real warming trend.' Fox, Justin. 2020. 'There Was a Warning About Climate Change in 1988. It Was Right.' 31 January, 2020. https://theprint.in/environment/there-was-a-warning-about-climate-change-in-1988-it-was-right/357032/.

10 Runciman, David. 2018. *How Democracy Ends*. London: Profile Books.

11 Wilkinson, Francis. 2018. 'Democracy Will Die, Maybe in Its Sleep: A Q&A with Political Scientist David Runciman.' Bloomberg. May 22, 2018. https://www.bloomberg.com/opinion/articles/2018-05-22/democracy-s-death-narrated-by-david-runciman.

12 Beauchamp, Nika Knight. 'Pope Francis: Capitalism Is "Terrorism Against All of Humanity"'. Common Dreams. August 02, 2016. https://www.commondreams.org/news/2016/08/02/pope-francis-capitalism-terrorism-against-all-humanity.

13 MacAskill, William. 'The Beginning of History: Surviving the Era of Catastrophic Risk.' *Foreign Affairs*. September/October 2022. https://www.foreignaffairs.com/world/william-macaskill-beginning-history.

14 Keane, John. 'How Does a Democracy Die?' July 1, 2021. https:// www.johnkeane.net/phantom-democracy/.

15 'A New Low for Global Democracy'. February 9, 2022. *The Economist*. https://www.economist.com/graphic-detail/2022/02/09/ a-new-low-for-

global-democracy. 'Democracy Index 2021: The China Challenge'. *Economist Intelligence*. https://pages.eiu.com/ rs/753-RIQ-438/images/ eiu-democracy-index-2021.pdf.

16 Deming, W. Edwards. 2000. *Out of the Crisis*. Cambridge: MIT Press. Deming was an American engineer and professor. He was credited with Japan's post-war economic boom in the 1950s and 1960s. He introduced fourteen key principles for business effectiveness in his book. This brief quotation is one of those.

17 Howard Gardner, in his book, *Leading Minds: An Anatomy of Leadership*, (1995. New York: Basic Books, A Division of Harper Collins Publishers) had defined leaders as 'Persons who, by word and/ or personal example, markedly influence the behaviours, thoughts, and/ or feelings of a significant number of their fellow human beings.' The definition here is derived from that root.

Chapter 2: Seven Billion Dreams and Aspirations

1 Marcos, Subcomandante. 2002. *Our Word Is Our Weapon: Selected Writings*. New York: Seven Stories.

2 The World Bank. 'Poverty.' October 17, 2023. https://www. worldbank. org/en/topic/poverty/overview.

3 Concern Worldwide US. 'The Top 11 Causes of Poverty around the World.' February 3, 2022. https://www.concernusa.org/story/ causes-of-poverty/.

4 Filipenco, Daniil. 'Homelessness Statistics in the World: Causes and Facts.' December 13, 2023. https://www.developmentaid.org/news-stream/post/157797/homelessness-statistics-in-the-world and SDG Indicator Metadata. December 20, 2021. https://unstats.un.org/sdgs/ metadata/files/Metadata-11-01-01.pdf.

5 'Global Inequality'. September 2023. https://inequality.org/facts/ global-inequality/ and Credit Suisse Group. 'Why Wealth Matters'. August 15, 2023. https://www.credit-suisse.com/about-us/en/reports-research/ global-wealth-report.html.

6 Compassion International. 'Poverty in Africa Preys upon the Most Vulnerable.' https://www.compassion.com/poverty/poverty-in-africa. htm.

7 United Nations Development Programme. 2023. 'Multi-dimensional Poverty Index.' July 2023. https://hdr.undp.org/content/2023-global-multidimensional-poverty-index-mpi#/indicies/MPI.

8 Ibid.

9 Ibid.

10 United Nations. 2023. 'Hunger Afflicts One in Ten Globally, UNReport Finds.' July 12, 2023. https://news.un.org/en/ story/2023/ 07/1138612.

11 Ibid.
12 Ibid.
13 Stasha, Smiljanic. 2023. 'The State of Homelessness in the US—2023.' March 23, 2023. https://policyadvice.net/insurance/insights/homelessness-statistics/.
14 Eurostat. 2022. 'Over 1 in 5 at Risk of Poverty or Social Exclusion in EU.' September 15, 2022. https://ec.europa.eu/eurostat/web/ products-eurostat-news/-/ddn-20220915-1.
15 Manral, Mahander Singh and Jignasa Sinha. 2023. '154 Farmers, Daily Wagers Die by Suicide Daily: NCRB Report.' *The Indian Express*. December 5, 2023. https://indianexpress.com/article/cities/delhi/154-farmers-daily-wage-laborers-suicide-india-ncrb-9054228/.
16 Eisinger, Jesse, Paul Kiel and Jeff Ernsthausen. 2021. 'The Secret IRS Files: Trove of Never-Before-Seen Records Reveal How Wealthiest Avoid Income Tax.' ProPublica. June 8, 2021. Accessed 10 November 2023. https://www.propublica.org/article/the-secret-irs-files-trove-of-never-before-seen-records-reveal-how-the-wealthiest-avoid-income-tax.
17 Ibid.
18 Banerjee, Abhijit and Esther Duflo. 2017. 'The (Not So Simple) Economics of Lending to the Poor.' October 21, 2017. Accessed November 2023. http://www.pooreconomics.com/sites/default/files/A%20PDF%20of%20the%20lecture%20slides_0.pdf Interest costs for micro loans in the formal sector in India are in the 25 per cent to 30 per cent range, but in the informal sector of moneylenders it is often as high as 100 per cent. Sometimes much more, e.g. fruit vendors in Chennai often pay 5 per cent interest per day. The landless pay interest rates varying between 28 per cent and 125 per cent, and cultivators pay between 21 per cent and 40 per cent. As against these, the interest rates for corporations that borrow in the millions varies between 11 per cent to 14 per cent per year. https://groww.in/loans/microfinance-institutions
19 Mander, Jerry. 2012. *The Capitalism Papers: Fatal Flaws of an Obsolete System*. CA: Counterpoint.
20 Piketty, Thomas. 2013. *Capital in the Twenty-First Century*.Translated by Arthur Goldhammer. Boston: Harvard University Press.
21 Crawford, Rick. 'What Lincoln Foresaw: Corporations Being "Enthroned" After the Civil War and Re-Writing the Laws Defining Their Existence.' Accessed 10 November 2023. http://www.ratical. org/corporations/Lincoln.html.
22 *Diary and Letters of Rutherford Birchard Hayes: Nineteenth President of the United States*. 2010. Edited by Charles Richard Williams. Montana: Kessinger Publishing.
23 Roosevelt, Theodore. 1912. 'The Progressive Covenant With the

People.' Accessed 10 November 2023. https://www.history onthenet. com/authentichistory/1898-1913/2-progressivism/5-wilson/19120800_Progressive_Covenant_With_The_People-Theodore_Roosevelt.html.

24 Civicus. 2020. 'State of Civil Society Report.' Accessed 10 November 2023. https://www.civicus.org/index.php/state-of-civil-society-report-2020.

25 Civicus. 2022. 'State of Civil Society Report.' June 27, 2022. https://www.civicus.org/documents/reports-and-publications/SOCS/2022/CIVICUS2022SOCSReport.pdf

26 The Soufan Center. 2021. 'IntelBrief: The Final Nail in the Coffin for Privacy? The Saga of the NSO Group's Spyware.' July 22, 2021. Accessed 10 November 2023. https://thesoufancenter.org/intelbrief-2021-july-22/.

27 Martin Luther King Jr., 1994. *Letter from Birmingham Jail.* New York: HarperCollins. Written on April 16, 1963, this is known as Martin Luther King Jr.'s most extensive and forceful statement against racial injustice.

28 'The Fuji Declaration: Awakening the Divine Spark in the Spirit of Humanity for a Civilization of Oneness with Diversity on Planet Earth'. 2015. Accessed 10 November 2023. https://fujideclaration. org/wp-content/uploads/2014/11/The-Fuji-Declaration.pdf.

Chapter 3: A New Vision

1 Johann von Goethe quoted in Chang, Laurence. 2006. *Wisdom for the Soul: Five Millennia of Prescriptions for Spiritual Healing.* Washington DC: Gnosophia Publisher.

2 William Butler Yeats (1865–1939) was an Irish poet, dramatist, prose writer and a recipient of Nobel Prize in literature in 1923. Mirza, Shikoh Mohsin. 2020. 'Charting the Ethical Landscape: Tagore's Vision of Nation in "Where the Mind Is Without Fear"'. November 29, 2020. Accessed 12 November 2023. https://thewire. in/culture/rabindranath-tagore-nation-gitanjali.

3 Tagore, Rabindranath. 1997. *Gitanjali: A Collection of Indian Poems.* New York: Scribner.

4 Aristotle. Accessed 12 November 2023. https://www.goodreads. com/quotes/1485252-in-a-democracy-the-poor-will-have-more-power-than.

5 Plato. Accessed 12 November 2023. https://www.brainyquote.com/quotes/plato_135639.

6 Sachs, Jeffrey. 2011. *The Price of Civilization: Reawakening American Virtue and Prosperity.* New York: Random House.

7 The World Bank. 2020. 'Exploring Universal Basic Income: A Guide to Navigating Concepts, Evidence, and Practices.' February 4, 2020.

Accessed 12 November 2023. https://www.worldbank. org/en/topic/socialprotection/publication/exploring-universal-basic-income-a-guide-to-navigating-concepts-evidence-and-practices.

8 Kung, Hans. 1998. 'Human Responsibilities Reinforce Human Rights: The Global Ethic Project.' In *Reflections on the Universal Declaration of Human Rights: A Fiftieth Anniversary Anthology* edited by Barend van der Heijden and Bahia Tahzib-Lie. Lieden: Brill.

9 Paul Sieghart (1927–1988), law reformer, quoted by Nani A. Palkhivala. 1994. *We the Nation: The Lost Decades*. New Delhi: UBS.

10 World Meteorological Organization. 2024. 'World Meteorological Organization Confirms That 2023 Is the Warmest Year on Record, by a Huge Margin.' January 12, 2024. https://wmo.int/news/media-centre/wmo-confirms-2023-smashes-global-temperature-record.

11 Wilson, Edward O. 2012. *The Social Conquest of Earth*. New York: Liveright Publishing Corporation, A Division of W.W. Norton & Company.

12 Office of the High Commissioner for Human Rights. 2022. 'Right to Healthy Environment.' April 12, 2022. Accessed 15 January 2024. https://www.ohchr.org/en/statements-and-speeches/2022/04/right-healthy-environment.

13 United Nations Environment Programme. 2022. 'UN Declares Healthy Environment a Human Right.' July 28, 2022. Accessed 15 January 2024. https://www.unep.org/news-and-stories/story/historic-move-un-declares-healthy-environment-human-right

14 'Right Against Climate Change a Distinct Fundamental and Human Right, SC Judgment.' 2024. *The Hindu*. April 08, 2024. https://www.thehindu.com/news/national/right-against-climate-change-a-distinct-fundamental-and-human-right-sc-judgment/article68041693.ece.

15 Kettley, Sebastian. 2019. 'Greta Thunberg Speech: Read the Powerful Climate Change Message to the UN—"Wake Up".' September 22, 2019. Accessed 12 November 2023. https://www.express.co.uk/ news/science/1181272/Greta-Thunberg-speech-full-climate-change-United-Nations-UN-global-warming.

16 James Madison to W. T. Barry, August 4, 1822, Library of Congress. Accessed 12 November 2023. Image 1 of James Madison to W.T. Barry, August 4, 1822. | Library of Congress (loc.gov).

17 McChesney, Robert. 1997. *Corporate Media and the Threat to Democracy*. New York: Seven Stories Press.

18 Galbraith, John Kenneth. 1958. *The Affluent Society*. New York: Houghton Mifflin Harcourt.

19 Korten, David. 2021. 'Ecological Civilization: From Emergency to Emergence.' May 25, 2021. Accessed 12 November 2023. https://davidkorten.org/ecological-civilization-from-emergency-to-emergence/.

20 Sen, Amartya Sen. 2007. 'Poverty, Evil and Crime'. October 5, 2007. Accessed 12 November 2023. http://economics-files.pomona. edu/andrabi/courses/econ126/senpoverty.pdf.

21 Banerjee, Abhijit and Esther Duflo. 2019. *Good Economics for Hard Times: Better Answers to Our Biggest*. New York: Hachette.

22 Raworth, Kate. 2017. *Doughnut Economics: Seven Ways to Think Like a 21st-Century Economist*. Vermont: Chelsea Green Publishing.

23 Basu, Kaushik. 2021. *Can Economics Keep Up?* August 30, 2021. Accessed 12 November 2023. https://www.project-syndicate.org/commentary/economics-contemporary-problems-need-for-new-thinking-by-kaushik-basu-2021-08.

24 Alexis de Tocqueville (1805–1859), a French political thinker and historian, best known for his work *Democracy in America*, quoted by Nani A. Palkhivala. 1994. *We the Nation: The Lost Decades*. New Delhi: UBS.

25 'Israel-Gaza War in Maps and Charts: Live Tracker.' 2023. Aljazeera. Accessed 10 June 2024. https://www.aljazeera.com/ news/longform/2023/10/9/israel-hamas-war-in-maps-and-charts-live-tracker.

26 Karatas, Dilara, Murat Karadag and Melike Pala. 2024. 'Pro-Palestine Protests at US Universities Continue to Grow in Europe, Worldwide.' May 6, 2024. https://www.aa.com.tr/en/americas/ pro-palestine-protests-at-us-universities-continue-to-grow-in-europe-worldwide/3211557.

27 King Jr., Martin Luther. 1963. *Strength to Love*. Boston: Beacon Press.

28 Chattopadhyay, Sahana. 2021. 'Crisis of Leadership.' 24 May 2021. Accessed 12 November 2023. http://www.whatisemerging. com/opinions/a-crisis-of-leadership.

Chapter 4: Crystallizing the Questions

1 Jonas Salk quoted in O'Brien, Bridget C., Karani, Reena, and Park, Yoon Soo, 'The Moment of Discovery: How Do You Know When You Hit a Question That's Pure Gold?' *Academic Medicine* 94, 11S. Accessed 15 November 2023. https://journals.lww.com/ academicmedicine/Fulltext/2019/11001/Foreword__The_Moment_ of_Discovery How_Do_You_Know.1.aspx.

2 United Nations. 'United Nations Charter.' Accessed 15 November 2023. https://www.un.org/en/about-us/un-charter/full-text.

3 United Nations. 'Universal Declaration of Human Rights.' Accessed 15 November 2023. https://www.un.org/en/about-us/universal-declaration-of-human-rights

4 Skidelsky, Robert. 2011. 'Life after Capitalism.' Project Syndicate. January 20, 2011. Accessed 15 November 2023. https://www. project-syndicate.org/commentary/life-after-capitalism-2011-01.

5 The concept of 'Triple Top Line' of joy, peace and contentment is comprehensively expanded in the author's book, *Quest for Exceptional Leadership: Mirage to Reality*. New Delhi: Sage Publishers. 2011 and 2016.

6 Business Roundtable. 2019. 'Business Roundtable Redefines the Purpose of a Corporation to Promote "An Economy That Serves All Americans."' August 19, 2019. Accessed 15 November 2023. https://www.businessroundtable.org/business-roundtable-redefines-the-purpose-of-a-corporation-to-promote-an-economy-that-serves-all-americans#.

7 Aquila, Francis J. 2020. 'Considering the Corporate Purpose.' February/March 2020. Accessed 15 November 2023. https:// www.sullcrom.com/SullivanCromwell/_Assets/PDFs/General/PLJ_ FebMar20_InTheBoardroom.pdf.

8 Goodman, Peter S. 2020. 'Big Business Pledged Gentler Capitalism. It's Not Happening in a Pandemic.', April 13, 2020. Accessed 15 November 2023. https://www.nytimes.com/2020/04/13/business/business-roundtable-coronavirus.html.

9 Whoriskey, Peter. 2020. 'Companies Furlough & Layoff Thousands of Workers While Continuing to Reward Shareholders in Dividends during Pandemic.' May 7, 2020. Accessed 15 November 2023. https://www.business-humanrights.org/en/latest-news/usa-companies-furlough-layoff-thousands-of-workers-while-continuing-to-reward-shareholders-in-dividends-during-pandemic/.

10 'Jamsetji N. Tata's Vision for India.' Accessed 15 November 2023. https://www.tatatrusts.org/about-tatatrusts/jamsetji-n-tata.

11 Gorokhovskaia, Yana, Adrian Shahbaz and Amy Slipowitz. 2023. 'Marking 50 Years in the Struggle for Democracy.' Freedom House. Accessed 15 November 2023. https://freedomhouse.org/report/ freedom-world/2023/marking-50-years.

12 Boyatzis, Richard and Annie McKee. *Resonant Leadership: Renewing Yourself and Connecting with Others Through Mindfulness, Hope and Compassion*. Boston: Harvard Business School Press.

13 Wells, H.G. 1922. *A Short History of the World*. London: Cassell.

14 Acemoglu, Daron and James A. Robinson. 2019. *The Narrow Corridor: States, Societies, and the Fate of Liberty*. New York: Penguin Press.

PART TWO

Chapter 5: The Human Story Till Now

1 Benjamin Jeremy Stein is an American writer and inventor. Accessed 5 November 23. https://quotefancy.com/quote/758089/Ben-Stein-It-s-amazing-what-ordinary-people-can-do-if-they-set-out-without-preconceived.
2 'The Great Migration: How Modern Humans Spread across the World.' 2009. *Independent*. February 11, 2009. Accessed 18 November 2023. https://www.independent.co.uk/news/world/world-history/the-great-migration-how-modern-humans-spread-across-the-world-1604966.html.
3 'Hunter Gatherer.' 2022. Nov 24, 2022. Accessed 18 November 2023. https://alchetron.com/Hunter-gatherer.
4 Maddison, Angus. 'The World Economy, II.' Development Centre of the Organization of Economic Co-operation and Development. https://doi.org/10.1787/9789264189980-en.
5 Clark, Gregory. 2007. 'Why Is the Global Divide Between Rich and Poor So Vast?' November 21, 2007. Accessed November 18, 2023. https://www.alternet.org/2007/11/why_is_the_global_divide_ between_rich_and_poor_so_vast/
6 'The Invention of Gunpowder and its Introduction into Europe.' Accessed 18 November 2023. https://www.encyclopedia.com/science/encyclopedias-almanacs-transcripts-and-maps/invention-gunpowder-and-its-introduction-europe#
7 Durant, Will. 2002. *The Greatest Minds and Ideas of All Time*. New York: Simon & Schuster.
8 Durant, Will. 1929. *The Pleasures of Philosophy: A Survey of Human Life and Destiny*. New York: Simon & Schuster.
9 The concept of the Five Phases of Human Enterprise was first articulated by the author in a paper titled 'Aligning Corporate Goals With Society's Needs: What Can Be Done?' presented at the BAWB Forum at Case Western Reserve University, Cleveland, USA, in October 2006. This was later elaborated in his book, *Quest for Exceptional Leadership: Mirage to Reality*. 2011. New Delhi: Sage Publishers.
10 Poshernik, Natalie Cvikl and Danau Posistruc. 2021. 'Ravi Chaudhry: Realistic Eating Fish Unrealistic Fish.' January 8, 2021. Accessed November 18, 2023. https://navdihni.me/ravi-chaudhry-realistic-fish-eating-unrealistic-fish/.

Chapter 6: The Advent of Wisdom Economy

1 Hesse, Herman. 1951. *Siddhartha*. Translated by Hilda Rosner. New York: Bantam Books.

2 This is the essence of the fifth and sixth verses in the sixth chapter of the Bhagavad Gita, the primary holy scripture of the Hindu wisdom tradition. For a more detailed elaboration, please refer to *The Holy Geeta: Commentary by Swami Chinmayananda*. 1992. Mumbai: Central Chinmaya Mission Trust.

3 This analogy was related by Swami Tajomayananda, the second Worldwide Head of Chinmaya Mission, in his discourses on the *Bhagavad Gita*, at the Chinmaya Vibhooti Ashram, near Pune, India, in December 2018.

4 Darwin, Charles. *The Origin of Species. On the Origin of Species* (more completely, *On the Origin of Species* by Means of Natural Selection, or the Preservation of Favoured Races in the Struggle for Life), published in 1859, by Charles Darwin. It is considered to be the foundation of evolutionary biology.

5 Dobson, Julian. 2010. 'From a Knowledge Economy to a Wisdom Economy.' March 3, 2010. Accessed November 20, 2023. https://www.thersa.org/discover/publications-and-articles/rsa-comment/2010/03/from-a-knowledge-economy-to-a-wisdom-economy.

6 Stebbins, Gregory. 2015. 'Sustainable Leadership Through Loving Wisdom.' March 16, 2015. Accessed 20 November 2023. http://www.susted.com/wordpress/content/sustainable-leadership-through-loving-wisdom_2015_03/. Stebbins, Gregory. 2017. 'Wisdom Economy White Paper.' PEOPLESAVVY. April 2017. Accessed 20 November 2023. http://peoplesavvy.com/wp-content/ uploads/2017/04/Wisdom-Economy_WP.pdf.

7 Daly, Herman E. 1996. *Beyond Growth: The Economics of Sustainable Development*. Boston: Beacon Press. In this volume, Daly outlines Earl Cook's nine characteristics of Wisdom Economy, described as the nine 'Neomalthusian Beliefs'. The first three have been quoted in the book; the next six are listed below:

- The appropriate human objective is the maximization of psychic income by conversion of natural resources to useful commodities and by the efficient use of those commodities, to generate psychic income for both—the human life-hour, as well as the yet unborn.
- Physical laws are not subject to repeal by men, and of all the laws of economics, the law of diminishing returns is closest to a physical law.
- The industrial revolution can be defined as the period of human history when basic resources, especially non-human energy grew cheaper and more abundant.
- The individual revolution so defined is ending.

- There are compelling reasons to expect natural resources to become more expensive.
- Resource problems vary so much from country to country that careless geographic and commodity aggression may confuse rather than clarify.

8 British Prime Minister David Cameron, when he was president of the G8 Group, in 2013, set up a task force, chaired by Sir Ronald Cohen, to recommend 'how to grow the social investment market to tackle our shared social and economic challenges'. The report, titled 'Impact Investment: The Invisible Heart of Markets', was released in September 2014. Accessed November 20,2023. https://www2.deloitte.com/in/en/pages/public-sector/ articles/impact-investment-the-invisible-heart-of-markets.html. Also see Bishop, Matthew. 'How We Can Be the Invisible Heart of Markets', September 29, 2014. Accessed November 20, 2023. https://unreasonable.is/invisible-heart-of-markets/.

9 This quote is from the author's review of Schwab, Klaus and Thierry Malleret. 2020. *The Great Reset*. Geneva: Forum Publishing. Accessed November 20, 2023. https://www.amazon.in/product-reviews/B08CRZ9VZB.

10 The conversation with Peter Senge took place as part of a global interview project with twenty-five eminent thinkers on leadership, sponsored by McKinsey & Company and the MIT Society for Organizational Learning. Scharmer, Otto and Jaworski, Joseph. 'Dialogues on Leadership.' Accessed November 20, 2023. www. dialogonleadership.org.

11 Prinzing, Michael. 2017. 'What is Wisdom?' February 21, 2017. Accessed November 21, 2023. https://practicalphilosopher.prinzing. net/what-is-wisdom-7c9fcb2a3a9c.

Chapter 7: The Traits of Wisdom Economy Leaders

1 This quote is commonly attributed to Ralph Waldo Emerson, an American essayist, philosopher, and poet. This could also be a paraphrase or a variation of Emerson's ideas rather than his verbatim quote.

2 Carolus Linnaeus, a Swedish zoologist, botanist, and physician, is known as the father of modern taxonomy. He gave this name to the human species in the tenth edition of his book, *Systema Naturae,* published in two volumes in 1758 and 1759.

3 Based on the author's notes during Swami Chinmayananda's discourses and his teachings in his book *Kindle Life*. 1982. Mumbai: Central Chinmaya Mission Trust. His Holiness Swami Chinmayananda (1916–1993) founded the Chinmaya Mission in India in 1953 and made

it the nucleus of a spiritual renaissance movement to provide the timeless wisdom of the Indian scriptures and a practical means for spiritual growth and happiness, enabling people from all over the world to become positive contributors to society. There are over 300 Chinmaya Mission centres, 250 in India and fifty overseas. http://www.chinmayamission.com/

4 Eliot, T.S. 1925. 'The Hollow Men.' Accessed 25 November 2023. https://www.litcharts.com/poetry/t-s-eliot/the-hollow-men.

5 Online Etymology Dictionary. Accessed 25 November 2023. https://www.etymonline.com/word/conscience

6 Sparks, Dana. 2016. 'Something to Think About: Listen to the Conscience.' July 7, 2016. Accessed November 25, 2023. https://newsnetwork.mayoclinic.org/discussion/something-to-think-about-listen-to-the-conscience/.

7 The quotation on conscience is by Anne Louise Germaine de Staël-Holstein, a French historian (1766–1817). Accessed 25 November 2023. https://www.thequotablecoach.com/the-voice-of-conscience-is-so-delicate-that-it-is-easy-to-stifle-it/.

8 The concept of 'wholeness' as one of the three traits of exceptional leadership was first expounded in the author's book, *Quest for Exceptional Leadership: Mirage to Reality*. New Delhi: Sage Publishers.

9 Davidow, William and Michael Malone. 2020. *The Autonomous Revolution: Reclaiming the Future We Have Sold to Machines*. Oakland: Berrett Koehler Publishers.

10 Suleyman, Mustafa. 2023. *The Coming Wave*. New York: Crown.

11 Professor Audrey Kurth Cronin of Carnegie Mellon University, Pittsburgh, PA, is one of the world's leading experts on security and how conflicts end. Accessed 20 January 2024. https://www. audreykurthcronin.com/

12 World Economic Forum. 2023. 'Future of Jobs Report 2023.' April 30, 2023. https://www.weforum.org/publications/the-future-of-jobs-report-2023/digest/.

13 Moodley, Keymanthri. 2017. 'Archbishop Desmond Tutu: The Essence of What It Means to Be Human.' October 20, 2017. Accessed 25 November 2023. https://theconversation.com/archbishop-desmond-tutu-the-essence-of-what-it-means-to-be-human-85402. For more insights on Ubuntu, I recommend the book by Mungi Ngomane, the granddaughter of Desmond Tutu. Ngomane, Mungi. *Everyday Ubuntu: Living Better Together, The African Way*. London: Penguin Random House.

14 Le Carre, John. 2011. *The Leaderless Revolution: How Ordinary People Will Take Power and Change Politics in the 21st Century*. London: Simon & Schuster.

15 The World Bank. 2023. 'Remarks by World Bank Group President

Ajay Banga at the 2023 Annual Meetings Plenary.' December 1, 2023. https://www.worldbank.org/en/news/speech/2023/10/13/ remarks-by-world-bank-group-president-ajay-banga-at-the-2023-annual-meetings-plenary#

16 Richard, Jinnie. 2023. 'Compassion Is a Verb.' Accessed December 10, 2023. https://www.humanedecisions.com/thich-nhat-hanh-said-compassion-is-a-verb/.

17 Jinpa, Thupten. 2015. *A Fearless Heart: Why Compassion is the Key to Greater Wellbeing*. London: Little Brown Group.

18 The Dalai Lama. 2019. 'Why Leaders Should Be Mindful, Selfless, and Compassionate.' February 20, 2019. Accessed December 10, 2023. https://www.dalailama.com/messages/compassion-and-human-values/why-leaders-should-be-mindful-selfless-and-compassionate

19 Seidman, Dov. 2014. 'Knowledge Economy to Human Economy.' November 12, 2014. Accessed November 26, 2023. https://hbr.org/2014/11/from-the-knowledge-economy-to-the-human-economy

PART THREE:

Chapter 8: Peopleism

1 William Arthur Ward (1921–1994) was an American writer.Accessed 28 November 2023. https://www.goodreads.com/author/ quotes/416931.William_Arthur_Ward.

2 Maslow, Abraham H. 1943. 'A Theory of Human Motivation.' *Psychological Review* 50, 370–396. Accessed November 28, 2023. https://psychclassics.yorku.ca/Maslow/motivation.htm.

3 Rawls, John. 1971. *A Theory of Justice*. Boston: Harvard University Press. The concept of social justice is derived from his writings.

4 John Stuart Mill, quoted in Ornstein, Norman. 1992. 'The Role of the Legislature in a Democracy.' November 1992. Accessed November 28, 2023. https://usinfo.org/enus/media/pressfreedom/ freedom3.htm.

5 Excerpt from Edmund Burke's Speech to the Electors of Bristol, 3 Nov. 1774, from *The Works of the Right Honourable Edmund Burke*. 6 vols. London: Henry G. Bohn. Accessed on November 28, 2023. http://press-pubs.uchicago.edu/founders/documents/v1ch13s7. html.

6 References relating to the comments on the role of legislators and the legislature:

a) Rosenthal, Alan. 'The Good Legislature.' *NCSL State Legislatures Magazine*. July/August 1999. Accessed 29 November 2023. www.leg.state.nv.us/Division/Research/LegInfo/Orientation/2010-11/Handouts/Jan19-24/1-19/05InstitutionHandouts.pdf

b) Ornstein, Norman. 'The Role of the Legislature in a Democracy'. accessed on 29 November 2023 https://usinfo.org/enus/media/pressfreedom/freedom3.htm

7 Somerset Maugham (1874–1965) was a British novelist. Accessed 28 November 2023.http://www.inspiration.rightattitudes.com/ authors/ w-somerset-maugham/.

8 Ferguson, Niall. 2011. *Civilization: The West and the Rest*. London: Allen Lane.

Chapter 9: Peopleism in Practice

1 Nagesh, Ashitha. 2019. 'Jacinda Ardern: "A Leader With Love on Full Display."' March 21, 2019. Accessed 30 November 2023. https://www.bbc.com/news/world-asia-47630129.

2 This quotation is attributed to Winston Churchill, but there is no definitive record of when and if he said it.

3 UNCTAD. 2023. 'A World of Debt: A Growing Burden to Global Prosperity.' Accessed 30 November 2023. https://unctad.org/ publication/ world-of-debt.

4 Drèze, Jean and Amartya Sen. 2013. *An Uncertain Glory: India and its Contradictions*. London: Allen Lane.

5 United Nations Development Programme. 'Human Development Reports.' Accessed 30 November 2023. http://hdr.undp.org/en/ content/ human-development-index-hdi.

6 Komanoff, Charles. 2015. 'A Call to Paris Climate Negotiators: Tax Carbon.' November 29, 2015. Accessed 30 November 2023. https://www.carbontax.org/blog/2015/11/29/a-call-to-paris-climate-negotiators-tax-carbon/.

7 Gibson, Carl. 2020. 'Workers Are Getting the Short End of the Stick from the Cares Act.' April 15, 2020. Accessed 30 November 2023. https://www.barrons.com/articles/cares-act-workers-companies-unfair-coronavirus-aid-51586983332.

8 Shrivastava, Aseem and Ashish Kothari. 2012. *Churning the Earth: The Making of Global India*. New Delhi: Penguin Books.

9 Shoshana Zuboff. 2019. *The Age of Surveillance Capitalism: The Fight for the Future at the New Frontier of Power*. New York: Public Affairs.

10 Vidyasagar, Aparna and Nicoletta Lanese. 2023. 'What is CRISPR, the Powerful Genome-editing Tool?' March 23, 2023. Accessed 30 November 2023. https://www.livescience.com/58790-crispr-explained.html.

11 Berreby, David. 2024. As Use of A.I. Soars, So Does the Energy and Water It Requires.' Published at the Yale Environment 360. February 6, 2024. Accessed 30 November 2023. https://e360.yale. edu/features/ artificial-intelligence-climate-energy-emissions

12 Ibid.

13 Ibid.

14 'The World Is Failing Girls and Women, according to New UN Report.' September 7, 2023. Accessed 30 November 2023. https:// www.un.org/sustainabledevelopment/blog/2023/09/press-release-the-world-is-failing-girls-and-women-according-to-new-un-report/.

15 World Economic Forum. 'Global Gender Gap Report 2023.' June 2023. Accessed on 30 November 2023. https://www3.weforum.org/ docs/WEF_GGGR_2023.pdf

16 Ibid.

17 Ibid.

18 'Message of the Holy Father John Paul II for the 30th World Communications Day.' May 19, 1996. Accessed 30 November 2023.https://www.vatican.va/content/john-paul-ii/en/messages/communications/documents/hf_jp-ii_mes_24011996_world-communications-day.html.

19 Goldin, Claudia. 2012. *Career and Family: Women's Century-Long Journey toward Equity*. Princeton: Princeton University Press. See also Goldberg, Pinelopi Koujianou. 2023. 'What Economics Was Missing.' Nov 21, 2023. Accessed 30 November 2023. https://www.project-syndicate.org/commentary/what-claudia-goldin-has-done-for-economics-and-policymaking-by-pinelopi-koujianou-goldberg-2023-11?barrier=accesspaylog.

20 Carli, Linda L. and Alice Eagly. 2007. 'Women and the Labyrinth of Leadership.' Harvard Business Review. September 2007. Accessed 30 November 2023. https://hbr.org/2007/09/women-and-the-labyrinth-of-leadership.

Chapter 10: Peopleism Fosters Responsible Entrepreneurship

1 'Ashoka's History.' Accessed on 3 December 2023. https://www.ashoka.org/en-in/story/ashokas-history.

2 Robinson, Jenny Perlman. 2014. 'How to Scale up Learning: Some Early Thoughts from the Millions Learning Project.' October 14, 2014. Accessed 3 December 2023. https://www.brookings.edu/blog/education-plus-development/2014/10/14/how-to-scale-up-learning-some-early-thoughts-from-the-millions-learning-project/.

3 ReachScale, an institution founded by David Wilcox. Accessed 3 December 2023. www.reachscale.com.

4 Green, Duncan. 2014. 'Why Social Entrepreneurship Has Become a Distraction: It's Mainstream Capitalism That Needs to Change.' August 2014. Accessed 3 December 2023. https://frompoverty.oxfam. org.uk/why-social-entrepreneurship-has-become-a-distraction-its-mainstream-capitalism-that-needs-to-change/.

5 Sanford, Carol. 2014. *The Responsible Entrepreneur: Four Game-*

Changing Archetypes for Founders, Leaders, and Impact Investors. New York: Jossey Bass.

6 Grameen Bank. 'Breaking the Vicious Cycle of Poverty through Microcredit.' Accessed 3 December 2023. https://www.grameen. com/breaking-the-cycle-of-proverty/.

7 Radjou, Navi. 2020. 'Wise Leadership: The Foundation of 21st Century Organizations.' October 13, 2020. Accessed 3 December 2020. https://www.linkedin.com/pulse/wise-leadership-foundation-21st-century-organizations-navi-radjou/.

8 'Layoffs during Pandemic Shows India Inc's Lack of Empathy: Ratan Tata.' *Business Standard.* July 23, 2020. Accessed 3 December 2023. https://www.business-standard.com/article/companies/layoffs-during-pandemic-shows-india-inc-s-lack-of-empathy-ratan-tata-120072301738_1.html.

9 Crandell, Roger. 2021. 'Standing Strong—and Standing with You—in 2020.' March 1, 2021. Accessed 3 December 2023. https://www.linkedin.com/pulse/standing-strong-you-2020-roger-crandall/.

10 'Yamaguchi, Goro.' Accessed 3 December 2023. https://kpmg.com/be/en/home/insights/2020/09/goro-yamaguchi-chairman-kyocera-corporation.html.

11 Sarkar, Christian. 2019. 'Patagonia: We're in Business to Save the Planet.' January 8, 2019. Accessed 4 December 2023. http://www.activistbrands.com/patagonia-were-in-business-to-save-the-planet/. —Ørsted. 'A World That Runs Entirely on Green Energy.' https://www.responsibilityreports.com/HostedData/ ResponsibilityReportArchive/o/OTC_DOGEF_2017.pdf.—Moore, Darrel. 2018. 'IKEA Launches New People & Planet Positive Strategy.' June 14, 2018. Accessed 4 December 2023. https://www. circularonline.co.uk/news/ikea-launches-new-people-planet-positive-strategy/. —'Buy a Pair, Give a Pair.' Accessed 4 December 2023. https:// www.warbyparker.com/buy-a-pair-give-a-pair.

12 AIM2Flourish is a programme of the Fowler Center for Business as an Agent of World Benefit at the Weatherhead School of Management, Case Western Reserve University, Cleveland, USA. Accessed 4 December 2023. https://aim2flourish.com/about-us.

13 'The Family Business Network (FBN).' Accessed 4 December 2023. www.fbn-i.org/about-us.

14 Jacobs, Garry et al. 2018. 'The Future of Democracy: Challenges & Prospects.' May 28, 2018. Accessed 4 December 2023. http://cadmusjournal.org/article/volume-3/issue-4/future-democracy-challenges-prospects.

15 SEE Learning™ provides educators with the tools they need to foster the development of emotional, social, and ethical intelligence for students

and themselves. Accessed 21 December 2023. https://101. seelearning. emory.edu/. See also 'Social, Emotional and Ethical Development (SEE Learning): Educating the Heart and Mind.' Accessed 21 December 2023. http://www.secularethics.net/assets/ files/seelearningframework-english.pdf.

16 Steiner, Claude. 2003. *Emotional Literacy: Intelligence with a Heart.* California: Personhood Press.

17 Prahalad, C.K. 2004. *The Fortune at the Bottom of the Pyramid: Eradicating Poverty Through Profits,* Philadelphia: Wharton School Publishing.

18 About 30,000 people gathered in Cochabamba, Bolivia, in 2010, to draft a proposed UN Universal Declaration of the rights of Mother Earth. It was formally submitted to the UN on April 22, 2010, with the backing of Bolivia, Ecuador, and many environmental and indigenous-rights organizations, notably the Pachamama Alliance, Global Exchange, Council of Canadians, and the Indigenous Environmental Network. South African environmental lawyer,Cormac Cullinen, was the primary organizer in drafting the Declaration. See also UN Secretary General. 2017. 'Harmony with Nature: Report of the Secretary-General.' July 19, 2017. Accessed on 4 December 2023. https://digitallibrary.un.org/record/1299301/?ln=zh_EN.

19 Mander, Jerry. 2012. *The Capitalism Papers: Fatal Flaws of an Obsolete System.* CA: Counterpoint.

20 Rifkin, Jeremy. 2010. 'The Empathetic Civilization: Address at the British Royal Society for the Arts.' March 15, 2010. Accessed on 4 December 2023. https://bsahely.com/2012/06/24/the_empathic_civilization/.

21 UNEP. 'Five Young Entrepreneurs Embracing Sustainable Business Models.' Accessed 4 December 2023. https://www.unep.org/news-and-stories/story/five-young-entrepreneurs-embracing-sustainable-business-models.

22 Hazel Henderson (1933–2022), a futurist, an economic iconoclast, and an author, was the founder of Ethical Markets Media LLC. (Disclosure: The author is also the co-chair of the EthicMark Awards panel of judges.) Accessed 4 December 2023. http://www. ethicalmarkets.com/.

23 Winners of the EthicMark® Awards for both 'For-Profit' and 'For Not-Profit' categories, over the years, recognize socially responsible advertising that uplifts the human spirit and society. Accessed 4 December 2023. https://www.ethicmark.org/about/.

24 The movement of Future500 was first conceptualized by Tachi Kiuchi and Bill Shireman, over two decades ago, to shift the focus from mere size and statistics to the quality of responsible corporate leadership. For a short while, I was also on their advisory board. Somehow, it did not

evolve as envisaged; the original movement took alternative routes to promote similar missions.

25 For an in-depth analysis of this new approach, readers may like to refer to the paper by Lubberink, Rob et al. 2019. 'Responsible Innovation by Social Entrepreneurs: An Exploratory Study of Values Integration in Innovations.' March 95, 2019. Accessed 4 December 2023. https://www.tandfonline.com/doi/abs/10.1080/23299460.2019.1572374.

Chapter 11: Peopleism Aligns Business and Civil Society

1 Margaret Mead (1901–1978) was an anthropologist and author in the mass media during the 1960s and 1970s. Quoted in an article by McMickle, Marvin. 2014. *The Passion of Individuals*. June 4, 2014. Accessed 9 December 2023. https://www.democratandchronicle.com/story/opinion/guest-column/2014/06/04/web-essay-passion-individuals/9925707/.

2 'The Roots of Democracy and Sustainable Development: Europe's Engagement with Civil Society in External Relations.' Accessed 9 December 2023. https://eur-lex.europa.eu/legal-content/EN/TXT/HTML/?uri=CELEX:52012DC0492&from=EN.

3 Fullerton, John. 2014. 'Limits to Investment: Finance in the Anthropocene.' Accessed 9 December 2023. http://www.great transition.org/publication/limits-to-investment.

4 'The State of Tax Justice 2023.' Accessed 9 December 2023. https://taxjustice.net/reports/the-state-of-tax-justice-2023/.

5 Inman, Phillip. 2021. 'UK Overseas Territories Top List of World's Leading Tax Havens.' March 9, 2021. https://www.theguardian. com/business/2021/mar/09/uk-overseas-territories-top-list-of-worlds-leading-tax-havens.

6 Drucker, Jesse. 2016. 'The World's Favourite New Tax Haven Is the United States.' January 27, 2016. Accessed 9 December 2023. https://www.bloomberg.com/news/articles/2016-01-27/the-world-s-favorite new-tax-haven-is-the-united-states.

7 Partington, Richard. 2021. 'G7 Tax Reform: What Has Been Agreed and Which Companies Will It Affect?' 7 June, 2021. Accessed 9 December 2023. https://www.theguardian.com/world/2021/jun/07/ g7-tax-reform-what-has-been-agreed-and-which-companies-will-it-affect.

8 'Civic Space in Numbers.' March 16, 2023. Accessed 10 December 2023. https://monitor.civicus.org/facts/.

9 Ibid.

10 'Civicus State of Civil Society Report 2023.' Accessed 10 December 2023. https://www.civicus.org/documents/reports-and-publications/SOCS/2023/state-of-civil-society-report-2023 en.pdf.

11 B Lab is a non-profit network transforming the global economy to benefit all people, communities, and the planet, to 'Make Business a Force for Good'. Accessed 10 December 2023. https://www.bcorporation.net/en-us/movement/about-b-lab/
12 Danone became the first listed company to adopt the 'Entreprise à Mission' model created by French law in 2019. '"Raison d'Être" Danone: From the "Dual Project" to "Societe a Mission".' Accessed 10 December 2023 https://www.danone.com/about-danone/sustainable- value-creation/danone-entreprise-a-mission.html.
13 Radjou, Navi. 2020. 'CEOs: Forget V-Shaped Recovery. Lead Y-Shaped Reinvention to Be Better.' November 26, 2020. Accessed on 10 December 2023. https://www.forbes.com/sites/ naviradjou/2020/11/26/ceos-forget-v-shaped-recovery-lead-y-shaped-reinvention-to-be-better/?sh=442258f11e7a.
14 'Danone's CEO Has Been Ousted for Being Progressive—Blame Society Not Activist Shareholders.' The Conversation. March 19, 2021. Accessed 10 December 2023. https://theconversation.com/ danones-ceo-has-been-ousted-for-being-progressive-blame-society-not-activist-shareholders-157383.
15 'Difference between Harvard College and Harvard University.' Accessed 11 December 2023. http://www.differencebetween.net/ language/words-language/difference-between-harvard-college-and-harvard-university/.
16 Raval, Anjli. 2023. 'The Struggle for the Soul of the B Corp Movement.' *Financial Times*. Accessed 11 December 2023. https:// www.ft.com/content/0b632709-afda-4bdc-a6f3-bb0b02eb5a62.
17 World Economic Forum. 2013. 'The Future Role of Civil Society.' Accessed 11 December 2023. http://www3.weforum.org/docs/WEF_FutureRoleCivilSociety_Report_2013.pdf.
18 The World Business Academy was founded in 1987 by Rinaldo Brutoco, along with Willis Harman and Jagdish Parekh. (Disclosure: The author is also a Fellow of the World Business Academy). Accessed 11 December 2023. https://worldbusiness.org/founding-the-world-business-academy/.3
19 Ibid.

PART FOUR:

Chapter 12: Life Is Beautiful

1 Chanakya, also known as Kauṭilya or Vishnugupta, was a philosopher, and a royal advisor to ancient Indian kings. He authored the ancient Indian political treatise, the *Arthashastra*, around the 3rd century BCE.
2 Clear, James. How to Be Happy: A Surprising Lesson on Happiness from an African Tribe. Accessed 14 December 2023. https:// jamesclear.com/how-can-i-be-happy-if-you-are-sad.

3 Robert, Gilman. 1993.'Between Oder and Chaos: The Dynamic Realm between Individualism and Mystical Unity.' (An interview with David Spangler). Context Institute. Accessed 5 December 2023. https://www.context.org/iclib/ic34/spangler/

4 Gore, Al. 'Nobel Lecture.' Accessed 14 December 2023. https:// www.nobelprize.org/prizes/peace/2007/gore/lecture/.

5 Archbishop Desmond Tutu wrote this in his foreword to Scilla Elworthy's book "*Pioneering the Possible: Awakened Leadership for a World That Works*" (North Atlantic Books, USA, 2014) https://scillaelworthy.com/activating-change/ accessed on 14 December 2023

6 Pearson, Catherine. 2014. '7 Secrets of Wise People.' Accessed 14 December 2023. https://www.huffpost.com/entry/wisdom-tips_n_5086606.

7 Murray, Alan and Katherine Dunn. 2020. 'Guiding Principles for the New Decade.' January 6, 2020 Accessed 14 December 2023. https://fortune.com/2020/01/06/2020s-guiding-principles-business/.

8 The theme of interconnected holism is expressed in the opening verse of Ishavasya Upanishad which is a part of the Vedanta texts in the Indian spiritual tradition. Transliterally, it means: This is the whole; that [part] is a whole. The whole (part) emerges from the whole. Even if the whole (part) is taken away from the whole, the whole still remains.

Chapter 13: The Inevitable Ascent of Peopleism

1 Hannibal Barca (247–183BCE), one of the greatest military commanders in world history, commanded Carthage's forces against the Roman Republic during the Second Punic War. Accessed 18 December 2023. https://jonathangifford.com/we-will-either-find-a-way-or-make-one-hannibal-crosses-the-alps/.

2 Tickell, Phoebe. 2019. 'We Need a New Story of What It Means to Be Human.' March 25, 2019. Accessed 18 December 2023. http:// www.whatisemerging.com/opinions/we-need-a-new-story-of-what-it-means-to-be-human.

3 Rowson, Jonathan. 2019. 'Twelve Tribes of Transformation: Awakening the Active Ingredients of a New Civilisation.' March 25, 2019. Accessed 18 December 2023. http://www.whatisemerging. com/opinions/twelve-tribes-of-transformation-awakening-the-active-ingredients-of-a-new-civilisation.

4 Rushkoff, Douglas is the host of the Team Human podcast and author of *Team Human* and many other books. https://teamhuman. fm/ and https://rushkoff.com/.

5 Ibid.

6 Godin, Seth. 2008. *Tribes: We Need You to Lead Us*. New York: Portfolio.

7 Georgescu, Peter, *Capitalism Is Slowly Committing Suicide,* in article by David Leonhardt, April 1, 2019 accessed 18 December 2023, https://www.nytimes.com/2019/03/31/opinion/peter-georgescu-capitalism.html
8 Wolf, Martin, 2023, *The Crisis of Democratic Capitalism*, Allen Lane, U.K., Review by Bill Emmott, 16 February, 2023, accessed 20 December 2023—https://www.ft.com/content/c75ea417-3baf-46f8-ab3a-252657c57b9c & Martin Wolf, *In Defence of Democratic Capitalism*—20 January 2023. https://www.ft.com/ content/877d1a2d-67df-46a4-a3af-8e28198b944a.
9 Sharma, Ruchir. 2020. 'The Rescues Ruining Capitalism. Wall Street Journal. July 2020. Accessed 20 December 2023. https:// www.wsj.com/articles/the-rescues-ruining-capitalism-11595603720.
10 Green, Matthew. 'Time for an Upgrade: A New Operating System for the Global Economy.' Accessed 20 December 2023. http://www.whatisemerging.com/profiles/katherine-trebeck.
11 Scharmer, Otto. 2014. 'Transforming Business, Society, and Self.' July 24, 2014. Accessed 20 December 2023. https://www.youtube. com/watch?v=gF8wV9OlUHc.
12 Björkman, Tomas. 2020. 'We Can No Longer Save the World by Playing by the Rules.' Accessed on 20 December 2023. http://www.whatisemerging.com/opinions/tomas-bjorkman-kyiv. Björkman is a Swedish social entrepreneur, author, and co-founder of the Ekskäret Foundation in Stockholm, which aims to catalyse higher levels of individual and societal consciousness by bringing change agents together.
13 Ibid.
14 Schmachtenberger, Daniel, in dialogue at the Rebel Wisdom Festival. 'Making Sense of the Downward Spiral.' June 2, 2020. Accessed 20 December 2023. http://civilizationemerging.com/media/making-sense-of-the-downward-spiral-daniel-schmachtenberger/.
15 Fullerton, John. 2020. 'A Multisystemic Response to Covid.' May 4, 2020. Accessed 20 December 2023. https://capitalinstitute.org/blog/a-multisystemic-response-to-covid-19. See also Fullerton, John. 2015. 'Regenerative Capitalism How Universal Principles and Patterns Will Shape Our New Economy.' Accessed 20 December 2023. https://capitalinstitute.org/wp-content/uploads/2015/04/2015-Regenerative-Capitalism-4-20-15-final.pdf.
16 Rees, Tobias. 2020. 'From the Anthropocene to the Microbiocene.' June 10, 2020. Accessed 20 December 2023. https://www.noemamag. com/from-the-anthropocene-to-the-microbiocene/.
17 Ibid.
18 O'Brien, Karen. 2020. 'You Matter More Than You Think.', 16 October 2020. Accessed 20 December 2023. https://journal ofbeautifulbusiness. com/you-matter-more-than-you-think-2e15e2bd6797.

19 Ibid
20 Witt, Susan. 2011 'Informed by Place, Guided by Wisdom, a New Economy Is Emerging.' September 2011. Accessed 20 December 2023. https://centerforneweconomics.org/publications/informed-by-place-guided-by-wisdom-a-new-economy-is-emerging/
21 Ibid.
22 Butler, Benjamin J. 2021. 'A New Dawn Awaits.' February 1, 2021 Accessed 21 December 2023. https://www.benjaminjbutler.com/a-new-dawn-awaits/.
23 I cross-checked what my grandson told me, and found his wisdom well documented in this book. Blauvelt, Christian. *Be More Yoda: Mindful Thinking from a Galaxy Far Far Away*. New York: Penguin Random House.
24 George Lucas Jr. (born 1944) is an American film director, producer, screenwriter, and entrepreneur, best known for creating the Star Wars and Indiana Jones franchises and founding Lucasfilm, LucasArts, and Industrial Light & Magic
25 Popova, Maria. 2022. 'The Remedy for Despair, from Gabriel Marcel to Nick Cave.' April 5, 2022. Accessed 21 December 2023. https://www.themarginalian.org/2022/04/05/gabriel-marcel-nick-cave-hope-cynicism/
26 Noam Chomsky is an American linguist, philosopher, cognitive scientist, and historian. Accessed 21 December 2023. https://www. goodreads.com/author/quotes/2476.Noam_Chomsky.
27 Bull, Hedley. 2012. *The Anarchical Society*: *A Study of Order in World Politics*. New York: Columbia University Press.
28 Hass, Richard. 2020. *The World: A Brief Introduction*. New York: Penguin Press.
29 Cleary, Sean. 2015. 'Sharing the Norms and Values That Enable Global Co-existence While Respecting Cultural Differences.' September 19, 2015. Accessed 21 December 2023. https:// futureworldfoundation.org/Content/Article.aspx?ArticleID=15477
30 Varoufakis, Yanis. 2024. *Technofeudalism: What Killed Capitalism?* New York: Melville House Publishing.
31 Ibid.

Chapter 14: Collective Wisdom Outshines Collective Ignorance

1 'Futuro Possivel: Co creation and Community Can Help Us to Build a More Resilient World.' May 26, 2020. Accessed 22 December 2023. http://www.whatisemerging.com/opinions/cocreation-and-community-can-help-us-to-build-a-more-resiliant-world.
2 'Research on the Commons, Common-Pool Resources, and Common Property.' Accessed 21 December 2023. http://dlc.dlib.indiana.edu/ dlc/contentguidelines.

3 'Divine Right of Kings.' Accessed 21 January 2023. https://www.britannica.com/topic/divine-right-of-kings.

4 Oxfam. 2024. 'Inequality Inc. Executive Summary: How Corporate Power Divides Our World and the Need for a New Era of Public Action.' January 14, 2024. Accessed 18 January 2024. https:// webassets.oxfamamerica.org/media/documents/Inequality_Inc._Executive_Summary.pdf.

5 Extract from 'Speech by World Bank Group President Ajay Banga at the 2023 Annual Meetings Plenary.' December 1, 2023. Accessed 21 December 2023. https://www.worldbank.org/en/news/speech/2023/10/13/remarks-by-world-bank-group-president-ajay-banga-at-the-2023-annual-meetings-plenary#.

6 Boehm, Sophie and Clea Schumer. 2023. '10 Big Findings from the 2023 IPCC Report on Climate Change.' March 20, 2023. Accessed 21 December 2023. https://www.wri.org/insights/2023-ipcc-ar6-synthesis-report-climate-change-findings.

7 Huxley, Aldous. 1962. London: Chatto and Windus. *Island* is the final book by English writer Aldous Huxley, published in 1962. It is the account of Will Farnaby, a cynical journalist who is shipwrecked on the fictional island of Pala. Island is Huxley's utopian counterpart to his most famous work, the 1932 dystopian novel Brave New World.

8 Juma, Norbert. '25 Arthur Ashe Quotes about Life, Sports, and Success.' Accessed on 21 December 2023. https://everydaypowerblog.com/arthur-ashe-quotes-2/.

9 Dante Alighieri, (1265-1321), was an Italian poet during the Late Middle Ages, quoted in *Wisdom for the Soul: Five Millennia of Prescriptions for Spiritual Healing,* by Laurence Chang (Gnosophia Publisher, USA, 2006)

10 Drucker, Peter F. 2006. *The Practice of Management.* New York: Harper Business. First published in 1954.

11 William James, (1842-1910), an American philosopher and psychologist, was the first educator to offer a psychology course in the United States. Accessed 21 December 2023. https://www. goodreads.com/quotes/37097-act-as-if-what-you-do-makes-a-difference-it.

12 'The Universal Declaration of Human Rights.' Accessed 4 March 2023. https://www.un.org/en/about-us/universal-declaration-of-human-rights.

13 'Statistics about Mothers around the World.' Accessed 17 May 2024. https://www.soundvision.com/article/statistics-about-mothers-around-the-world

14 Patanjali was a renowned writer and scholar of Indian scriptures and wrote several famous works in the 2nd century BCE. He is credited as the author of this inspiring verse; even though this does not appear in any of his published writings. It is believed to be a part of his teachings in person.

Gratitude

This book on leadership is a labour of love, nurtured over years with the support of some very special people in my life, and inspired by many brilliant minds who have been my 'personal board of mentors'.

First, I owe it to my late parents, Prof. Kewal Ram Chaudhry and Durga Rani Chaudhry, who instilled in me a non-negotiable set of values, a love for learning, and the importance of leading a life of harmony and balance. My wife, Sumir, played an anchoring role in not only strengthening those beliefs, but also infusing them with her compassion and brilliance. Together, we embarked on the most important journey of our life: an attempt to understand and seek what matters most in life.

In our shared quest, we had the great fortune of being blessed and guided by three of the most realized souls one could encounter. Providence gave us the unique opportunity to learn at the feet of the greatest master of Vedanta in the 20th century, Gurudev Swami Chinmayananda. This extraordinary experience continued with unconditional love from his most learned disciple, Guruji Swami Tejomayananda. More recently, the sacred teachings of Sri Mooji Baba have enormously enriched our understanding and helped us embrace a truly holistic view of life and leadership.

My affectionate appreciation for our precious children—Shivani, Ashwin, and Monika, and grandchildren—Arnav and Arunima. While accompanying us on our life mission, they have also supported my passion for writing, with great love and joy.

I would like to acknowledge a few special people, who I knew well, but are sadly no more; they had a lasting impact on my approach to leadership: J.R.D. Tata, Hazel Henderson, Jean-Pierre Lehmann, C.K. Prahalad, Edward de Bono, Ramesh Sarin, and Rahul Bajaj.

I am thankful for the opportunities to interact with some very inspiring people, who not only aroused my curiosity on a wide range of issues, but also generously shared their wisdom with me: Ratan Tata, Azim Premji, Farhad Forbes, Naushad Forbes, Anand Mahindra, Nandan Nilekani, Kiran Mazumdar Shah, Mallika Srinivasan, Harsh Mariwala, Ajay Shriram, G.M. Rao, Nadine Hack, Sergio Lub, Tachi Kiuchi, Georg Kell, Anil Sachdev, Tomoyoshi Noda, Dominic Barton, Peter Wuffli, Oliver Zipse, Martin Brudermueller, Stephan Contius, Stephen Kanitz, and Alejandro Litovsky, among several others.

The many co-travelers on this path—with whom I have had the joy of close association—enriched many of the ideas explored in this book. I have already acknowledged some of them as the 'voices of corroboration'. I would like to especially thank Rinaldo Brutoco, Thierry Malleret, Dennis Snower, Sean Cleary, Philippe Bourguignon, Tomas Bjorkman and Arun Maira.

I value the meaningful interactions that followed my lectures and the stimulating conversations with experts in diverse fields, as I started writing this book. My gratitude to Ashok Khosla, Eberhard von Koerber, David Korten, Garry Jacobs, John Fullerton, Winston Nagan, Pradeep Mehta, Ted Souder, Olivier de Richoufftz, Chandran Nair, Peter Grk, Joshua C. Ngoma, Philippe Welti and Michael Yeoh, for their support and friendship.

My appreciative thanks to professional colleagues and business associates who were always ready to listen and share their experiences: Edward Saltzberg, Frederic Barge, Jonathan Cave, Frederik Otto, Francis Sermet, Ana P Assis, Sonja Klopcic, Ali Borhani, Patrick Cowden, Tičo Zupancic, Marjetka Kastner, Peter Ilgo, Feisal Alibhai, Mehmet Buldurgan, Yusuf Soner, Meredith Sumpter, Peter Matthies, Penelope Morin and Liselotte Hagertz Engstam.

I gratefully acknowledge member-colleagues of the Community of Climate Governance Experts of the World Economic Forum for deep-dive learnings during our incisive dialogues: Pim Valdre, Sarah Barker, Simon Learmount, James Cameron, Michael Sheren, Jane Nelson, Luke Fletcher, Emily Farnworth, Sebastian Vos, Rebekah Cheney, and Richard Barker.

Deliberations among Fellows of the Salzburg Corporate Governance Forum were always enlightening and thought-provoking, particularly the lively interactions with Dottie Schindlinger, Stephanie Bertels, Anastassia Lauterbach, Christopher Lee, Melissa Obegi, Katrina Scotto di Carlo, Irene Chang Britt, Stacy Baird, Byron Boston, Andrew Corbett-Nolan, Barak Orbach, Seda Roder and Charles Ehrlich.

I am deeply grateful to my close friends and family associates for their continuous encouragement and support while I was writing this book: Ashok Chopra, Adarsh Chaudhary, Sangeeta Mamgain and Promod Chawla.

My sincerest thanks to my office colleagues—Swati Bisht for research assistance and Prashant Swain for administrative support. For collectively taking care of the many routine but vital tasks that helped me devote a major part of my time to writing, I extend my gratitude to Anoj Kumar Sharma, Surya Prasad Bashyal, Jagannath Sharma, Jyotsna Kundu, Ishranti Honhaga and Bahamani Burh.

I would like to make a special mention of the extraordinary support from my daughter, Shivani Chaudhry. Despite her busy work schedule earlier, and forced sabbatical on health grounds later, she always found time to patiently go through my various drafts and engage in a dynamic ping-pong of ideas with me. Her substantive inputs and editorial advice have been immensely useful. I have no doubt that she is all set to author many books of her own.

Most importantly, my profound gratitude to Rahul Srivastava, Managing Director of Simon and Schuster India, who has been instrumental in bringing my vision to reality. His personal support and discerning guidance at every stage of the project have been invaluable. My earnest admiration for Elizabeth Kuruvilla, Publishing Director, for her incisive inputs and for being a pillar of support in every stage of this endeavour.

My heartfelt thanks to my excellent editor, Anurag Basnet, whose diligence, enthusiasm, keen eye for detail and insightful suggestions helped shape my manuscript into a compelling narrative of great substance. My sincere appreciation for the remarkable team at Simon and Schuster India, for their superb contributions during each phase of publishing and marketing: Abhay Singh, Senior

Marketing and Publicity Manager; Aayushi Jain, Digital Marketing; and Tanvi Shivam, Designer. I must also mention the team that works behind the scenes, while taking care of the many critical tasks. My sincere acknowledgement and praise for their pivotal role: Richie Maheshwary and all his colleagues.

Finally, a word of welcome to readers around the world. I hope you enjoy reading this book as much as we enjoyed working on it. Thank you for being a part of the 'global family' that is committed to bring forward a future where wisdom leads and Peopleism prevails and life is beautiful for everyone.

Index

O

P